THE GLOBAL MAF

THE GLOBAL MARKETPLACE

Capitalism and its Future

John Redwood

HarperCollins*Publishers*

FOR MY FAMILY

HarperCollins*Publishers*,
77–85 Fulham Palace Road,
Hammersmith, London W6 8JB

Published by HarperCollins*Publishers* 1993

2 4 6 8 9 7 5 3 1

Copyright © John Redwood 1993

John Redwood asserts his moral right to be
identified as the author of this work

A catalogue record for this book is
available from the British Library

ISBN 0 00 255135 7

Photoset in Linotron Sabon by
Hewer Text Composition Services, Edinburgh

Printed in Great Britain by
HarperCollinsManufacturing Glasgow

BUSINESS

AUTHOR'S NOTE

This book was written between April and July 1992. Since then a new administration has been elected in France, a Democrat president chosen in the USA, and the conflict in Bosnia has intensified. This book tries to describe the background to these and other momentous events.

Contents

ONE

Building a World Brand

The idea of trading internationally or globally is an old one. The Phoenicians traded along the coasts exploring ever more territories. The Viking raiders travelled long distances in search of areas to settle and goods to seize or trade. The patterns of trade in medieval Europe were quite sophisticated with well-manufactured products travelling long distances. A substantial trade in gold and precious stones developed.

World trade grew dramatically from the fifteenth century onwards when westerners started to travel more widely in their improved sailing ships. The discovery of the Spice Islands, of the silver lands of South America, and the rich natural resources of the Asian and American continents in general, created many new patterns of potential trade. The faster and larger sailing ships, with more capacious holds, reduced the risk involved in transporting goods, as well as shortening sailing times between continents. Another important element in the development of international trade was the increase in the numbers of risk-bearing private enterprise companies.

The true progenitors of the large multinational corporations of today can be found in the British and Dutch East India Companies of the seventeenth century. Founded with a joint stock capital these companies bought ships and ventured their stockholders' money in cargoes which they plied between the East and the West. They started a traditional pattern of trade where the West imported the raw materials and luxury items it sought from Asia and in turn exported back some of the manufactures and temperate products that they were capable of producing.

In the twentieth century the search for natural resources and the growing demands of voracious western industry created a new scale of global enterprise. Starting from modest beginnings the

I

large multinational oil companies sprang up, spanning the world in their quest for crude oil and in their trade in oil and refined products. Shell, British Petroleum and the Seven Sisters of America which sprang out of the original US oil conglomerate, soon came to be dominant companies trading worldwide with assets and interests in a host of foreign territories. The oil companies in the 1930s and 1940s developed the concept of world brands, seeking to sell Esso and Exxon petrol or Shell or BP petrol under a clear brand name with its own separate logo, colours, corporate loyalties and alleged magic ingredients and superior properties. Similarly, the large exploiters of gold, diamonds and other mineral deposits developed into large multinational corporations capable of owning and mining in a range of territories where their raw material was found, processing it and exporting and marketing it to the world's outlets. The natural resource companies lived in a largely satisfactory relationship with their host countries. Whilst there were times when the national sentiments of the host country were upset by the dominance or presence of multinational corporations, they were usually welcomed because of their access to technology and capital which the developing country needed in order to exploit its own natural resources. In the wake of the large resource corporations came a flurry of other western businessmen providing services to the expatriate resource company staff and establishing stronger trade links to help spend the profits of the natural resource exploitation.

The early large companies were primarily concerned with trade and the next wave with natural resource exploitation. The development of large multinational manufacturing companies tended to come later. This is most manifest in the twentieth century in the evolution of the motor car market which gradually became dominated by a handful of large multinational corporations based in the United States, Japan and a few European centres.

In the 1950s American customers bought Ford and General Motors cars, British customers bought Austins and Morrises, French people bought Citroëns and Peugeots and Germans bought Volkswagens. Each major car-producing nation had distinctive designs for its motor vehicles, and each primarily supplied its motor vehicles to its own domestic market; those countries without indigenous motor production tended to concentrate on importing or buying products from just one or two sources established in their country. Cross-border trade was only just developing, inward investment was in its infancy, and the idea of the global car had not even been dreamt of.

The later 1950s and 1960s saw a tidal wave of American investment around the world, especially in the crowded and active European car market-place. Ford and General Motors' trading as Vauxhall and Opel, quickly established large manufacturing plants in the principal western European countries. They soon accounted for a sizeable proportion of domestic market sales. In the 1960s and early 1970s these American majors, although acting in a way which created some commonality of parts and design across borders, still recognized national characteristics and differences. The best-selling car in Britain, the Ford Cortina, was different in body shape during this period from the popular Ford Taunus, its counterpart in engine size and seating capacity, which was sold in continental Europe.

By the end of the 1980s things had changed considerably. The major manufacturers had streamlined their model ranges, and had started producing similar cars throughout a broad market area as large as western Europe. There might be national variations in specification, trim or finish, but the basic body shell and engine specification was now identical and many of the parts came from a common source. There were still, however, sharp differences between, on the one hand, the cars that Ford and General Motors would offer in the European marketplace, and, on the other, the vehicles they would offer in the American marketplace.

The advent of the Japanese as global traders and investors at the end of the 1980s and in the early 1990s took the argument on one stage further. Japanese inward investment into the United Kingdom was designed to put on the streets of Europe vehicles similar to those that were common in Tokyo. At the same time the Japanese were assaulting the American citadel, exporting a large number of vehicles from Japan into the United States, particularly along the west coast.

The successive oil crises of the 1970s and 1980s, coupled with the mounting traffic problem on the freeways of the United States, had led to a growing demand in America for smaller and medium-sized compact cars. This gave a market opening to the Japanese and to the German manufacturers who had the products and the wherewithal to offer their cars widely in the US market. The relentless pressure towards compact cars and greater fuel efficiency, coupled with strong environmental controls in many states, started to influence the design of the mighty American car itself. Out went the huge trunks, large fenders and the extravagance of the all-American motor car of the 1950s and 1960s. In came parts and styles that looked more in place in a modern world moving towards the global vehicle. True American ostentation could still have its occasional fling in revivals of 1950s style but practical considerations were putting more and more smaller vehicles onto American highways.

During the course of the 1990s the motor industry will complete its journey from the production of different types of motor vehicle in different countries with strong contrasts between American, Japanese and European styles, to the production of a family of global vehicles from the same manufacturer. Whereas the Volkswagen Beetle, the Citroën 2CV and the Morris Minor were distinctively German, French and British respectively, the new generations of Fiestas, Golfs, Polos, Metros and Unos are all much more interchangeable – a similar response to common design and customer pressures throughout the different market-places. Nevertheless, these cars still need to gain the confidence of overseas investors.

Each manufacturer is moving towards providing one basic car in each of five different saloon categories. At the bottom end of the scale are the very small cars, pioneered by the Japanese. The Europeans come into production at the Mini car level with the Fiestas, Metros and Unos. The small car ranges include the Escort & the Polo. In the middle range manufacturers produce their Mondeo equivalent, and in the large saloon category the Granada and its competitors. Styling and specification have become common around the continents and between the manufacturers as they employ similar market research and design consultants, and as national differences and requirements are eroded. The Japanese, manufacturing in the United Kingdom for export throughout Europe, hire English design consultants, absorbing UK design work into their global product. As Japanese industry set about improving its style and design in the late 1970s and early 1980s, it turned deliberately to European and especially to Italian designers as its market research showed that having established a reputation for quality it needed to supplement it by having a reputation for good design.

As the large global companies fight it out for the market share, so they have discovered that participation in world motor sport and in the development of specialist vehicles is part of creating the right image which will appeal to customers worldwide. Japanese participation in motor sport was designed to give an impression of Japanese vehicles as having a strong sporting connection and the technical strength to be able to take part at the highest level under the most stressed conditions.

The development of sports cars by the Japanese industry was designed not only to tap the market niche that can be lucrative worldwide, but to strengthen the image of Japanese vehicles as being in the lead in the development of world style. Traditionally people had thought of Britain and Italy as producing the main sports cars, the British specializing in the open-top throaty cars like the MG and the Austin Healey, with the Italians specializing in the luxury expensive coupes. Today the Japanese have taken on the mantle of designing and producing many of the sportiest looking coupes in the world market, having picked up many of their original ideas from Italian design houses. The British sports car was in sharp decline in the 1970s and 1980s, as MG was allowed to languish under British Leyland ownership. In the late 1980s and early 1990s a clutch of small manufacturers in the UK sprung up again, producing interesting sports cars, but not on a significant enough scale to become world competitors.

Perhaps the first truly world vehicle was the British-designed and produced Land Rover. This ubiquitous, rugged, all-purpose vehicle was popular in Africa and Asia as well as in Europe. It served many a farmer's turn, was adopted by many armies and was often purchased by international organizations like the Red Cross and the United Nations for service in difficult areas. The Japanese recognized the importance of this style of development and turned themselves to producing more durable vehicles for world service. Seeing the popularity of the more luxurious variant of the Land Rover, the Range Rover, they soon proved capable of designing, producing and marketing several different off-road vehicles to the Range Rover standard. The Americans too were interested in this market, building on the success of the military Jeep in the Second World War, and designing a number of large Land Cruiser-style vehicles for American and export demand.

The Japanese ability to develop the idea of the four-wheel-drive vehicle and exploit this market niche, to improve styling, specification and cost performance of this type, and to market it worldwide, was an important lesson for the British, European and American industry in the 1980s. It was a classic case of how successful large corporations could refine and develop a product, using their widespread marketing outlets to create a world brand in a new area. Just as they had lifted their performance in saloon car manufacture, so they demonstrated as the 1980s wore on the ability to gain attention in areas like sports cars and offroad vehicles where before they had had no recognized product.

The colossal success of the Japanese industry is an integral part of the story of the development of the world marketplace and the world motor vehicle. In the early 1970s Britain, Germany and Japan all made around the same number of vehicles – about two million vehicles per annum. During the 1970s the British motor industry, largely in public ownership through the Government purchase of British Leyland, lost its way. Its products did not suit international or domestic tastes and it saw its UK and world market share plummet. Following British entry into the European Economic Community, the German and French industry took advantage of the weakness in the UK and by the end of the ten-year period the German industry was making more than four million cars per annum and the British industry was down to one million. In the 1980s the Japanese industry surged further, the German industry made steady progress and the British industry started to rebuild following the disaster of the 1970s. As the 1990s dawned, Japanese industry was producing twelve million cars per annum, the German industry six million cars per annum and the British industry was struggling back to two million cars per annum.

These huge divergencies in car output had knock-on effects throughout the engineering sector. So important had the motor industry become to sophisticated economies that the relative performance of Japan, Germany and Britain in motor car assembly had widespread ramifications, which affected significantly the demand for domestically produced steel and the output and work of a large number of car component suppliers. International competition had dictated that the Japanese were going to be the best in engineering, that the Germans were going to be the best of the major European countries in engineering, and that the British industry was the one which was to suffer. The problems arose primarily because the British industry in the 1970s had not recognized changing styles and preferences and had produced model ranges of cars that did not suit the evolution of taste. This, coupled with the strong Japanese reputation for quality and reliability and the British reputation in the 1970s for the reverse, led to the sharp changes in market share. The American industry too was suffering from the Japanese attack. Because the American industry was slow to recognize the growing demand in the States for small and compact vehicles and was slow to adapt to the new high quality standards the Japanese were pioneering, the American manufacturers also came under sustained competitive attack and many American buyers decided to turn to the Japanese vehicles to satisfy their needs.

Part of the evolution of the world car resulted from and fed the process of evolution in the world component marketplace. The large integrated motor manufacturers were able to draw on component product and ideas worldwide. It became accepted in the 1970s that disc brakes should be the norm in saloon car manufacture. The development by GKN, a leading UK component manufacturers, of the constant velocity joint produced in Britain a world-class product that became incorporated in one way or another in many globally produced cars. We have already seen how four-wheel drive pioneered for military vehicles spread into the consumer civil vehicle sector. Fuel injection, automatic transmissions, better electrical and electronic controls, new styles of instrumentation and better in-car audio, heating and air-conditioning facilities became standard on many vehicles as the 1980s progressed. The Americans liked automatic transmission: their preferences started to spread to other markets. Customers worldwide sought higher quality stereo and radios: their wishes were met by the manufacturers. People expected higher safety standards and so manufacturers and component manufacturers experimented with methods of construction that produced higher resistance to impact, better performance in crashes and greater protection of the passengers in their seats. Neck and headrests, cushioned steering-wheels, collapsible steering columns, strong steel body shells around the passenger compartment all became more common as world designers sought a world solution to a general problem in the age of mass transport by motor car. As the 1990s dawned designers started to turn their attention to the problem of car security as the growing number of vehicle thefts in the Americas and in Europe drew their attention to the need to reassure people that their car would not be so easy to break into.

The development of mass customization, dealt with in the discussion of modern manufacturing systems in chapter 2, ironically has powered the move towards the common global car. If the individual manufacturer can offer the individual customer, wherever he may be, forty or fifty different variations on his main theme, it becomes that much easier to offer a single main theme globally. The customer is spoilt for choice, and so he can accept the underlying car product and component range produced for the world market rather than for his own domestic national or regional market. The new age is one of mass production with the individual customer in mind, rather than market segregation at the level of the nation, the state or the continent.

The development of the world market is also clear in the pharmaceutical industry. Here the United Kingdom has performed extremely well, through the development of major research products by Glaxo, Beecham, Fisons, Reckitt & Colman and others. The UK has discovered that it is world class in pharmaceuticals and has managed to achieve a high rate of performance in developing new compounds, identifying medical problems that permit a pharmaceutical solution and employing the right range and quality of scientists capable of experimenting on and developing those products. In the 1980s the successes of Glaxo and ICI Pharmaceuticals in particular made a strong impact upon the world market. UK drug companies had produced compounds which led the world in tackling problems with the heart, asthma and viral infections.

It was natural for the pharmaceutical industry to develop a global presence. Its products are small and light in weight, easily transported by air with high value relative to the weight being transported. The problems of infection, disease and organ failure are global problems and the body of basic science on which much of the work is founded is an international process fuelled by the exchanges in journals and conferences between the scientists of the world. Even during the schism between East and West created by the presence of communism, there was still an international community in pure science where American, British and Japanese scientists would read the research findings of Russian ones and vice versa through scientific journals. There was always more scope for exchanging ideas in the medical field than in those fields of pure and applied science related to military activity. The basis of pure science is a collaborative endeavour, fuelled in part by some competition between individual schemes to make a reputation, but furthered by the exchange of ideas through publication and the development of research teams in universities and other institutions of learning. The process of developing particular compounds is a competitive activity undertaken by large research-based companies. Employing their own teams of scientists, they would draw on the corpus of fundamental research and would develop their own compounds, testing programmes and ideas which target particular therapeutic areas located through both market and scientific analysis of the problems. Substantial sums of money and large amounts of brainpower are expended on the development of a single compound or on the solution to a single therapeutic problem. The cost and elaborate nature of the work are intensified by the understandably high standards required by the national regulators before approving any particular drug. In order to meet these regulatory requirements companies have to go through analysis with field work, animal and human testing before a drug can pass into accepted use – all of which demands considerable time and attention. The problems that Distillers encountered by allowing a drug to be marketed which had very bad side-effects illustrated how devastating to a company's reputation, as well as to the unfortunate people who take the drug, the marketing of an insufficiently tested product can prove.

The Japanese have made their own contribution to the pharmaceutical industry, just as they have in the world motor industry. It has taken them longer, but they have now reached the point where they have their own intellectual capability to make a contribution to the development of new compounds and to the advancement of fundamental pharmaceutical research. The American houses have always been powerful players producing a large number of therapeutic ideas. Recently there has been, across the board, a trend of merger as the companies have come to see the advantages of having detailed sales forces in each of the different marketplaces and the benefits of pooling research and ideas across the oceans. The Smith-Kline Beecham merger was one of the largest and showed the way in which large corporations on both sides of the Atlantic had come to see the need for mutual support in the development of the world pharmaceutical industry and marketplace.

Because therapeutic products are global in their implications the large companies that think them up do need international marketing forces. Having spent all the money required to produce a successful new treatment a company must be able to sell it not just in the UK, not just on the continent of Europe, but in the Americas and Asia as well. This in turn requires large marketing forces with a specialist knowledge of products, who are capable of talking to doctors worldwide about the advantages and the risks of the particular treatment. To tackle this problem of scale and to provide the economies needed to cover the overheads of research and development of the treatment, the companies have naturally turned to the development of large international sales forces who have the ability to market a product worldwide.

Products that are heavier and less valuable have also developed a world market presence – primarily through advertising and strong brand leadership. Whilst it may have seemed natural that pharmaceuticals would be sold worldwide once they had established themselves as good treatments, it was less obvious that soft drinks, ice-creams, cheeses and other food products would be developed, produced and marketed on a global basis. In the case of drinks products, like colas and mixer drinks, it is rarely the case that the company draws benefits from manufacturing all in one place and then shipping worldwide. The product is too heavy and it does not usually make good business sense to spend a lot of money packaging water in elaborate bottles and cartons and then sending it on ships around the world. Instead what is sold worldwide is the idea through a system of international licensing and marketing. The companies may retain ownership of all the production facilities, building production plants in each major territory it wishes to penetrate, or it may simply license the recipe or method of making the product to others, collecting the royalties. The Coca-Cola company and its chief competitor, Pepsi-Cola, showed early on how the world market for a consumer product could be exploited skilfully. A special recipe was developed and then marketing created the demand for this product on a worldwide basis. Coca-Cola and Pepsi-Cola soon went into production in a wide range of countries and discovered that they had hit a winning product. Coca-Cola has recently strengthened its global approach to marketing by becoming one of the official sponsors of the Olympics, seeking to associate its product with health, fitness and success in the world's premier athletic sporting event.

Whilst we are a long way off the world menu for most people, the development of international business and tourist travel and the franchising or construction of large international hotel chains has produced a global menu for the international traveller. The food offered in the Hiltons of the world is very similar from hotel to hotel, regardless of the country and continent you happen to be in. The world menu may be a pastiche of different dishes drawing on the strengths of Asian and European cuisine, but it is also a small but important force towards the globalization of the food industry. Wherever you go in the world people expect to be able to buy French wines which are successfully exported and have built up a strong brand image. France is now under strong competitive attack from Australia and California, who are succeeding in building an image for quality in their wines, which are now also commonly available in many different countries. Cheddar cheese has built an international reputation and many other food products are attempting to follow the same road.

The vital part of the creation of the world market is the development of international communications. The origin of telephone systems usually lay in the development of a national monopoly in each country. People thought demand for communication would be mainly between people of the same city or town, or possibly for trunk calls up and down the country; they saw international telephone traffic as a relatively small part of the process. Being also the most difficult technically, requiring the spanning of oceans and the crossing of national borders, it developed less quickly than local and national trunk traffic in most countries. As the global market expands and as more and more companies operate on a global basis, so the demand for international telephone traffic has mushroomed. The development of new satellite links and the ability to route messages across large distances without the need for subterranean cables has helped the growth. Much swifter switching mechanisms have also facilitated the complicated routings often required to complete an international telephone link and conversation. The world market is data and communications driven. It is not possible to run large global businesses unless communications are first class. The businessman running a company from New York wants to be assured that he can pick up a telephone and talk to his Australian, Japanese, German and Canadian subsidiaries. He wishes to be sure that he can fax them documents and instructions and can receive back from them detailed fax or telex reports on their performance. The communications revolution is critical to the development of business confidence in the growth of the large corporation and the exploitation of the world market.

The explosive growth of international telephone traffic is beginning to erode the traditional national monopoly systems. Technology itself is proving more potent a force for change than many imagined, now beginning to affect the structures of the industry. Whereas the early technology based upon copper cable and large complex switching was arguably geared to the investment and maintenance of the large national monopoly, the newer technology based on radio links, microwave connections, cell patterns and digital switching is more compatible with competitive marketplace developments. The rate of technical change was so great that no single monopoly was able to embrace all of the ideas and to keep up with the challenge of competitors. Those countries which adopted the competitive structure earliest, like the United States and the United Kingdom, developed their markets the quickest and became the testing grounds for a glittering array of new technology. This demonstrated that technology can affect the marketplace. However, for technology, and its consequences, to be a success governments and other influential powers have to be prepared to make the necessary changes to facilitate and permit its development.

Creating the digital highway around the world is the goal of several leading British and American corporations. The main impediment in the way of completing the system – through the monopoly defence of international telecommunications rights country by country – is a political one. The United States of America is as guilty of this as many other territories, seeking market entry to other people's markets whilst restricting the terms on which foreign competitors can come into the United States to use networks there to link up with the ultimate customer. Gradually trade negotiations and other pressures will erode the current attempt by some countries to provide a monopoly break to the developing international market. Some alert companies are already finding ways around the restrictions, setting up domestic companies in the territories they wish to penetrate, building national links there and then using them in the development of an international network. Cable and Wireless, the UK company, has already spent a great deal of money on completing a global highway across the Atlantic and Pacific, and satellite capacity has been expanded by several consortia providing considerable scope for growth in international telephony.

Linking the world by satellite, cable and radio is important. Much of the pressure for the development of the global marketplace has come about through television and radio links. Listeners and viewers in remote countries are able to see American films and to hear the BBC World Service which provides some common experience and a means to understand very diverse cultures. It creates pressures for uniformity and common economic ambitions. American television has done more than any other single industry to create similar aspirations. It is the sight of American living standards on television screens in India and Africa and in the Far East and South America that has led to so many demands for political and economic systems similar to or capable of competing with the American dream. Now telephony is following in the wake of broadcasting, bringing businessmen from different continents into contact with one another, minute by minute during the working day and at the touch of a few buttons on a telephone. The fax machine makes simultaneous receipt of information in offices around the global empire a matter of common practice; the telephone and audio-visual links make it possible for managers to discuss business problems even if they are separated by three or four thousand miles of water. The development of open network systems in computing means that on the desk of the successful business executive in the middle 1990s will be a piece of equipment capable of transmitting and receiving video tape, voice messages and data, or any mixture of them around the offices of his group worldwide. Information is crucial to the control of businesses and to the spread of the service-driven culture of the 1990s. The information revolution is now providing more computing power more cheaply than ever before, and in a more accessible form, so that even those with limited computer skills are able to use the machinery.

Businesses have the opportunity and capability to talk to one another around the world. The motor industry has displayed how the world brand is developing out of the national brand. Similar things are happening in a number of other business and product areas. The Japanese consumer electronics industry has shown what can be done when a group of businesses is serious about world penetration of the market and patiently works away at distribution and marketing systems on a global basis. Thirty years ago names like Hitachi and JVC were unknown outside Japan. Today they are global giants supplying much of the world's requirement for televisions and video recorders. Their progress has not always been easy. In the 1960s when Japanese goods first started to arrive in reasonable quantities in western Europe, they dressed them up under European-sounding brand names and sold them at the cheaper end of the market. In the 1970s they set themselves the task of establishing the Japanese names as important brands in their own right. They gradually moved their products up-market, selling them under a reputation for quality sometimes at a premium price. By the later 1980s this practice was well established, with the Japanese brand names strongly identified by consumers with high quality and technical excellence.

Japanese companies have experienced more and more difficulties since success breeds jealousy and often leads to protectionism. To counter this they started to invest substantial sums of money in manufacturing plants in America and western Europe. The United Kingdom, during the course of the 1980s, became a net exporter of televisions again, having suffered greatly from the attack of both continental European and Japanese manufacturers in the 1970s. The re-establishment of high quality, leading-edge manufacturing in the UK owed a great deal to the presence of new Japanese investors who were prepared to set up plants in a friendly territory within the European Community, and from there produce for export throughout the Single Market area.

The establishment of world brands is now clear in a range of consumer durables, consumer products, travel, communications and financial services. National governments are ambiguous in their attitude towards all this. They equivocate between, on the one hand, encouraging it and on the other, denigrating and trying to stop it. This is very clear with the French administration. They spent considerable time and energy trying to attract the Disneyland project for Europe to a site near Paris, and were ultimately successful. They often offer all kinds of help and inducements to foreign investors to spend money in France rather than elsewhere within the European Community. Conversely, the French socialist administration was very shrill in its criticism of Japanese and American companies and often expressed great hostility to the actions of the competitors they were trying to woo as inward investors. The French do not favour cars made by Japanese companies in western Europe which circulate freely within the Single Market area. Nor do they favour a big influx of Japanese video and TV products. They are very worried about, as they see it, American cultural, political and economic imperialism. Yet at the same time even the French administration recognized the commercial logic of moving in the direction of larger accumulations of capital and international businesses which can operate without any great sense of frontiers and borders, and are keen to be part of that process.

The United Kingdom has been less ambivalent. It has made it clear that it recognizes the growing tendency towards global business, and wants to be part of that process. It has flung open its doors by offering a liberal regime for mobile capital and by trying to ensure that the United Kingdom is an attractive base in which to invest. Taxation, industrial relations and social policies all concentrate on ensuring a skilled and flexible work-force and an atmosphere in which profits can be made and monies remitted by any investor with a good product to offer. The result of Britain's inward investment policies has been to secure two-fifths of the stock of Japanese and American capital in the European Community – about twice the United Kingdom's share of Community gross domestic product. Footloose international investors do want political safety; they want reassurance that there will not be penal taxes imposed upon them; they want the knowledge that they can repatriate profits and dividends or even investment itself should circumstances change; and they want to have access to the skills and talents of the people in the country in which they are investing. Good communications help: ready access to international standard airports, telephones, roads and rail links are of inestimable value to such an investor.

The financial services marketplace, and business services generally, is another area where rapid progress is being made towards global business. Banking has to be international as the surpluses and deficits between the different countries of the world are enormous, giving banks the huge and vital task of recycling surpluses to finance deficits. Over the last ten years Japan has run a very large trade surplus and has, as a result, gradually become the most important banking nation in the world using the money it has accumulated through trade as the banking reserve from which to re-lend money around the world. Where the United States once dominated through the creation of the dollar area and through the work of its banks in creating the Euro-dollar pool, in the late 1980s it was the Japanese who provided the main sinews of world trade through the financial muscle of their banking system. Banks have traditionally been organized on national lines and in some countries have been nationalized and protected institutions. The emergence of the large American and Japanese banks has transformed provincial and national centres into international centres. Those who wish to be ahead in the banking business have to welcome to their cities and towns the large banks of Japan and the United States.

London has been foremost in this process. There are more foreign banks in the City of London than in any other financial centre around the world: well over 500 different names can be found within the square mile or just beyond. The City of London demonstrates how concentration and competition stimulate business development. Some have thought that the way to business success is to try to find an area or a business niche away from the madding crowd. Yet even casual observation illustrates that this strategy is a less successful than locating in a business area or in a region where others are practising the same type of activity. If you want to buy a high-quality suit you go to Savile Row; if you want to shop at a multiple store you go to Oxford Street; if you wish to produce high-tech products you locate in the Thames Valley or Silicon Glen where there are many suppliers and competitors. The excitement and the competitive pressure mean more ideas in circulation, more opportunities for purchasing from high-quality and low-priced suppliers, and better access to the market. Modern competition theory is based upon the premiss that research and development, quality and price competitiveness come from a concentration of a large number of businesses jostling with one another in the same area. The City of London, which attracts many companies because it is a centre where there is already a concentration of businesses to trade and compete with, shows how true this is.

Financial services, just like banking, is becoming a global business. The three large stock markets of the world – London, Tokyo and New York – dominate. Trading runs continually, twenty-four hours a day, beginning in Tokyo, then moving to London and ending up in the New York time zone. The large global and international shares are now traded in each of the three big markets and companies have to consider very carefully where they make their announcements, what format they use, and what impact it might have upon the trading patterns in their shares on a round-the-clock, global basis.

Just as big banks are being created because of the pressures of Japanese trade surpluses and the need to syndicate and manage ever bigger sums of money, so too businesses offering financial services are being set up out of the wish on the part of many investors to invest and operate worldwide and receive a global service from their investment house. Investing globally has always been more attractive in London than in Tokyo or New York. The depth, breadth and liquidity of the domestic markets in Japan and the United States have meant that investors there have been happier for longer to maintain all or most of their assets in local currency-denominated local company assets. For many decades people in London have been used to investing around the world, laying off their risk and going for the most attractive businesses and the best-value securities on a worldwide basis. This habit of mind is now spreading to both New York and Tokyo: increasingly, investors are realizing that they have to compare the values between companies within the same sector on an international basis, and that the business trends and economic forces which have the main bearing upon the value of the companies in which they have invested are now regional and global ones, not merely national.

The world is talking itself into three main economic blocs or groupings – one in North America, through the free trade area of Canada, the USA and Mexico; the second in western Europe, through the growing Single Market area between the European Community and the EFTA countries; and the third in the Pacific Basin, where the Japanese are exerting more and more economic and technical leadership over the Asian tigers of Taiwan, Hong Kong and Singapore. The poverty, inflation and high indebtedness of South America and of most of Africa have relegated these two continents to the sidelines. South Africa, the most prosperous country in the whole African continent, has been somewhat marginalized because of its apartheid policies and thus has found it increasingly difficult through the 1970s and 1980s to maintain or develop links with the three big economic areas of the world. The 1990s could see a change for the better if political events begin to unlock the South African problem. If the new democracy can create peace and stability it could become Africa's link to the global market.

The financial markets have done their bit to organize the world into a three-cornered triangle. Investment managers specialize in the Pacific rim, America or Europe. Investment strategists and portfolio managers make asset distributions in relation to yen block, deutschmark block and dollar block investments. Equity is now raised or sold on a worldwide basis in the largest issues. United Kingdom privatization issues pioneered the concept of the international sale for a proportion of the shares. It has now been developed in primary and secondary offerings of larger company securities with the investment brokers and merchant bank advisors of London, New York and Tokyo collaborating in issues that span the globe.

It is none the less easy to exaggerate the extent to which the world has become an international financial marketplace. Much business is still done domestically within individual nation states. Although English is the international business language, most people still speak a different language and wish to talk to their savings advisor in their own language, and buy a product developed for their own particular market. Tax differences often reinforce national differentiation of savings products. What we are witnessing is the creation of a two-tier financial services industry. On one level there are the large international houses and investors who move very large sums of money about and provide finance for the global companies; and on another there are the millions of individual savers country by country, who route their savings through their own domestic financial advisors, often into products that are made, sold and managed locally. Very often the large multi-national financial service businesses and banks discover that the only way to run a profitable activity in a given territory is to do what the locals do, as there is a limited amount of global business, and only a few centres are really playing the game for all it is worth. Often in lesser centres the main type of investment and financial business is that which circumvents legally (or even occasionally illegally) exchange controls and other government-imposed regulations. In a weak currency country, which is desperately trying to hold its money in by artificial regulations, substantial business can be done by directing the money out of the country or by depositing and saving it once it has been moved. Any international banking centre has difficult moral political dilemmas: should it assist in the process of encouraging the free movement of capital, taking the view that if a crime has been committed it has been committed by the depositor and not by the receiving bank, or should the financial centre try to stamp out the deposit of illicitly moved monies? This problem has become more acute with the laundering of large sums of dirty money from drugs and crime, a case where reputable centres and businessmen have decided that they do wish to co-operate with the authorities in rooting out this kind of abuse.

Technology has been the driving force behind many of these changes. Financial technology has been applied on a worldwide scale. The ideas of debt-swap, privatization, bond and convertible issues and the provision of global capital to global companies, have spread around the world bringing with them new business opportunities. These in turn have reflected the underlying realities of global capitalism. More and more companies want access to money on a worldwide basis; more and more companies want access to common service from common personnel who oversee their accounts in the three or four corners of the world. Managements attempting to operate on a far-flung basis out of New York, Chicago, London, Frankfurt, Tokyo and Osaka want the reassurance that comes from knowing the financial side of their businesses are being looked after or from being advised by world-class financial institutions who speak the same language of business common sense in the different territories in which their companies are operating.

The General Agreement on Tariffs and Trade round in the early 1990s, called the Uruguay talks, attempts to extend its principles to intellectual property and to capital flows. Conscious that the world is now skill based and service driven, the GATT is attempting to provide worldwide the same freer framework for trade in services and movement of investment monies that it has succeeded in providing for trade in goods over the 45 years since the Second World War. It is much easier to block trade in services and stop capital flows. Many countries have strong controls against the movement of capital and many use a variety of protectionist means to prevent the provision of services on a cross-border basis. The language barrier is more acute than with traded goods. Professional qualifications can be used to restrict entry into areas like accountancy and law. Local knowledge and contacts may be far more crucial in winning business in areas as diverse as advertising, marketing, sales consultancy and professional services than it is in traded goods. It is more difficult to compare quality and price in the service sector than when buying a fairly simple industrial product like screws or batteries or copper wire. In many cases the price of the service is not known before it is completed. Charging bases include charge-out rates per hour and estimated sums for a complete job, but rarely does the client know in advance exactly what he is going to pay because the job often turns out to have complexities and changes in specification not envisaged when the contract was first signed.

None the less some global service providers are now in evidence. The Anglo-Saxon-based accountancy practices have been very successful, expanding the number of partners, setting up offices in different territories of the world, and providing cross-border accountancy services for the global companies and the large overseas investors. Some lawyers are now specializing in cross-border work across the Atlantic, across the Pacific and within the European Community. A large company needs to know the basis of its contractual relations, employee terms and conditions of employment, product liability, environmental exposure and tax obligations across the multitude of jurisdictions in which it is trading. Good legal and financial advice in an accessible form is at a premium. In order to persuade employees to move round the different territories of their global companies the groups have to offer internationally competitive fringe benefits – pensions, cars, insurance facilities, bonuses and remuneration. The mobile executive breeds the portable pension. The footloose company breeds greater harmony of treatment in different territories over employee rights and participation. The global company will seek out those jurisdictions that are most tolerant or most compatible with its traditions and culture.

How much business is being conducted on this global basis and how much is likely to be in the future? We have seen that motor car assembly, pharmaceutical production, international financial services, banking and a number of consumer product areas are now organized on a global basis by large companies. They may use dozens of individual suppliers in separate national territories from competitive market-places, and their customers may still be geared in whole or in part to their national traditions when it comes to purchasing the goods available and the type of distribution used to sell them. Even so, there is a perceptible and growing shift towards global business and global themes. Advertising around the world is becoming increasingly homogenous. Anglo-Saxon-based companies do not always bother even to change the script on their adverts, let alone the photographs and themes. Other companies using French or German as their first language sometimes simply translate their adverts into English for use in other territories.

There are waves of global styling emanating from London, Paris, New York and Tokyo. French *haute couture* and design houses, along with the Italians, more or less determine the length of hemlines and the colours and fabrics that are used worldwide. English and American financial services businesses and telephone companies exercise considerable influence over the type and range of service and the style of product to be launched in their respective fields of endeavour. Japanese car and electronic companies now lead the world in design and engineering concepts. They push them out through global adverts and through their global assembly companies, selling them through a host of agents and licensees in the different countries of the world. They market them through the diverse distribution systems of Pacific, Europe and America. As they do so there are more and more pressures to conform and more and more pressures to form global businesses that can compete with them and supply them on a like for like basis.

The large car company breeds the large accountancy firm and advertising agency; the large advertising agency and accountancy firm breeds international standards and international approaches to common problems. These in their turn generate a climate in which more products are likely to be produced for a world market rather than a domestic market. Change is now rapid. The ubiquitous television set spreads the message of consumerism from territory to territory and from house to house. Once a family has a television they have a window on the world of western and Japanese consumer durable goods. Once seen they are often smitten. The consumers themselves then clamour and pressurize for the global companies to arrive and satisfy their newly defined requirements. This was most recently demonstrated in East Germany. When the Berlin Wall came down the East German consumers, fed on a diet of western adverts but for so many years starved of the products they represented, voted with their purses and pocket books for a big surge in western imports. It didn't matter whether the western goods were better or worse than the eastern goods they were to replace: what mattered was the brand, the image and the knowledge that they had joined the western club at last.

The new heroes of western materialism are the strong branded goods. Buy a Honda car, a JVC video, a Toshiba television, a Pringle sweater, a Chanel perfume, go to an American theme park and drink an American soft drink: these are the passions of the modern consumer world, these are the forces that underlie the world's political and economic drama in the latter part of the twentieth century. The politics of the world are about the relationships between the haves and the have nots, and the struggle between the free traders and the interventionists. We must now turn to the impact the global market is having on the style of manufacturing and the nature of industrial progress.

TWO

Making It Modern

Modern manufacturing is about timeliness, quality and innovation. Successful modern manufacturers understand the connection between manufacturing and service. Far from seeing service as a separate mickey-mouse economy, they see it as an integral part of their success and of their new processes. The globalization of manufacturing is dragging with it the service sector. The new large integrated manufacturer producing motor vehicles or washing machines requires worldwide services. He needs access to good-quality legal advice, financial advice, marketing, advertising, corporate promotions and other skills on a worldwide basis. The nature of manufacturing has shifted dramatically in recent years with the advent of the microchip, transnational telecommunications links and the development of global brands.

Timeliness is one of the keys to the system. Western European motor manufacturers thought it was fine to take six to eight years to design and test a new model before launching it into production. It was the Japanese who revolutionized this approach to time, discovering that they could design, test and bring a new vehicle onto the market within three years. They did not cut the thinking time, but they slashed through the number of consecutive functions and made more consecutive functions take place simultaneously. Control of time can also help control cost. In a fast-moving world, where images and consumer values shift rapidly, being closer to the market and being able to launch a product quickly can make all the difference between success and failure. As soon as someone demonstrated it was possible to design and build a car in three years it seemed very old-fashioned to do it in eight. Before the Japanese did it many argued it was impossible. It was thought that only the large integrated motor manufacturer with his secure but plodding procedures could mount enough people and money to design and build a new model that would satisfy all the regulatory requirements and meet the sophisticated consumer demands. By carefully analysing the flow charts and time diagrams of the typical car design process and rationalizing them in an efficient way, the Japanese came to believe otherwise. Timeliness is also at the core of improved manufacturing performance on the factory floor. If you go to a badly managed factory you will see a great deal of stock and work in progress all round the factory. There will be a large stock room of components and raw materials. There will be haphazard stock levels at different stages in the production process of semi-assembled and semi-finished goods. There will be another large stock room containing the finished product. Many millions of pounds will be tied up in stock and in work in progress and it will take many days, if not weeks, for the product to get from being a gleam in the production manager's eye to being completed and on the stock shelf ready for dispatch.

The first question any successful modern marketing manager needs to ask of the production side is how long will it take if he secures an order for goods to be produced and dispatched? With modern manufacturing systems it is possible to produce a product as sophisticated as a motor car within two days of the order being lodged and for the car to be dispatched and made available to the customer within the week. Most western car manufacturers failed to hit these exacting deadlines in the 1980s and lost market share partly as a result.

The second question the marketing manager should ask is how customized can the final product be? Traditional manufacturing has not only relied upon substantial stocks at the beginning and the end of the process, but has attempted to combat the extra costs these impose by firm disciplining of the number of different options made available. In the early days of mass production the customer was told he could have any colour of car or telephone he liked as long as it was black. Cutting out a range of colours meant a substantial reduction in the amount of stock the factory and the stockists had to hold in order to satisfy consumer demand.

The modern customer will not put up with this discipline and limitation of choice. He wants to be able to choose from a wide range of colours and, in the case of a sophisticated product, a wide range of options. The car buyer will want to decide whether to have the saloon or the estate or the drop-head convertible version. He will want to decide which of several different engine specifications and performance tuning is most suitable to his needs. He will want variations of trim and will be able to decide for himself what kind of stereo system, car telephone, instrumentation and other finishes he would like within his budget. The result is a whole host of different permutations for hundreds of different vehicles which are produced to the same basic design. All this requires careful production management to prevent the final stocks from mushrooming and, at the same time, to ensure prompt delivery to the final customer of the exact vehicle he has chosen from an attractive and wide range of options.

The finance director will want to ask a different type of question. He will want to be reassured that the proliferation of choice does not lead to a proliferation of stocks of raw materials, components and final products. He will want to make sure that frequent changes in the style of vehicle being manufactured lead neither to excessive down-time on machines nor to too much disruption of the production line as employees find it difficult to get up to speed with all the different varieties going through the factory. He will need to realize that modern manufacturing is the ally of efficiency as well as of customer choice. The idea that producing a single product in very long runs is the optimum from the financial point of view will need to be relegated to history.

Technology is assisting the modern plant manager in creating flexibility and cutting stock costs. Many companies have now had a blitz on the component and raw material store. They are demanding much more rapid high-quality supply from their component and raw material suppliers than they have been used to receiving. The Japanese 'just-in-time' system is becoming not only popular but essential to manufacturing success. A large assembly factory will now have a series of satellite company suppliers capable of matching its specification and delivery deadlines. In a successful car plant the question now is not on what day or week of the month do you wish to receive the parts but at what hour of the day. Once the factory is streamlined to work upon supplies arriving by the hour or daily, the stock costs of raw materials and components can be slashed, as can the associated costs for the store man, the store computer system and the physical space previously required to handle the incoming goods. The nearer the modern factory gets to the parts coming straight off the lorry onto the assembly line the better from the point of view of cost and quality control. Keeping too many parts and raw materials in a separate store and then moving them around as and when they are needed just increases the likelihood of damage and decay.

Tackling excess stock and work in progress on the shop floor also requires firm action from production management. Old-fashioned factories often have jagged and zigzagging production flows. It is a useful experiment in each factory to try to follow the flow of raw materials and components through to the final goods and to see how many times the semi-manufactured item needs to be shifted and how often it has to pause on the shop floor between processes. The good modern factory has straight flow lines. You see the raw materials and components coming in one end and the finished goods going out at the other. The flow is as constant as the various processes permit. The more successful the factory the less likely you are to see large quantities of semi-manufactured produce sitting around waiting. In a bad factory a nightmare series of controls has to be imposed to keep track of the meandering product as it advances across the factory floor in an effort to reconcile orders and specifications with the work being done. The longer semi-finished products hang around the more likely they are to be damaged in transit: something is more likely to go wrong with its quality as people compare which processes it has been through and which it has still to complete.

It is not always possible for manufacturers to produce only against orders received. If they can do so then they need have no final stock problem at all. If the production process is well controlled and automated and if the production flows smoothly then it is possible to quote to final customers twenty-four or forty-eight-hour delivery schedules and, at the same time, manufacture a product only once the order has been received telephonically or by fax. The best factories have order queuing and production planning and marketing systems combined. When the customer rings up the quote, which is given over the phone, includes provisional allocation of production line space so that a date for completion can also be given. As soon as the order is confirmed the machine time is booked and work only carried out against an order.

The ability to produce to these tight schedules means that the manufacturer can then himself become part of the 'just-in-time' chain. If he is able to control his production processes he can dispatch and supply to his final customer by the hour or by the day rather than weekly or monthly. This then opens up new business vistas, and means that he will be capable of supplying the finest final assemblers who demand the narrowest tolerances on time. The new assembler/supplier relationship is central to the development of new industrial activity. Whilst seeking value for money from suppliers the informed manufacturer does not necessarily award each contract to the lowest bidder. Instead he is likely to build customer/supplier relationships with a handful of well-placed manufacturers whom he trusts and then to engage in collaborative work in many cases. The final assembler may work with the component supplier to see how the latter's systems can be improved to reduce the waiting time and to increase the smooth flow of work through the factories of both processes. The final assembler may meet surges in final demand which he needs to respond to or he may go through periods of sluggish customer requirements. He will want to work with his suppliers to sort out how he can shield them from the impact whilst simultaneously responding quickly to the demands of the market-place. It is in his interest as well as that of the component suppliers that the variable costs can be adjusted rapidly.

Modern manufacturing is learning the wisdom of the adage, 'if you want something done quickly give it to a busy man.' Delay breeds inefficiency. The longer something hangs around the more likely it is to be done badly or inaccurately. If a business has no sense of urgency in meeting its customers' needs it may also lack a sense of quality or precision. It is difficult to see what you can do better tomorrow that you put off today.

Quality is the second watchword of modern manufacturing. Traditional mass production in some ways improves quality over handmade goods in that it can standardize and machine things to fairly fine tolerances. But, throughout the era of mass manufacturing, there has been and still is a general feeling that if you wanted something really good you had to turn to a craftsman who would produced a unique product for you and would discard anything that was not up to standard. Manufacturing standards were average but not necessarily high. Products were tested in a primitive way or were subject to a rapid visual inspection and most of the bad products were winnowed out by these processes. People always took the view that they got what they paid for and that if you wanted something reasonably priced and mass produced you had to accept that it would not be as good as the more individual product.

Modern manufacturing technology permits the production of the highest quality goods that can be customized from mass production lines or techniques. Machining tolerances have improved since the early days of mass production. Controls have been introduced into kilns, ovens, distilleries and other processes involving the use of heat, so that they can now be very precisely monitored and, by a combination of chemistry and trial and error, the characteristics of the product going through them can be very accurately predicted. As a result, quality has increased by leaps and bounds, along with an understanding of the product. This has enabled savings to be made on raw material and component input as the chemistry and physics of properties involved have been better controlled, allowing the manufacturer to select the standard required to meet needs without being unduly expensive.

These improvements in technology have been buttressed by the development of quality systems. One such system in the United Kingdom is the BS5750 which is a two-part quality standard. It relies for its success upon the establishment of proper procedures for monitoring raw material and product flow through the factory and for handling complaints. A good manufacturer logs every batch, quickly corrects and withdraws any batch which has gone wrong and if there are generic problems with a series of batches works closely with the customer to improve the specification and design out any fault. Partnership between supplier and customer is critical as both become used to working to much greater degrees of accuracy. Cost can be reduced as the one gains confidence in the other. In a good manufacturing system the final assembler should take for granted the high quality of the product arriving at his factory from his supplier. He can dispense with much of the inspection and paraphernalia of quality control that he used to need if his supplier's factory operates to high standards. The ambitions of the best manufacturers have improved dramatically.

Where it would have been common for manufacturers to have accepted three or four per cent waste from failed products, they are now trying to achieve much less than even one per cent waste through better production systems. Where a manufacturer might have been prepared to accept ninety-nine per cent reliability of the goods going out of his factory they are now arguing over the third or fourth decimal point of the last one per cent. Rigorous inspection and checking during the course of production is critical to maintaining the standards of finished product and to ensuring the correction of errors as the processes go along.

All these stages have a direct impact upon the quality and attitude of staff. It is not possible to run a modern factory working to these very high tolerances and regarding design as an integral part of successful manufacturing with staff who take no interest in the final result. Higher levels of training are essential and a degree of commitment by each employee is important. Instead of people performing repetitious tasks on piece rates, working rather as if they were an adjunct to the machinery, there is now a much greater emphasis on teamwork, joint problem solving and greater variety and job interest. The simple repetitious processes are rapidly being automated. Packing the product into boxes, moving the product from one part of the line to another during assembly, screwing and welding components one to another are functions now being done not by people but by machines, extended automated lines and by robots. Machines are always going to be better at these processes than human beings as they will be more precise and more capable of dealing with the boredom of repetition. The most crucial question in each production process is the relative cost and, given the sharp reduction in unit cost of automated control equipment, more and more jobs of this kind are being done by machinery.

People are needed to watch over machinery, remedy any defects that develop in the machine lines and to keep an ever vigilant eye over the product flow and the quality of product being produced. The integration of design and management teams with the production controllers is a growing feature and many industrialists have experimented with removing the more obvious physical and grading barriers between the old white-collar and blue-collar staff as the jobs become less distinct. A production line specialist who may need to put right defects has to be able to work closely with, or supplement, the product design team when tackling generic errors. The marketing people need to liaise with production management to ensure that the 'just-in-time' principles can be reflected in the output for dispatch. There has to be a sense of collective achievement, often generated by the establishment of production and sales targets and by the clear publication of results hour by hour and day by day for all in the factory to see. This may be related to a combination of quality and output bonuses going to teams or to the whole of the staff.

Equally important in modern manufacturing is how a company handles innovation. There are two extreme models of how to innovate – one Japanese and the other Anglo-Saxon. The Japanese tend to proceed by incremental improvement. They take an existing product, pull it to pieces and think through how it would be possible to simplify or improve it. The number of working parts are examined to see if the same results could be achieved with fewer, thereby reducing the cost of assembly, the capacity for error and the cost of components. The range of features and performance of the product are looked at (taking a video machine, they might wish to extend the number of programmes that could be put into its memory or they may wish to improve the remote control system, the picture quality or sound output), as are the appearance of the final product and its compatibility with related TV and sound systems.

Their questioning would always be related to market research and market testing. They would look very carefully at customer preferences to see what they were keenest to have altered or improved in the product. The way in which Japanese designers have completely transformed the styling of their motor cars over the last twenty years illustrates how very successful this incremental process can be. Twenty years ago few would have bought a Japanese car in Britain for its stylistic quality, where-as now it is the Japanese motor manufacturers who have used the best design schools of the world to produce curvaceous coupes and clean-lined saloons. Their work on television and video has also brought rewards. They have moved their industry from being a down-market, cheaply-styled one to being an expensive up-market, high-quality one. The TVs and videos the Japanese are producing now are totally different from the products they were selling in the early 1970s. They have developed technically in a dramatic way, but much of the product improvement was done incrementally.

The Japanese also believe this cuts the risk of new-product launch. If they make frequent changes to their product each individual change does not represent a huge alteration. Customer research is followed by a period of market testing when they will see through experimental outlets and locations whether the customers like or dislike the improved facility they have designed or incorporated. It also gives them the chance to remedy any technical defects before launching the revised product more generally. Once they are satisfied the customers like it and it works they will launch the improved product through their global outlets. Meanwhile, teams are already working on the next possible improvement or series of improvements.

The Anglo-Saxon style can be crudely characterized as the mad-professor approach. Some of the best Anglo-Saxon inventions have come from individual moments of genius and clear thinking. The hovercraft, the jet engine, some pharmaceutical compounds, the small-wheeled bicycle were largely the work of one person's genius, or that of a small team, who had developed a more radical view of a problem traditionally solved in other ways. Such a system can make dramatic leaps forward, but it also carries with it substantial risks. There is a possibility that the designer is well ahead of public opinion and demand: there is rarely an immediate requirement for a revolutionary concept as it does not form part of people's perceptions of what they should or do need. There is the danger that the creative leap will be too great and that the first volume of a product will be dogged with a whole host of technical problems which will prejudice people's reception of the idea when it assumes a reality in hardware. Alternatively, the change could be so dramatic as to fuel a huge marketplace demand and could supersede the existing generations of the product from around the world. Keeping up with it becomes a problem.

Many large companies have tried to replicate the mad-professor approach to creativity and design with limited degrees of success. In practice most large companies are too bureaucratic to employ the individuals most likely to make the breakthroughs. As soon as an individual researcher is employed in a company and has to account for how he spends his time, writing long reports on how his thinking is developing and how it is contributing to the corporate goals, it is quite likely that he will lose that important radical spark or that he will be put off from working for the company altogether. There is also a general belief, in part reflected in the actuality that modern technology is so complicated, that it is beyond the capabilities of one person or a small team to make a real contribution and that modern mad-professor design has to be done by large targeted teams of researchers working away over a concentrated time period.

Sometimes these managed research teams do produce very good results. The case of the British pharmaceutical industry is a good one. It has assembled a large number of talented scientists in big research teams and asked them to resolve particular or general medical problems through the application of new chemical compounds. Exhaustive, well-documented and well-controlled research work has produced some remarkably good results, with Fisons, Glaxo and Beecham all making major contributions through the discovery and development of new compounds in a wide range of medical fields. In other areas the application of large amounts of money and large numbers of people has been less successful. Over many years the joint European Taurus project has worked hard to try to generate power from fusion as an alternative approach to nuclear fission. To date nothing has come of this research other than the expenditure of vast sums of money. European Taurus has yet to find its Crick and Watson capable of thinking through the basics in a way which permits a technical solution.

These simple caricatures of the Japanese and Anglo-Saxon research styles partially distort reality. In practice the large British and American company of today has elements of the Japanese style in it. It will have patient teams of designers and researchers thinking about what the market wants and going for some preliminary testing. Conversely, sometimes the Japanese will make a more dramatic change with the past. There is evidence that Japan now thinks it is a weakness that in its very strong industrial base it does not have the same capacity for basic science as America and Britain and that it has not always shown enough flair in radically changing designs. Japanese car manufacturers are now being more flamboyant and are prepared to make bigger creative leaps in the reskinning or redesigning of cars. At the same time British and American companies are doing more painstaking work on market testing to try to avoid the launch of wholly new products that backfire.

The dangers and advantages of the dramatic breakthrough can best be seen through the career of a talented entrepreneur like Clive Sinclair. Sinclair's ability to produce cheap electronic consumer products, especially calculators and small computers, transformed the way we looked at those products. When he tried something similar in the transport field through the launch of the Sinclair C5 the product flopped because it did not meet a need in the marketplace.

The importance of design can be seen in many industries. It is not good enough these days just to have a product that fits the purpose or works: it has to look good, be part of an image or style that people enjoy. Over the 1970s and 1980s the British ceramic tile industry, dominated by Pilkingtons and Johnsons, came under strong competitive attack from Italian and then, subsequently, Spanish and Brazilian tile manufacturers. For a long time leading experts in the tile industry felt that the competition was unfair, believing that the problems lay in subsidized gas, hidden industrial subsidies and other areas which were advantageous to the Italian and the Spanish producers. The natural reaction was to seek a government-related answer to the problem: was it not possible to impose tariffs, instigate anti-dumping practices, take up with the competition authorities, domestically or in Europe, the control of the surge of product into the UK market? Was it not possible to replicate some of the alleged benefits to the Italian and Spanish industries here at home?

In practice the problems of the British industry were more fundamental – a microcosm of the problems of many traditional British industries struggling to compete in a world where suddenly the competitors had greatly improved. There were two main strands to the Italian competitive advantage which had nothing to do with subsidy or unfair trade practices. The first was that the Italians had spent a great deal of capital on developing a new competitive tile industry which was far more modern than the British. The kiln transit times of the Italians were faster than the British, cutting the gas cost. The flowlines were straighter and the handling much reduced. The production process was much less energy and people intensive. The cost base of the Italian industry was in practice a lot lower, and was kept down by intense competition between a host of smaller producers, most of them equipped with the latest style of single-firing kilns.

The second competitive advantage was the Italian designs. It was the Italian industry which pioneered the move from 4¼ × 4¼ tiles to 6"×6", and who then went on to even larger sizes. It was the Italian industry which offered the public real choice away from the traditional geometric patterns and floral designs of the British ceramic industry to more adventurous features. It was the Italian industry which recreated the use of tiles of different sizes and shapes as part of the same pattern. It was the Italian industry which developed the idea of creating pictures through a grouping of ceramic tiles.

The British industry had to fight back and overhaul the Italians on their own terms. It had to spend a great deal of money on modernizing so that it too had processes that were not labour and energy intensive. It needed greater flexibility in its production runs, the ability to achieve high potting rates against a background of frequent changes of colourway and design. Above all, it needed the infusion of new design talent to capture the imagination of the European and world buyers of ceramic products.

The British industry had on its side one great resource which had been little used in the 1970s and early 1980s – its pattern book which included the work and creation of many years. At the height of Victorian prosperity British ceramic producers had been highly innovative, marketing a range of exciting designs and colours which were dominant in their day. The revival of some of those designs was part of the method of arresting the decline in market share. Experimentation with tiles of different sizes and shapes and the recreation of some of the Victorian ceramicists' successes did improve the image and acceptability of the British product.

The story of the ceramic industry, where the market came under progressive attack from new competitors abroad, is a common one in the British industrial experience. Something similar happened in textiles. Here some of the success of the competitors did come from cheap labour areas abroad where it was possible to undercut because the costs of the labour-intensive part of the textile operation could be slashed. Yet, whilst the British industry concentrated upon the dangers of cheap competition from the Far East, a bigger threat was materializing from the high-wage economies (based on superior design and better understanding of market characteristics) of the USA, Germany, France and Italy.

The French attacked the garment market drawing on the strength of their close links with the French fashion houses: they were able to project an image of style which attracted many customers. The Americans through heavy mechanization mounted an important challenge in thread, and cotton and woven fabric markets. The Germans and Italians also entered both the fabric and the garment marketplaces with a vengeance.

The British industry had to respond in the same way as the ceramic industry. It had to employ better designers, had to find market niches where its good designs and reputation could be strengthened and had to automate so that its mills and garment manufacturing was up to the best modern standards. In the early 1970s a trip through the textile lands of Lancashire and Yorkshire was like a visit to an industrial museum. There were still many two-and three-storey mill buildings with old machinery, highly labour intensive, turning out product that was gradually ageing. By the 1990s successful manufacturers were in modern, purpose-built, single-storey buildings with high-quality modern machinery which was far less labour intensive and capable of producing modern fibres and fabrics to high-quality tolerances.

In the service area Anglo-Saxons have been more creative and innovative than they have been in some traditional industries. Whilst the Japanese have taken the lead in car video and TV design it is the American and British banks who have provided the lead in innovative financing systems and the development of new financial technology. The leverage buy-out, privatization, syndicated loans, the management consultancy contract, and new methods of accounting are the areas that the creative talents of the West have concentrated on. It has created a new relationship between service and manufacturing, creating a new type of manufacturing conglomerate.

Where a traditional 1950s or 1960s multinational manufacturer would think it necessary to have the bulk of the facilities he needed in-house, the modern manufacturer is much more inclined to contract out or buy in the skills and services he needs. The carefully structured and layered corporations of 1960s global capitalism would have included lawyers, accountants, investment specialists, designers, engineering specialists, and the like, on the central payroll. Very often the thinking of the company was jealously guarded as a commercial secret and layer upon layer of management was employed to ensure coordination of the thoughts of one department with another and to ensure all conformed to a general collective company plan. A typical multinational of the 1960s was rather like a collective government still tries to be: it had to speak with one voice, have a common policy wherever it was speaking or acting throughout the world and try to ensure that all its actions were actually controlled and compatible with one another. Finance was a central function where the bank balances and cash flow of each subsidiary and operating unit had to be consolidated daily and the treasurer at the centre had to be sure of where he was. Important legal cases had to find their way up to group headquarters so that the company could come to an overall assessment of the risk of the law suits around the world. American multinational car companies expected design teams working on the Asian or European car to report to the American parent and although local variations were part of the marketing strategy the ultimate decision-making powers would lie at group HQ.

Whilst it is still true that a large multi-national corporation needs to have a corporate philosophy and some central controls, especially over its total financial risk, there has been some relaxation of the general proposition that everything has to be done in-house, tightly controlled and thought through for its compatibility with everything else that is going on. We now live in an age of cutting management structures and hiring in the skills needed to solve problems often on a piecemeal basis. A large industrial company in Britain or America would naturally turn to consultants to solve quite difficult problems that one would have thought the management themselves would wish to solve. If a subsidiary or factory unit is no longer operating successfully or profitably the natural reaction is to call in the consultants to do a thorough review and present conclusions to the board on whether the factory should be closed, fundamentally altered or improved by some other means. If a new product needs designing the group is as likely to turn to external design specialists as it is to strengthen its in-house team. If a difficult legal case crops up the telephone line to the best Wall Street or City lawyers will be red hot whatever the cost per minute. If the company needs to raise additional money for a project it will naturally turn to merchant or commercial bank advisers and City specialists.

The whole range of problems may well be contracted out. The works canteen is usually operated now by a specialist catering firm. The offices and factories are usually cleaned by an outside contractor; maintenance, site security and gardening would also usually be done by outside contractors. Large specialist conglomerates have built up a good source of revenue by supplying a range of business services to the main manufacturers.

It is this strong link between service and manufacturing which makes the debate about whether service or manufacturing creates wealth so bizarre. The modern manufacturing conglomerate cannot survive without a healthy service sector around it. If there is no one there to clean the factory, to design the advertisements, to assist in the design of the product, to solve difficult technical problems in the production process or to come up with conclusions on how to turn round an ailing subsidiary, how could the modern manufacturing conglomerate survive in anything like its current form? The service component in manufacturing is expanding all the time.

As a market becomes more mature so the service element naturally increases. In the heady pioneering days of explosive growth in computing the prime task was to sell as much hardware as possible. The business was designing, manufacturing and retailing computer boxes. Every large company needed to have a computer, then every medium-and small-sized company and then the home itself had to be invaded by the all-conquering product.

As the market expanded and developed so the service element started to become more important. People wanted more and more software so that they could use the computers they had been talked into buying for a greater range of functions. And as the market growth slowed, as more and more people had access to a computer, so the demand for replacement, repair and service built up at the expense of growth in demand for an entirely new product. In the space of a few years computer companies saw their business change: whereas seventy or eighty per cent was supplying new equipment, they moved to a situation where seventy per cent or more of turnover was in service and software.

Physical change on the ground mirrors the move from high-manufacturing to high-service content. In an advanced economy two-thirds of the employees work in what is defined as service sector activity and only one-quarter in manufacturing. As an economy develops so the basic engineering and assembly factories of the 1950s and 1960s shut down and are replaced by the new high-tech office factories of the 1990s. If steel can be produced by computer-controlled furnaces and poured into moulds by automated machinery and if motor cars can in no small measure be bolted and screwed together by robots, people have to move on to add value to the process in other ways. They do so by providing a better service to the customer and by devoting their energies to product improvement, design, marketing and repair and maintenance.

The service sector itself is now going through a technologically driven revolution. In the 1970s and 1980s big gains in employment came in the banks, building societies, thrifts, mutual funds, lawyer and accountancy firms. The demand seemed insatiable. As technology drove greater prosperity in the 1980s, as manufacturers were able to produce more and more with fewer and fewer people, so people had a surplus to spend, save and invest. Large sums of money needed routeing through financial intermediaries and the process of technology-led growth needed financing with more and more credit- and equity-based financing schemes. Especially in the Anglo-Saxon economies, the process of growth was rapid and was fuelled by a major expansion in credit and banking activity. Japan too throughout the 1980s enjoyed the blessings of cheap money and its banking system lent on ever larger sums, backed by the asset values created through the remorseless upward movement of Japanese share prices.

In the early 1990s things changed dramatically. Growth disappeared in the principal economies. Money was tightened to control inflation and the financial and service sector businesses faced a serious reduction in their revenues and profitability. This has triggered a major pursuit of technological and productivity improvement in the service sector itself. Banks and building societies in the United

Kingdom have been forced to ask whether they need the very large retail chains that they built up and whether there is room in each High Street for so many competing outlets, each representing substantial costs in property and staff. Back offices of financial service businesses are discovering that automation can replace large numbers of people and do the job efficiently and at lower cost. There is a tidal wave of technology replacing people in financial services in the 1990s similar to that which hit manufacturers in the 1980s. Many banks, building societies and thrifts are having to adopt a much more prudent attitude towards their lending, whilst at the same time making substantial write-offs for bad business opened in the headier days of the 1980s expansion. Large holes in bank balance sheets around the world lead to a much tighter regime for credit and further pressure to find cost reducing measures in the performance of business.

Management styles have evolved over the years through this period of change. In the United Kingdom the 1970s was the decade of management capitulation. Management found the problems too great. A hostile macro-economic climate combining high inflation, low-activity and low profitability generally made the management task difficult. In some cases it was made almost impossible by union intransigence and by the failure of the political process to get to grips with the endemic lack of competitiveness and confrontational attitudes within British society. The early 1980s saw the establishment of what people called macho management. The government was prepared to change the terms of the debate between management and unions and to provide a new legal framework which empowered union members at the expense of the union leadership and gave management an opportunity to reassert itself. The country became gripped by the new awareness that major changes had to be made in manufacturing. Whole types of industry had to be closed down as they were old-fashioned, no longer capable of producing products people wanted at a price they were prepared to pay. A new generation of industry had to be installed and this fundamental change took firmness and required the reassertion of management control.

Confrontation is not, however, a basis for creating a modern successful industry. Once the early battles were won it was possible for more enlightened businesses to understand the need to build a new style of industrial management founded on partnership, consultation, co-operation and a belief in quality. As the 1990s dawned this more collaborative management style was bringing great rewards to those companies that had adopted it. The major constraint upon its successful adoption throughout the economy is the ability of the educational and training system to produce the large number of high-quality individuals which such companies require to make their philosophy a success. Throughout this time period there were notable examples of companies that had always put quality and co-operation at the top of their agenda and with the advent of the 1990s there were still examples of companies where management was craven or too aggressive in the face of difficulty. None the less, the broad characterization of the three eras reflects the changing mood of the times and the evolving experience of companies generally. I visited a lot of companies in the 1970s and used to spend a great deal of time discussing what could be done, which then meant asking what the unions would accept. People both took it for granted that there was a right answer to their problems and that that right answer could not be implemented at once, if at all, because of the union difficulties. In the early 1980s the accent was always upon cost-cutting and major basic change, often to the detriment of thinking about the longer term and the need to spend on research and development, and on new products. Since the 1990s conversations have been much more about how to survive in a fast-changing market and how to harness the energies and talents of all of the employees. Only the best understand how competitive things have become and how rapidly a business has to improve to survive.

At the same time as massive sea-changes were washing over and through British industry the government took on the challenge of remodelling and renovating the public sector. In the post-war world the public sector was growing like topsy. The experience of total war between 1939 and 1945 had taught people to look to the government for solutions to practically every problem. The immediate enthusiasm in the post-war period for the National Health Service combined with the acceptance of the need for strategic planning in key industries that were to be brought into public ownership. These ideas influenced the mood of the nation from 1945 right through until the early 1980s. Socialists, planners and intellectuals were in agreement. Transport required a planned view: there needed to be a co-ordinated strategy between buses, trains, planes and motor cars. They were all agreed that the commanding heights of the economy like steel, energy, water and crucial engineering sectors were best planned or influenced, and preferably owned, by the state. Only the government could take an Olympian vision of how people should travel to work, how they should receive their energy, how much water they should need to drink. They thought it was better the government should own all these businesses and oversee them properly.

The popularity of the idea was based both upon a general principle and upon a specific success. It was natural to look to someone else to blame and to someone else for leadership. The government, thanks to the charismatic leadership of Sir Winston Churchill, had made a vital contribution to the winning of the war. The underarmed and rather chaotic defence system of the late 1930s was transformed into a tough, fighting machine, capable of producing a large number of highly effective aeroplanes, ships, tanks and small arms so that a significant contribution to the allied war effort could be made. Whilst it may have been the might and strength of America that was the eventually critical factor in the allied victory, no one doubted that the resolve, determination and flashes of technical genius and bravery of the British people were equally important in seeing the allies through.

If the government could make such a major contribution to winning a war, uniting a nation against its enemies, surely it would find the challenges of peacetime that much easier? If we could beat Hitler, we could beat poverty, ill-health, bad housing and unemployment. The scourges of all previous eras could be wiped away with a little more concerted government planning, a little more concerted government investment and a little more public sector effort.

I have yet to meet politicians of any major party who would rather the sick were uncared for, who would rather that people lived in poor housing or who would rather see people unemployed. There is a great deal of unanimity across the political spectrum in most advanced democracies that ill-health, poverty, bad housing and joblessness are wrongs that should be beaten by any means possible. The problem is that no country has yet found a means for the government to take on and overcome all these scourges in a way that lasts and is satisfactory. The argument is about means rather than ends; it is also about feasibility and how perfectible the human condition might be.

The first post-war government was elected to provide answers based on this intelligible and readily acceptable principle that responsibility could be passed to ministers. The government would be able to win because it had won the war. The attractiveness of the principle was buttressed by the popularity of the National Health Service amongst politicians of both major parties. The single most important reason why people looked to the government for an answer was that it backed the principle of the free provision of medical and dental care for all those who needed it. One of the most frightening features of life for all those on low incomes in the pre-war period had been the dread of the doctor's or dentist's bill when they needed treatment. Everyone wanted access to the best treatment possible for those family members who were in pain or suffering. Yet the pre-war system meant that if you did not have the money you had to be extremely careful before committing yourself to a doctor's visit.

The Labour Party showed great resolve and energy in putting the principle of free care into effect. The Conservative Party had accepted the principle but did not wish to ally to it the nationalization of the hospitals, which became the important difference between the two main political protagonists. The early days of the National Health Service were a great success. Many teeth were drilled and filled, many pairs of reading spectacles dispensed and people grew to love their access to free health care. It soon posed an insuperable problem for the Labour government. Far from there being a temporary surge in treatment as everyone caught up and then a sharp falling off as everyone got healthier, the demand just rose and rose. Labour discovered that if something is free its demand can rise exceedingly rapidly. They discovered that you never win with health for if someone is healthy today thanks to preventive or curative treatment he may be even less healthy tomorrow having lived to an older age. The Labour government felt itself forced into the introduction of prescription charges and charges for spectacles and false teeth, which split the party and led to resignations. But the principle of payment for some items of service and treatment was there to stay and, subsequently, has never been altered by either Conservative or Labour administrations. None the less, the largely free health service had struck a chord with the British people and was one of the main reasons why many were prepared to give the benefit of the doubt or have faith in government solutions to other difficult problems like transport and housing.

In the housing field the answer was to have massive government investment programmes in so-called slum clearance. As the 1950s and 1960s developed the political pressure to speed up the process intensified. In order to hit the ever more exacting targets of the number of dwelling units to be supplied, councils and architects turned to the construction of partially prefabricated, rapidly erected, tower blocks. Some were infatuated with the notions of Le Corbusier. Some just thought it was a good way of making money, to stick up large blocks of flats quickly and relatively cheaply in order to share in the government honey pot. In the process whole communities of streets with pleasant brick houses were bulldozed simply because they lacked a coat of paint or the installation of central heating. In the transport field the 'answer' was the nationalization of buses, railways and airlines. The creation of monopoly carriers for each type of transport enabled politicians to plan centrally, to show largesse in dishing out subsidy and investment money and to control the standard of service offered to the public. Nationalized BR saw through a huge investment programme to switch from steam to diesel or different types of electric traction. The nationalized bus industry absorbed subsidy to keep routes going that had been in existence for many years. The airline also built up heavy losses. If the businesses lost money the answer was to give them more subsidy. Over the years millions and millions of pounds were poured in, but no single main new railway line was constructed, the numbers of bus riders plummeted and the airline lost out to overseas competition in those areas where competition was permitted.

The same notion that the government could and should provide dominated in the municipal, and then nationalized, water industry. Water, they said, was so important and the control of its quality so critical to life that it had best be entrusted to the public sector. When the industry came to be privatized in the late 1980s it was discovered that there was a massive backlog of investment that needed seeing to and that the standards of cleanliness in our streams and rivers left a great deal to be desired. In energy the government's tentacles extended through electricity and gas into oil and the coal industry. The might of government was used to preserve an important relationship between the British coal industry and the electricity generating industry, with the industry primarily building 660 megawatt coal stations despite their lack of thermal efficiency. Government clout was also used to drive through a nuclear power industry where large sums of money were spent on the development of different styles of nuclear reactor, and considerable political capital was spent on offsetting the environmental pressures against nuclear construction.

The dream that government could and should provide, and would improve lifestyles as a result, did not turn easily into reality. Whilst the public admired the pledge of access to health care free at the point of use they did not similarly back the principles that underlay the other public sector initiatives. They did not like their nationalized trains and buses very much and spent all their energies earning enough money to buy a car in order to travel by private means. Neither rail nor public road transport could compare with the ubiquitous success of the motor car. The public were not very enamoured with their nationalized fuel monopolies, finding them often unresponsive to customer complaints and demands and disliking the frequent price increases which they imposed. The public were not over pleased at the lack of cleanliness in the streams and rivers and grew tired of hosepipe bans and other interruptions to supply whenever there was a warm summer. Above all the public did not like the huge council estates built in the 1950s and 1960s in the name of slum clearance. Some of these large blocks disfigured our cities, discouraging investors and private house-builders from locating adjacent to them and causing tensions on the estates themselves.

The Conservative administration elected in 1979 decided to change all this. The missing ingredients in the government mix were competition and choice. If individuals had no choice of which transport they could use, of how they could buy their energy, of the style of flat or house they would be allocated, they felt alienated by the whole process. If there was no competition in the provision, if everything was produced by a monopoly, there were no pressures to provide better service, to innovate, to provide better answers, to be attentive to the customer's needs. The problem with a monopoly transport operator is that you cannot go down the road to get a better service. In consequence people took to their cars instead. The problem with monopoly energy provision is that if you do not like the price and terms of supply you do not get any energy. The problem with monopoly council housing is that if they are only offering flats in vertical villages you have to take a flat in a vertical village even though you would prefer a bungalow. If you fall foul of the providers of these services there is no escape. Your lifestyle may be badly affected because you dared to cross the local council housing officer or the local manager of the electricity business.

The Conservative idea of choice and ownership matched in popularity Labour's implementation of the pledge of health care free at the point of use. The promise that people if they chose could buy their own council house or flat and could then exercise their choice over how to decorate and improve it turned out to be a runaway success. The biggest privatization of them all, that of the housing stock, was very popular with the British people. The privatization of the large businesses was much more contentious, although many people became shareholders and attitudes did change. The transformation brought by the introduction of competition and choice has been wideranging, and there are still many more ramifications to be thought through and developed. Whereas a monopoly industry would only build coal stations that were dirty and lacked thermal efficiency, the privatized, more competitive industry is building power stations that are fifty per cent or more fuel efficient and as a result much cleaner. Technology itself did not change: management reassessed its attitudes to technology as a result of the competition. Whereas the nationalized industry kept quiet about water quality standards and the state of our rivers, the new privatized industry is subject to much greater scrutiny, regulation and the publication of performance against targets. Massive investment is now underway to try to improve water quality. Similarly, the nationalized railway did not build a single new line, but, as the railway emerges into an era of competition, already a number of schemes have come forward for major new rail investments which would provide links across London and from London to the Channel ports. The nationalized bus industry failed to see the full scope for exploiting motorway coach travel, whilst the deregulated privatized industry has established many successful new routes plying the motorway system of Britain.

Privatization of commercial and trading activities took up a great deal of political time in the 1980s. In the 1990s we must turn to improving some of the core services of government itself. Government has to learn from the experiences of the private sector. If the private sector is moving towards much-reduced management hierarchies and is challenging the notion that everything can or should be done in-house, so too the government should ask itself how much of its work should be done in-house and whether there are benefits to be gained from competition and contracting out. If the private sector is discovering that quality, flexibility, teamwork and co-operation are some of the watchwords of modern success, maybe the government too should be thinking along similar lines.

Much of government is a series of clerical factories. The largest employers in the government service are the revenue departments who collect money and the benefit departments who distribute much of that money back out again. It takes almost 100,000 people to collect VAT, excise, income and capital taxes. It takes around 80,000 people to distribute pensions and income support. These are crucial functions given the larger amounts of income that are redistributed through this system. Around four of every ten pounds earned in the economy is taken by the public sector. Around one in every three pounds taken from the tax-payer is given back through benefits.

This large operation can be automated and made more customer-friendly. The benefits distribution has been converted into a single agency under a chief executive. Government is trying to segregate the management of programmes from policy and ministerial responsibility. Whilst it is entirely right that a minister should be responsible to Parliament and the electorate for who receives benefit, how much tax is raised and for the general thrust of the policy that underlies the redistribution, it is important that the day-to-day implementation of the policy and the enforcement of the rules should be properly managed by professionals who are in turn accountable. The new agency is busily setting itself targets for the turnround of benefit claims, for courtesy of customer treatment and for accuracy in determining entitlement. In each of these areas there was considerable scope for improvement and the new agency is already achieving a better standard.

Numerous other activities of government can also be segregated and established as separate executive agencies. A separate agency responsible for receiving annual reports and accounts and annual returns from each registered limited company in the United Kingdom and responsible for keeping lists of directors has been set up called Companies House. Its creation as an executive agency led to the establishment of targets for dealing with incoming documentation and the processing of enquiries. Before it had agency status it took around a month before the incoming documents were placed upon the file for the public to gain access. The turnround times for public enquiries both in the reading rooms and by post were also unsatisfactory. Setting targets and managing against them soon led to dramatic improvement, with documents being turned round in less than a week and maximum waiting times established for people going into the offices or applying by post for access to records. Far from this being more expensive, it was discovered that efficiency and productivity were connected. If you handle the post on the day it arrives you need neither a stock room, nor more complicated control systems, nor people carrying the post backwards and forwards from stock to the postroom to be opened and processed. If you answer enquiries promptly you do not get so many queries and mistakes and complaints that are costly to handle.

Improved management across the public sector has been delivered in a number of agencies. Everything from the Queen Elizabeth Conference Centre through the Insolvency Service to the Radio Communications Agency have been suitable cases for treatment. Around half of the central government core staff have been transferred into agencies, and now have higher morale and a greater sense of what is expected of them. They are participating in a big drive to serve the customer and to understand his needs. Placing customers first was an important element in the transformation of the nationalized industries when they passed into the private sector. Persuading government to understand it too had customers and they should be treated well was an important first step in beginning the transformation of government service delivery. Some in the nationalized industries in the 1970s disputed the very idea that they had customers. They thought there was a thing called public service which was more amorphous and did not entail dedicated customer service in the way in which a competitive commercial business does. A similar culture shock needed to be administered to central government, which had long held the belief that it somehow was above the *mêlée* of the marketplace and that it responded to virtues different from those of being polite to customers and trying to satisfy their needs.

It is true that some elements of government are different from elements of a commercial competitive business. Many branches of government are not trying to make a profit. Some elements of government are concerned with regulating and enforcing the law rather than with pleasing the people they are handling. But this is to obfuscate the central issue that much of government is about providing service and that service should be as well provided and as sensitive to the needs of the users as any service delivered by competitive business.

If people are making use of the local housing office, benefit office, employment service or trade and industry services they should expect a level of interest and support from the counter staff and advisers comparable to that which they would get from a private sector business. They should also expect the continuation of the long-standing public sector's virtues of honesty, integrity and fairness.

Government in its role as regulator does have to be above the *mêlée* and does have to ensure that it enforces things fairly even if this means upsetting those who come before it in search of judgement or redress. It is not possible for a regulator to be universally popular: indeed, it could be undesirable, implying that he was too accommodating to the crooks and cheats as well as to the law abiding citizens. A regulator should instead aim to be respected. There is no excuse for a regulator to be sloppy about those elements of customer service where normal standards should apply. If someone is applying for planning permission the regulator should be friendly in all his dealings with the applicant. He should be courteous and timely in his responses and clear in guiding the individual through the system. Whilst he may well have to turn the applicant down because his application is outside the terms of the local plan, he should do so clearly, fairly and in good time so that the applicant knows where he stands. Even the police handling potential criminals can and do distinguish between the customer service elements and the regulatory and enforcement elements. The police are under a duty to explain to people their rights and wherever possible to be civil and not to use force unless they have to. However, their attention to customer service should not extend to letting criminals off because the criminals find being detained inconvenient.

At the heart of local authorities and central government lies policy making. This is often thought to be the most important element of all and is a jealously guarded secret of a handful of politicians and a number of senior officers or officials primarily concerned with the process of policy formation. Many argue that this process must remain firmly within the hands of staff on the core payroll, yet even here we see that practices are already evolving and changing despite the absence of any strongly articulated policy to do so. In many crucial policy areas now consultants are hired for a specific job. They play a big part in assessing public opinion on a range of issues through opinion polling and in mounting a series of options when the policy process has determined on a general aim. Consultants have done well out of both the privatization programme and an intractable range of social problems confronting Labour and Conservative administrations in local government as well as central government itself. Local government has been very reluctant when discussing the idea of compulsory contracting out of a number of core activities, yet something like it is already happening as individuals, communities and councils decide to hire in or contract out policy work.

What then will the new public sector world be like? It will be more productive and efficient than the old public sector world could ever be. Jobs in it will be more challenging and exciting because there will be some competitive pressure and because individuals will need to satisfy their customers and clients. There will be many fewer direct employees in Whitehall and Townhall and many more working for the government and the council under contract. There will be a greater range of ideas coming into the system and more openness in debating them because the process of policy formation will be more diffuse. The natural response of government to the loss of direct power over some elements of research and policy formation should be to respond to the public wish for a more open debate anyway. Democratic governments should wherever possible proceed by issuing consultation documents to encourage public response and to compel ministers and senior officials to enter into free discussion with interest groups and those with a specialist knowledge before any policy is finalized. Drawing on a range of private sector skills in policy formation can strengthen the process as different groups perceive and approach problems from different perspectives.

It does not mean that the size of government will necessarily be smaller. That is a political decision driven by the community's sense of how much it wishes the government to provide. For example, during the period of wholesale privatization of the nationalized industries the overall size of government continued to grow through the development of new policies particularly in health and social services. During the development of the enabling council the size of the local authority sector continued to grow in terms of the total amount of money it was spending and the amount of service it was delivering, despite the sharp change in arrangements. The numbers of employees directly employed will fall, but the numbers whose lives depends in whole or part upon public sector money marshalled from tax-payers and the financial markets may not decline at all unless forced to do so by political decisions.

For this reason opposition parties in the UK are coming to see that the enabling council or the enabling government concept is not necessarily a Conservative or right-wing notion. It has the capacity to deliver the range of services at the price and quality people want whatever their political judgements about that range of services. Those on the Left who want more and more provided by the state could still organize that through the enabling framework, one which many of them now believe sounder than the large directly employed monopolies pre-dating it. The cries for automatic renationalization and the recreation of monopolies have been more muted in recent years. Opposition politicians have concentrated on criticizing government policies for not introducing enough competition and choice into some of the areas that are now being treated in this way.

The dangers in this scheme lie in the capacity of the public sector to negate some of the benefits by elaborate and over-complicated procedures for tendering and compliance monitoring. Some have tried to defeat the object of competitions by producing rules and methods of analysis that tend to favour the in-house bidder. Some have offset the benefits by overcomplicated procedures and requirements that mean too much bureaucracy with insufficient service delivered. There will be times when it is cheaper and better to employ the people yourself on your own payroll and ask them to get on with the job, and there will be times when the marketplace does not provide a sufficiently competitive response because the area of treatment is new or there is some imperfection in the offer of service in that area.

These are matters which can be watched. A raft of rules to impede or prevent anticompetitive practices is being introduced. As the private sector adjusts to the new world so the range and competitiveness of the marketplace improves. In the areas with the best competitive response, like building management and refuse collection, the savings from contracting-out can be substantial, often more than ten per cent. Wherever contracting out is tried it leads to some savings: that is inherent in the process as if there are no savings no contract is let.

Contracting out and quality can be natural allies. Critics of the process like to say that it is a way of reducing quality, but all sensible contracts include quality clauses. Often councils and governments make a conscious decision to concentrate on quality in the new arrangements, whereas when they were delivering through a directly employed work-force they had not bothered about it. As a result, the quality can rise.

The UK's introduction of the Citizens' Charter, backed up by the introduction of competition and choice, offers the world as important and challenging a model for reform of government services as privatization has done for government-owned trading bodies. The Charter is based upon the principles of openness, reporting and auditing. Users of services are told what they should expect by way of a general service quality, and offered specific pledges concerning the handling of their supply or care. They are told how the service has performed each year against the general standards and have a right to complain if their specific cases are not adequately dealt with; ultimately, they have the right to compensation as well as rectification if a mistake has been made. To deliver public bodies are having to establish targets internally, slim down their chains of command, improve their rapport with customers and put work out to tender.

Charter principles lie behind the pledge to cut the price of telephone calls, to guarantee telephone installation times, to cut the time taken to process licence applications and a host of other improvements. The Charter revolution is evolutionary and has a long way to go. It is driven by competition and choice, by putting customers first.

THREE

A Sense of Community

The headlong rush towards global capitalism is making people more and more conscious of the local, the particular, and the comprehensible. As the Balkans plunges into war, as the great powers meet around the table to hammer out a new round of the General Agreement on Tariffs and Trade, as global businesses develop world products, so the typical British Member of Parliament's post-bag is increasingly filled with issues about individual streets, houses, pavements and animals. At the height of the Gulf War there was greater correspondence on sow tethers used for keeping pigs; during the course of discussions on Yugoslavia there were letters about the trade in live horses and ponies, and there is too a steady stream of correspondence about whales, badgers and planning problems at street and village level.

People naturally seek to belong to a community they can understand, and they then expect to be able to exert some control over it. The noisy neighbour, the housing developer who ruins the view over adjacent fields, the negligent or cruel dog owner, the foreign whalers seen on television screens, the local council that fails to maintain the footpaths: these are the villains of everyday life that have an intensity which the broader issues of war and peace and economic development cannot hope to match.

People have several different senses of community. Individuals are driven primarily by their own feelings, ambitions and fears, but many work closely within a family which at its best is mutually supportive and at its worst exerts considerable influence over the individual because of the tensions and conflicts it generates. Most people have some family sense of community, and will draw many of their ideas, their strengths and their weaknesses from that family background. The next strongest loyalty is usually to the village or town in which the individual lives. In the case of very large towns or cities the loyalty may be strongest for that part of the conurbation in which the individual lives or works. There may be a separate loyalty to the street or a small area within the village. When one villager asks another where he lives, the answer given would usually consist of the name of the street or general area – on the green or close to the church. Such a description may have more than geographical significance. There may be a residents' society. The residents may have to come together to fight a planning application or work for some improvement in their local services. The village as a whole will see its outward civic expression through the chairman of the parish council and the parish meetings, open to all those with an interest in parish affairs. The village will also have a sense of community through shared membership of the same church, support for village teams of football and cricket, and the development of more informal communities through pubs, clubs and societies.

In a large urban area like London loyalty is more commonly drawn to the borough or parish. Some of the boroughs are amalgamations of more than one settlement, as with the London Borough of Southwark which comprises at least three distinct places – Dulwich, Peckham, and Bermondsey. People living in Bermondsey or Dulwich are unlikely to say Southwark when asked where they come from, even though it boasts a cathedral and they share a common borough council. Bermondsey has its own separate tradition, a riverside, dock-based tradition. Dulwich is more mixed with substantial tree-lined areas and middle-class detached housing. In the centre of Peckham lies Southwark town hall which, to the south, is surrounded by the tower-block redevelopments of the 1960s that are different in style from Dulwich.

The smaller and more compact the town or city, the stronger the sense of loyalty tends to be to the single place. Brought up in Canterbury, I always felt part of Canterbury, whether at school to the north of the city or at home to the south. In contrast, people lying in the cluster of settlements around the edges of Birmingham or Manchester would wish wherever possible to differentiate between their own place of residence and the greater city.

Defining the city is one of the most difficult problems for electoral and local government purposes. The planners believe that the city should be as broad as possible taking in the outlying suburbs and settlements so that a more general planning judgement can be made about transport links and the location of new industry and housing. Yet those who go to live in the suburbs and villages coalescing around the edge of our great cities often go there in order to live in a different place from the city itself. They value their hedgerows and their green fields, the narrow green belts that divide them from the conurbation proper. They fight in many ways to prevent their identity being absorbed into the city and try to keep many of the features of village life going that were defined and developed in a former agricultural age. People feel happier with a village green and some common land, even once the need to graze their animals on it has long disappeared. Urban dwellers are coming to see farmers as rural gardeners on a grand scale, manicuring the fields, hedgerows and trees so that we can all enjoy the feeling of extended parkland and garden beyond the city edges. People's choice of house styles and the work of developers reflects the English historical romanticism at the heart of many people's feelings. In my constituency a new town of seven thousands houses was constructed. Some of the most popular house styles were those that picked up the Tudor tradition of half-timbered housing, even though the half-timbering was an external adornment to a brick-built house. Understandably people wanted something different, something more than just a simple brick box, and they wanted something that looked back as well as forward, that was part of the English tradition.

The shires and counties of England have a long-standing place in the story of our island. From the early days of parliaments, knights of the shires were elected to represent people's views. Since the late nineteenth century, when the great county councils were established, the county has often been used as a means of government. The Queen is represented in each county by a lord lieutenant who carries out civic and ceremonial duties on her behalf.

Counties and shires, some perhaps more than others, engender great loyalties, intense support and a sense of community (one obvious manifestation of this is in county sports). Woe betide the man who tries to move the border between Lancashire and Yorkshire. It was tried in the 1973 reform of local government and many signs had to be replaced as people, unprepared to accept the change in territory, took to removing the new ones. Whilst Lancastrians and Yorkists no longer fight the Wars of the Roses, to this day Lancastrians wear the red rose of Lancaster and Yorkshiremen are fiercely proud of their county.

The 1973 reforms of local government showed how difficult it is to change people's underlying sense of community. Managerial criteria were laid down for sweeping changes to the map of England and Wales. Each county was to have around 500,000 people, and each district to have 75–100,000 people. Hundreds of smaller councils were to be demolished so that services could be provided on a bigger scale with resulting economies expected. Herefordshire was combined with Worcestershire as a new joint county, Rutland and Huntingdonshire were removed from the map, too small for the modern era, and the large cities were lumped together with the villages and towns that lay beyond them in large new urban counties in Humberside, Cleveland and Avon. Merseyside, West Midlands, Greater Manchester, and Tyne and Wear also brought together numerous urban centres.

People did not take kindly to being bossed around by management theorists and planners. The new counties found it difficult to engage the loyalty of their resident population. There are many people still using Huntingdonshire and Middlesex on letters and cards sent through the Post Office. People in Berkshire are still not entirely reconciled to having lost the White Horse of Berkshire to Oxfordshire, and some people in North Somerset still find it difficult to express support for new Avon.

The theory behind the changes was as questionable as planners' understanding of human nature. The idea that larger units would be more economic and more accountable did not always prove to be true. Larger units meant employing more people in the hierarchy at higher salaries. The creation of both counties and districts to serve the same area often confused people about who was supplying the service, and in some cases led to unnecessary duplication or expensive rows between the different levels of government. Far from settling the government of England for one hundred years, the 1973 reforms left many questions unanswered and many tensions latent in the system. Large councils tend to have large ambitions, and those which represent differing communities that do not feel they belong together encounter higher spending pressures than those that represent natural communities. In some districts or counties, where different towns and areas were pulled together, the councils often found that those parts away from the centre and away from the principle town which contained the district or county headquarters pressed for more and more expenditure. They felt neglected and left out and, however much was spent, they resented the main town. Many districts and counties reproduced the problem across the Scottish border, where the Scottish minority within the United Kingdom claim to be hard done by when it comes to the distribution of resources from remote London, yet in practice they receive substantially more than England as the government attempts to reassure them and to compensate.

All these issues are being re-examined. The 1993–98 Structure Review of local government starts from the two propositions that good borders must define natural communities, and that where possible local government should be conducted through a single council rather than a multiplicity.

Each layer of government has a tendency to dislike most the layer just above it, and to appeal or ally with the layer two away from it. Large parishes often compete with districts to attend the same function, to influence the same planning issue, to establish the leadership of their communities. Districts and counties have been known to antagonize one another, and counties have sometimes seen their role as providing a rival centre of government to Whitehall. Relationships between national capitals and Brussels have at times flared into disputes.

Alliances between levels of government tend to be at one remove. Counties and parishes are inclined to unite. Districts ask central government to look after them, whilst the European Community sees regions wherever they exist as natural allies for its policies. Governing bodies seek power, and they often perform pincer movements on other levels of government. The idea that there should be regional government in the United Kingdom could be damaging to county, city or rural district authorities, taking power away from them and imposing new burdens on them. Yet it is regional government that the European Community is currently looking for and it is regional government that some parties in the domestic political debate are currently suggesting.

Once upon a time England was governed as several different kingdoms – Wessex, Mercia, Northumbria – but it would be curious today to hear someone say they were Mercian. That would be an archaism way beyond the usual strong sense of tradition. The media may have succeeded in creating Essex man, but they would be hard pressed to resuscitate Wessex woman.

Scotland and Wales are another matter. The constitutional arrangements within Britain are flexible with different administrative structures where history, tradition and a sufficiently strong sense of cultural identity require it. In Scotland a very separate identity has been maintained since the Union of 1707. Scotland has its own legal system, its own education system and its own churches. There is a separate department of state running Scottish affairs, led by the Secretary of State and his ministers, and in the House of Commons a Select Committee on Scottish affairs has been established. Scottish views are expounded in a forthright way by elected representatives to the UK Parliament.

The question of whether Scotland should be self-governing or have its own Parliament or executive within the UK in order to give fuller expression to its distinctive identity has been widely debated over the past twenty or more years. In a referendum in 1979 on proposals for a Scottish Assembly, only one-third of those entitled to vote gave their support. More recently, only around a fifth of the votes cast in Scotland at the general election of 1992 were for the SNP which wants total separation for Scotland. The Conservative Party campaigned strongly against a Scottish Parliament believing that all the opposition party proposals posed a threat to the maintenance of the UK as a united nation. The Conservative Government's commitment to the Union is unequivocal: so too is its wish to reflect Scotland's distinctive traditions and interests in the way it is governed.

Wales too has a special identity within the United Kingdom. Wales is a principality rather than a kingdom. It placed kings on the English throne earlier than the Scots. The House of Tudor received a better press than the House of Stuart. Welshmen abounded at the court of Queen Elizabeth I. The patterns of settlement are very different. The largest part of the Welsh population is along the southern coastal strip from Newport through Cardiff to Swansea and its valleys behind. Many of these people, while rooting for

Wales, do not spend effort on portraying England as the 'old enemy'. Though some speak Welsh, the proportion which does so is small. Many are the families of comparatively recent inward migrants from the time of rapid industrialization in the nineteenth and early twentieth centuries.

A different spirit is alive in the Welsh-speaking parts, concentrated largely on the rural areas of West and North Wales. As in England, the old small counties are remembered with affection, but several super counties created in 1972–73 attracted little support and there has been persistent pressure for reversion to the older pattern. In future, Wales will be governed at the local level by units closer to its feeling of natural community based upon the former counties, different valleys and main towns. In 1964 a separate Welsh Office was created, and Wales now also has its own local government structure. The passion behind Welsh nationalism, mainly in the rural areas, is less strong in industrial South and North-East Wales where trade and employment flows across the border.

It does not follow that England should be similarly divided up into large regional units. It is never wise for governments to seek to take away all of the local and national differences that characterize people and places. Planners may have logic on their side, but rarely do they carry the heart as well as the mind. The absence of an easy translation of 'nooks and crannies' into French shows the difficulty.

Regional identity is elsewhere in England. The European Community believes it has found it in its NUTs regions, the planners in their planning regions. Planners have tried to create regions by defining large blocks of the country described by the points of the compass. I live thirty-five miles to the west of London and am designated by planners to be part of the South-East. So too is someone who lives 120 miles from me in East Kent, someone who lives on the south coast, and someone who lives in Bedford. The planners see some commonality which those living in Newbury, Luton and Dover fail to notice. Kent is very different from Berkshire. East Kent is a picturesque patchwork of hop gardens and fruit farms looking both to Calais and London. Rural Berkshire consists of undulating, cow-grazing countryside with pretty villages and new hi-tech developments spreading westwards along the Thames Valley.

The contrasts are equally sharp between Sheppey and Southampton. When asked where they came from people rarely answer by saying the South-East. They would usually refer to their county or town. As a 'South-East' MP I have never once had a letter from anyone suggesting that there should be a South-East government or that their sense of South-Eastern-ness is being frustrated. Planners see the South-East as London's commuter belt, yet people commute to London from Bristol and the Midlands, as well as from Surbiton and Southend, and at the edge of the South-East few look to London.

It might be thought that the planners have a better point in the north of England. When Southerners travel north they are made to feel different, with Northerners stressing that their visitors come from the South. They like to jest at how ill equipped we are to deal with the rigours of the Northern climate or the bracing Northern commonsense views. The Pennines, once a major obstacle to travel especially in winter, still divides the North in two. The division between Yorkshire and Lancashire reinforces the barrier of the Pennines. The Wars of the Roses rallied people to the alternative banners of the House of York and the House of Lancaster, brought the red roses into battle with the white; it underpins divisions between the two counties to this day. The attempt to create an economic region bigger than the old Lancashire has been less successful. Travelling south from Lancashire into Merseyside, attitudes change. Liverpudlians have a special sense of identity and may not feel Lancastrian even though Liverpool was part of historic Lancashire.

The division of the centre of the country into the East and West Midlands has been no more successful. The beautiful towns and villages in a county like Warwickshire – Stratford-on-Avon, Henley-in-Arden and so on – have little in common with Birmingham, the heartland of the British engineering and manufacturing industry. The division between the East and West Midlands is more one of convenience than actuality, scarcely reflected in the attitudes of people or in the topography. Taken all in all, the creation of economic planning regions has not struck a chord with the peoples of England. The maypole music of rural English communities is more melodic than the computer notes of the planning regions.

Some might argue that to create true regional areas in England it is important to go back further in our past to a time when England was not a united country. It is still possible to sketch on the map the rough outlines of Wessex, Mercia, Northumbria, the kingdoms of more than a thousand years ago which were unified into one following the Norman Conquest. The strongest claim to an individual historical regional identity must lie with the most powerful and most successful of those kingdoms, Wessex, and perhaps this is reflected in the survival of the name by the Wessex Water Company. Living in Wessex and being conscious of its long historical tradition, however, I have never met anyone who spontaneously says he comes from the place. More than a thousand years have led to a failing of the memory and an erosion of that sense of identity. There has been no recent upsurge in Wessex nationalism!

In England, London is the best example of an area being controlled by special arrangements made on a regional basis. Some people see a separate London identity covering the area of the old Greater London Council, which was disbanded in the 1980s despite campaigns to keep it going. Any discussion with people from outer London demonstrates that loyalties are much stronger to those local boroughs, towns or villages which have become absorbed into the large urban area than to the conurbation itself. Recently on a visit to Richmond I noticed the Mayor quite carefully say to me, 'I presume you are returning to London shortly.' When I asked her about her choice of words she agreed that they felt Richmond, which used to have a postal address in Surrey, was outside London. She accepted that Richmond was now an outer London borough and that many people travelled from Richmond into the centre of the urban area for their jobs, but none the less felt it still had an important separate sense of place. People from Wimbledon, Sutton, Croydon and many other areas feel the same.

Inner London is different. Many from Hackney, Lambeth, Wandsworth and Westminster see themselves as Londoners. Yet the focus of London life is still as complicated as the pattern of settlements which make up the conurbation. London has two centres: the City of Westminster and the City of London. The City preserves the old form of nonpolitical Common Councillors and aldermen with a prestigious mayoralty. Westminster has a much bigger local population and contains within its perimeters the political capital of the nation. The Government has established a cabinet committee to take those decisions that need a London-wide view (transport, planning and development are just three areas which require such a perspective). The private forum on London will promote the metropolis as an international centre for business, trade and inward investment.

There are those who claim that certain things can best be done at a regional level by regional government. It is one thing to identify a natural community, as we can do in Scotland and Wales, but quite another to find a government function that is so successfully handled at a regional level in England to justify the imposition of an additional layer of government burdens upon people. Natural communities can survive without expression through government. As we have seen the new districts and county councils created in 1974 did not succeed in destroying the sense of loyalty to Bristol in Avon or to Herefordshire in the combined county of Hereford and Worcester. These loyalties can live on and can be expressed in other ways.

Advocates of regional government in England usually wish to see the regions take on a variety of tasks in strategic planning, transport and economic development. Those arguing the case often do not appreciate the difference between an island nation and a continental one. Major highways and railways are best planned strategically at a national level. Roads in Scotland and Wales remain the responsibility of the Secretaries of State for Scotland and Wales but their position within the unitary UK cabinet allows for the full co-ordination of the planning of cross-border routes.

Britain is bounded by the natural frontier of the sea. Breaking planning up into artificial planning regions may have administrative convenience for officials, but it creates its own border problems which would get in the way of sensible strategic planning if those boundaries had electoral significance. Major strategic road and rail routes tend to cut right across these artificial boundaries. If such decisions have to be made it is more sensible to make them for the nation as a whole than to leave them to regional governments who between them might end up with incoherent answers.

I estimate that eleven regional governments in Britain would need at least £200 million for staff and offices. They would then undoubtedly wish to spend additional sums on social provision, industrial support and transport, probably leading to extra spending of more than £4,000 million or 2p on income tax quite quickly. The Greater London Council, a redundant upper-tier authority, spent £1,500 million alone in its last full year of operation – more than 1p on income tax at that time.

They would antagonize local authorities, compete with the national government and bring little of value for people. Countries with land frontiers are in a rather different position. People travelling south across the Danish border or travelling west or south across the Dutch or Belgian borders want to know that there are equivalent standards of rail and road transport on either side. There may be a case for some co-ordination of national efforts and some joint planning. There could even be a case for joint planning of settlements, as the construction of a large town on the edge of a land border would involve strain and costs upon the adjacent country.

New regional economic development powers are even more difficult to support in a unitary nation the size of Britain which has a single currency, with a single set of interest rates, a single central bank and note issue and a single economic policy. Where planning problems arise as they may do in the inner cities, a series of targeted measures are produced to harness the partnership between the private sector, central and local government. The main tools of economic policy are in the hands of the central government and it is difficult to see how that could be split. Yorkshire could not enjoy separate interest rates from Lancashire. There is no question of a different exchange rate when passing from Cheshire to Liverpool. There are common rates of benefit and nationally agreed wages in many occupations especially in the public sector. The main way that the terms of trade can be altered between Liverpool and London is through differential degrees of productivity growth and product development.

What could regional government add to the story? It could impose a new set of regulations, producing different rules in Wessex from Mercia, in Liverpool from London. This would add to the cost and burdens of business and make cross-border trading that much more difficult, at the very time when national governments are coming together to try to get greater regulatory clarity and commonality across national frontiers. It could raise additional taxes from business, burdening them further, to pay for its administrative superstructure and perhaps to channel grants back in to its local community. Unless the central government was prepared to raise national taxation and divert it from one region to another it would not add to the net amount of money in any regional community. What they spent would have to be raised from their local businesses and people.

The biggest block of money which is distributed regionally is the annual grant to local government. In 1992–93, in the areas outside London and the big conurbations, grant and business rates amounted to £707 per adult. In the metropolitan areas it was £920, in outer London £1,019 and inner London £1,615. These figures reveal large benefits to urban areas. In total, therefore, outside London the big cities receive £1,700 million extra. Outer London receives £1,000 million extra, and inner London £1,600 million – a total of £2,600 million for London, and a grand total of £4,300 million extra for the urban areas. Regional shifts are also important. The North, the North-West and Yorkshire and Humberside receive more than £100 a head above the level of the southern shires.

Besides these figures, totalling over £33,000 million of grants and business rates, all other regional policies pale into insignificance. They mostly reinforce the redistribution of local grant. Specific government programmes as a whole direct over £4,000 million into inner city areas.

The total regional funding from British tax-payers via the European Community is only about £415 million per annum. This is not surprising. There is no Objective 1 region on the mainland and 80 per cent of EC monies goes to Objective 1 regions. Out of this £415 million, approximately £35 million goes to the rural areas of Western Scotland, South Wales and the South-West. Most of the remaining £380 million goes to urban areas in the North, Midlands, South Wales and the Scottish lowlands. Under £5 million goes to London and the South. The £415 million which is distributed via Brussels compares with £33,000 million of Exchequer support for local government and a further £4,000 million on urban regeneration programmes: or just £1 in every £90 spent is routed via the EC from British tax-payers, the rest is routed direct.

Many people in Britain have a false perspective. They think the total of regional EEC aid is much larger as a proportion than it is, and they feel we ought to benefit more. They forget that for every pound we receive from Brussels we have sent £1.50 to Brussels and been charged a handling fee. Some begin to believe the false propaganda about our alleged poverty. An EEC map dividing the regions of Europe into six bands of wealth shows Britain with no region in the bottom band, yet the whole of Greece, Ireland and Portugal and most of Spain and Southern Italy are in that band. The Community has a southern and western belt that will absorb most of the regional monies. That is why Germany, the UK and France, the three large rich countries of the EEC, will continue to send more money to Brussels than we receive back. The Labour Party favour big increases in regional funds, but they also have the difficult task of persuading British voters, since the primary purpose of the regional EEC and social funds is to take money from tax-payers here and other prosperous countries and to promote schemes in the Community's poorer areas. Given the demands for such funding arising elsewhere in the Community, we cannot expect to have many winning tickets.

Could all this money be better spent if there was regional as well as local and national government? This is unlikely. Good government needs roots and loyalties, so that it has a feeling of community behind it, and it needs to separate policy from provision. The task of government is to regulate, and to enable services to be provided where democratic decisions judge that the market should be supplemented or overridden. The idea of the Citizens' Charter and the enabling authority represent the future, where government decides on standards and qualities of service, and others provide it.

The creation of extra bureaucracies and new tiers, the ideas of government as omniscient lawmaker and omnipotent provider, offering a cornucopia of policies are too reminiscent of the past: 'Grants for social justice, grants for industrial success, services for all – a few billions more will buy happiness.' If only it did. If you take that strategy to its logical solution you end up with communism – everything planned centrally, nothing working properly.

There is no case for regional government; but there is a strong case for local government. This has to build on the sense of natural community and on the recognition that there is a requirement for one or two levels of local government to deliver service, to provide a focus for community loyalty and expression, and to maintain civic and county life. Central to this function is the planning and regulatory function which has so much impact upon the urban and rural landscape. The British are particularly sensitive to planning issues as Britain is a densely crowded island where people have a great veneration for the past, and for the pleasant development and redevelopment of their countryside. Recently there has been considerable discussion in government circles, in village pubs and in the press about hedgerows. The landscape of Britain has been transformed in many agricultural parts of the country, particularly in East Anglia and in southern arable areas, by the development of much larger farm machinery. This has created the need to do away with the patchwork quilt of small fields bounded by hedgerows that were characteristic of the English countryside from the enclosure movement of the seventeenth and eighteenth centuries, through to the second half of the twentieth century. It is one of the most welcoming sights on returning from abroad as the aeroplane gets lower over the English countryside to see those remaining areas of deeply green fields bounded by variegated and exciting hedgerows.

The prairie farming of the new arable world, based upon major use of fertilizers, limited rotation of crops and access to substantial price support and subsidy arrangements under the Common Agricultural Policy, has created considerable controversy in recent years. People have been worried about leaching all of the good properties out of the soil by not having a sufficiently varied rotation. They have worried about the consequences of chemical fertilizers seeping into the water courses and rivers, and they have worried about soil erosion as wind and rain have a bigger impact on prairie fields than on the smaller enclosed fields of nineteenth-century rural England. The Government has recently responded with an initiative to encourage the replanting of hedgerows. Back will come the ash, beech, holly and hawthorn, to provide a habitat for mammals, butterflies and other insects, and for wild flowers and berries that characterize the typical English hedgerow.

The agricultural world often finds itself in conflict with suburban and urban dwellers' ideas and ideals of the countryside. Farmers point out that they are running a business and they are not just there to be grand gardeners making available their fields for those few hot days in the summer when urban dwellers wish to spill out and to enjoy the natural beauty of the rural scene. Urban and suburban dwellers for their part see the land as a common inheritance and regret over-mechanization of farming methods or the planting of alien crops in true English fields. As farmers discover that they can produce more than enough food on the acres they possess, the problem arises of how to convert some of the over-farmed acres for other uses. The Government has stepped in with proposals for new national forests to provide areas of traditional English deciduous tree planting. The aim is to recreate some of the grandeur of Sherwood and Windsor as they were before eighteenth-century industrialization and the felling of the mighty oaks.

Applications for rural industry pose different types of problem. There are many redundant farm buildings, many constructed without planning permission and some of them built in an unattractive style. Whilst most people are keen to conserve the tithe or dutch barn, the half-timbered property or the red-brick farm structure, there is less of an attachment to the concrete and metal fabrications of the later twentieth century. Very often the fine old barns are converted readily to domestic use, whereas applications to use the concrete or steel structures for a variety of low-value industrial or commercial purposes, ranging from plant hire for heavy plant through repair and mechanical engineering to second-hand dealing and scrap, cause all kinds of outrage in rural communities.

As farmers look for new ways to use their land they turn to the idea of servicing the burgeoning leisure industry, especially golf courses. Rural communities are divided about this development. Farmers, golf players and some village and suburban supporters see the golf club as a delightful half-way house between rural wilderness and suburban development. Others fear that it is a halfway house to more intensive development. Some leisure complexes have already shown the path that can be trod. The planners accept a rural golf course. Then the applications go in for a bigger clubhouse, flats for the club staff, soon to be followed by a demand for houses abutting the course. The clubhouse can be used for other facilities in the evenings which means more lighting, extra car-parking and an extension of hours for late-night parties and dances. These are the new planning issues that most divide suburban and rural communities.

As the global market rushes on its way, as the international statesmen jet from five-star hotel to five-star hotel, talking about the big issues of war and peace and the regulation of the market, so the local communities of England increasingly look inwards on themselves. It is a natural reaction for people to have. Their own individual quality of life is most affected by who lives next door, by whether there is a field or a housing estate opposite, by whether there is dog mess in the park, and whether the club has a night-time extension for drinks. In a crowded island like England planning will always lie at the heart of many disputes.

England is not wholly a nation of village or suburban dwellers dreaming a rural idyll, but neither is it solely dominated by its agricultural traditions. There are many English people who live in towns and would feel unhappy in the village. There are often times when the rural ideal does not live up to urban expectations when people move out of the towns. They come expecting peace and quiet and discover the countryside abounds with new kinds of noises. They were not expecting to be woken up at five by the milking machines or at six by the tractors and heavy plant moving onto the arable fields. They were not aware that crop-spraying, ploughing, muck-spraying and other features of modern farming are now heavily mechanized and noisy. They may have been unaware of the way that the English rural landscape is peppered with military aerodromes, and scrambling low-level fighters which, as they practice, roar over the valleys and the villages. The sound of the countryside in summer is not just the sound of leather on willow or the clip-clop of horses' hooves on the metal bridleways of the village centre. The new sound of the village in summer is the sound of loud pop music coming from powerful transistors, the sound of throaty sports cars in village lanes, and of agricultural machinery in fields.

Nor is the rural and suburban landscape as perfectly manicured as some urban dwellers think. The farmyard itself is usually untidy and may be characterized by a pile of old tyres, assorted bric-à-brac, metal junk, bits of old tractors, railway sleepers and many other things that may come in useful. The modern agricultural building is as likely to be a concrete or wooden lean-to as it is a classic English barn. There may not be many of the apocryphal town dwellers who arrive to complain about the mud on the lanes left by the tractor tyres, but there will be those who are offended by some of the sights of rural industry and farming.

There will be other rural dwellers who do not wish to see the countryside and the suburb become too much like the town centre. A suggestion to put in pavements, street lights, car-parks and other urban features to suburban or rural England can often evoke protest from those who wish to keep the rural aspect of their lives. Similarly, urban dwellers often seek a small haven of the countryside in the town itself. The best parts of our English cities are laid out around squares and parks containing well-maintained English lawns and the deciduous trees of the English landscape.

A sense of identity grows when people feel it is under threat. Being brought up in England in the 1950s and 1960s I was never too conscious of the separate English identity. The English flag is rarely flown and Englishness was something most people took for granted. Recently when a friend was travelling the English canals on his narrow boat flying the Cross of St George, people stopped him and asked him which country he came from: many thought it was probably somewhere in Scandinavia. Contrast this with the attitude of the emerging countries and regions of eastern and central Europe. As soon as the Berlin wall came down and communism was on the retreat, the carefully preserved flags of fifty or sixty years earlier were brought out and waved vigorously. The Czechs and the Slovaks, the Poles and the Serbians, the Macedonians and the Hungarians were all there with their national flags, their national songs and their feeling of national and regional identity. Despite being suppressed for so long, it could not be wiped out.

A sense of English identity is strongest when we are challenged to a game of rugby by the Welsh or Scots, or when there are fears about the way some people in Brussels are trying to lead us. The dominant partner in a union is usually happier with the flag and the national anthem of the union than the other partners in the union itself. In Scotland and Wales people are more conscious of the symbols of the Scottish nation and the Welsh principality themselves because they value the differences as well as the union within the United Kingdom.

These questions of identity become that much more important with the progress of global capitalism. As the large multinational corporations produce their own culture which runs across borders, many people feel subconsciously an even stronger urge to protect and preserve something of their own roots and origins. As many welcome the common fare of McDonalds across the continents, the development of international beer brands, the globalization of fun through Disney and the big film companies, and the development of all the different international consumer durable products, so too people need to revert to their origins at the village fête, in the local pub or through their choice in the local tailors or dress shop.

There are some who think that the global market will win out and that these separate identities, customs and cultures will merely become small differentiations catered for by the all-embracing global company. To such commercial minds the fashion in England for drinking a special kind of warm bitter can be accommodated as one variant in their brewing and marketing strategy worldwide. With any luck they may discover other people in other parts of the world who will want to do it the English way, at least occasionally when the mood takes them, or they may convert all the English to cool lager. Different sports will be tried out in the world marketplace and the most successful will be played everywhere. Each successive world Olympic games adds new sports to it to allow for the wishes of different countries of the world. Worldwide football, rugby, basketball, golf, billiards, darts and other major sports battle it out for audience figures, and their success or failure in capturing the television ratings is reflected in how many young people want to take them up and in how much product the sports suppliers can sell.

The fashion houses too can absorb it all. Out of the same Paris fashion house may come the Indian ethnic look or the English well-tailored style, or the French *haute couture* product. Cultural difference is just one more product variation in the advance of global style and the global marketplace. Instead of being deep-rooted features in our lives, the regional and local variations become competing fads and crazes in the product launches of the global corporations. Each may have its moment of glory on the stage or may be absorbed as one of the winning brands or lines for global exploitation.

But man is not made for and of commerce alone. Whilst there is some truth in the argument that global capitalism can absorb and exploit cultural and regional differences, it never overwhelms them nor takes away the underlying strength of many of these passions in men's souls. The fact that people coming to London will want to buy model red buses and bags made out of the Union Jack does not mean that they will go home and root for British teams in international competitions, or begin to think like an Englishman in their approach to world problems. The fact that an English lady may buy French *haute couture* clothing and enjoy going to Paris and speaking French does not mean that when it comes to making decisions about political issues like immigration, the future of the European Community or where Britain should stand in world events, she will have automatically joined an international rather than a national consciousness on these issues. Nor should we over-estimate the numbers of people who are truly involved in the global game of the international corporations. Those who manage and run them, those who move from country to country to take on a new management challenge, those who are most involved in incorporating local differences into their product range, may well have an international mind and a global approach to more problems. But they will not be more than a small proportion of the large populations who tend not to move from country to country and who are predominantly creatures of the time and place and circumstances of their birth and life.

The tension between the all-successful global market economy and local and cultural sentiment is at its most obvious with the great religions of the world. Christianity has found a way of living with capitalism, but many elements of the modern church are unhappy with some elements of the global economy. Few churchmen see free enterprise as the best means of lifting people out of poverty or spreading riches and income around. They instead turn instinctively to a more paternal or socialistic way of thinking as evidence that they care. There are some religions who find the whole process of wealth creation and greater prosperity distasteful, and who naturally choose a lifestyle sheltered from the full rigours of the wealth-creating process. The religions of the Middle East, India and Pakistan often see American capitalism as a corrosive influence that should be resisted. The Catholic Church battles against some elements of global economy in Latin America and elsewhere where it is strong. The Church of England regarded itself as one of the central pillars of opposition to a doctrine critics called Thatcherism. There is a reluctance in many a clerical mind to understand the benevolent power of the creation of wealth and freedom. Far better, many would say, that there should be fewer people really well off and a more equable distribution of misery than that some should become very rich in the process of others becoming a bit richer.

An equally important modern strand of opposition to global capitalism has emerged in the environmental movement. Here the argument is not one about the poverty of individuals or groups of people in a society but about the impact which the whole global market process is having upon the built environment, upon the water and the air of our planet. The assumption of the environmentalist is that the more modern and richer a society, the bigger the adverse impact it must have upon the environment. This leads to the belief that not only is the adverse impact increasing, but that it has reached, or will soon reach, the point where the planet's remarkable capacity for renewal is overwhelmed by the power of global capitalism to destroy or to render dirty.

In the 1970s the main fear was the exhaustion of certain raw materials. When the oil crisis put the price of oil up fourfold in 1973/74 the forecasters of the apocalypse rode out to tell us all that this was what we should expect when we got too greedy, and that the world was to be plunged into a new dark age short of the raw materials it needed to remain prosperous. This belief was intensified in the early 1980s when the oil price more than doubled again. The environmentalists could argue convincingly that there was a limited amount of oil hydrocarbon in the ground. One day they said, sooner or later, all the exploitable oil would have been pulled out of the ground and then industry and motor cars would grind to a halt.

This argument has been greatly weakened by what has happened since. Far from oil going from $20 a barrel to $50 a barrel, as many gloomsters were predicting in the early 1980s, the oil price has sunk back into the teens. For the British purchaser of oil, at its worst oil cost almost £30 a barrel, whereas today it costs less than £10 a barrel. The marketplace has responded. As the price went up, so exploration companies found it more worthwhile to spend more money to improve their techniques and consequently discovered more oil. They found it was possible to spend money on enhanced recovery: where before they had left more than two-thirds of the oil down the hole in many an oil well, the recovery rates rose with the application of more brain power to the problem. At the same time the high cost of oil led many to think of alternative ways of delivering the energy they required. It turned out that the problem was rather like the apocryphal problem in London at the end of the nineteenth century when people feared that London was going to decay under a mountain of horse manure because of the rapid growth in horse traffic. They had not foreseen the technological breakthrough that would render the horse redundant and banish him from the streets of the city.

Technology is available and can be more widespread to introduce renewable sources of energy. Man knows or will be able to know how to harness the renewable energy of the sun, the wind and the waves, should the need arise. It is all a question of price. When oil is sufficiently expensive, so more renewable energy will be used. Already the higher price of energy has encouraged very worthwhile conservation schemes, with more effective ways of generating electricity, doubling the thermal efficiency of plants. Many people now invest in insulation materials to curb the heat loss in their homes, shops and factories.

A similar case can be made for many of the other natural resources of the world. None of the individual metals or fuel stuffs on their own are essential. Many of them are still in abundant supply as their relatively weak prices demonstrates. In many cases renewable substitutes are already available. Energy can be generated from plants like sugar, which can be easily grown. Alcohol is a largely untapped industrial fuel source. There is a surplus of ore for many metals. Many metals can be recycled and re-used as with steel. As people become more conscious of some limitations in resource, and as the desirability of re-using rather than casting away increases, so recycling will come to play an evermore important role in ensuring good use of the scarce resources of the planet.

As environmentalists began to see that the argument about energy did have its defects they shifted the ground of the discussion to the impact that certain industrial processes and techniques had upon the air, water and land of our planet. They were right to point out that many industrial processes and some forms of transport do make the air and the water dirty. They were right to point out that there must be limits to the amount of fouling that individuals and companies should be allowed to carry out. They were right to point out that if the scale of industry expands too dramatically using dirty processes, so the dirtiness will intensify to the point where it can be damaging to the health of those who live nearby.

This was no new perception, although the intensity of the argument conducted on a worldwide scale was. It was well-known to those who introduced the clean air legislation in the 1950s and 1960s in Britain. It was an argument that the great pioneers who put in the Victorian sewers would have fully understood. It was an argument which the social reformers of Victorian Britain were putting about the impact of smokey factories upon the mill towns and steel cities of northern Britain.

History shows that concerted campaigns to get people to clean up dirty processes and practices do succeed and that there are periods of concentrated activity in human history when man decides to clean up his game. Recent attention on the need for cleanliness is wholly admirable and already major programmes are being put in place so that the later twentieth century will go down in history as another period like that of the big Victorian reforms when advances were made in improving the cleanliness of parts of the planet.

But the campaigners are wrong to think that dirtiness is a direct result of prosperity and sophistication. Whilst it is true that the richer a country becomes per head, the more per head people consume which can add to the amount of by-product and waste, it is also true to say that the richer a society becomes the more conscious they become of the need to recycle waste, and the more they spend on environmentally-friendly processes and activities. A comparison of East and West Germany, as it was, illustrates this well. At the time of re-unification West Germany was several times richer per head than East Germany, yet East Germany was several times dirtier than West Germany. The East German processes for making steel, basic chemicals, metals and fabrication allowed large quantities of harmful pollutant to belch out of factory chimneys or to run out of factories through the drains and into the rivers. The united Germany soon found that it yielded many more results from spending the extra deutschmark on cleansing the river sources of eastern Europe than it could get from spending the extra deutschmark on further cleaning in the west. Prosperity brings with it the money and the will to curb the excesses and to control the waste.

Richer societies can afford to spend on re-using materials that are wasted from the production processes. They can afford to spend money on scrubbers and other devices in factory chimneys to extract harmful particles before they are vented into the atmosphere. They can spend on segregating harmful waste through the drainage system of the factory to ensure that liquid waste is transported away to be looked after in properly constructed tips.

The environmentalists would counter by saying that there are none the less elements in the western lifestyle which are still far more damaging to the planet than in poorer societies. They would probably draw attention to the impact that the American motor car can have on the ozone layer and the world atmosphere in general. Whilst America may have got further in fitting catalytic converters and in controlling lead and other harmful pollutants from exhausts, it is undeniably true that American cars do vent a large amount of carbon dioxide into the atmosphere. It is also true that they vent more than the vastly burgeoned population of Asia, although every pair of human lungs takes in oxygen and passes out more carbon dioxide.

The battleground in the world economic debates lies between, on the one hand, those in the poorer countries who wish to limit the West's capacity to use the motor car and build more factories, and on the other hand, those in the West who would rather see the developing countries keep more forest and crop land busily taking in carbon dioxide and passing out more oxygen. No one has yet suggested that the balance between carbon dioxide and oxygen is going to be so distorted as the American motor car outguns the

Brazilian rainforest, that we will start to suffer from a shortage of oxygen, but there are those who argue that the ozone layer is going to be damaged, causing skin cancer and increasing the likelihood of dangerous sun radiation getting through. Whether advanced or developing, all countries need rules and regulations to ensure that water supplies and water courses are clean. There has to be some global control on what people can put into the atmosphere.

There is some relief in sight. Newer technologies are less dirty technologies. The new computer businesses do not churn out the number of harmful substances that the old steel mills and engineering shops produced which they have supplanted. In the large cities the sheer lack of space to accommodate the growing number of motor cars is leading to renewed interest in travel by trams, rapid transit systems, monorails, which are less fuel intensive per passenger carried. As an economy matures it switches people and resources away from heavy industry which tends to be dirtier, and towards leisure and services which are much less intensive in their use of dirty and harmful processes. More and more information and messages travel by telephone wire and radio wave, reducing the need for greater growth in the traffic carrying people. The world market had to solve the transport problem. Many wanted to enjoy the Olympics but it was not possible for them all to travel to Barcelona to see the games in person. The market creates the wish to see the Olympics and the market solves the problem of how people can through the growth of television. Everyone with a TV set can now be there at the ringside to see the best jump, the best shotput, the fastest run. Many an armchair traveller can sit at home and see and feel what it's like to be in the Brazilian rainforest or to visit the temples of Asia without the cost and inconvenience of having to go there in person.

None the less, the creation of bigger markets and global interest can produce a wear-and-tear problem in some areas. The British love of history and past achievements has meant that the major tourist attractions in Britain were all too well trodden. The steps in Canterbury Cathedral, the floors in the Tower of London, the pathways around Stonehenge or the favourite walks through the Lake District National Park have all needed strengthening or protecting from the impact of millions of pairs of feet.

The argument is not, therefore, primarily one between those

who would go for growth at any price and those who see all growth as inimical to the survival of the planet. These extreme positions contain within them a sliding scale of more carefully differentiated views. Those of us towards the growth side of the spectrum would argue that it is growth which can develop the technology and the resources to solve the problems. There may well be a need for governments to intervene and regulate, but they should do so conscious of the pace at which businesses and economies are capable of changing and conscious of the balance between cost and benefit. Others more towards the no-growth end of the spectrum would argue strongly that regulation should be tough and effective from day one, even if that means closing down a large number of plants and stopping many people from using their preferred form of transport. The present evidence is that the people who favour increased prosperity and growth are still in the ascendancy. There is no evidence in recent international conferences of a headlong rush to dramatic world controls that could threaten the engines of prosperity. The market itself has recuperative powers just as surely as the planet does.

If big business moves away from an area leaving an old plant on a derelict lot, however serious the contamination of the soil, weeds, wild flowers and even shrubs and trees soon start to take root again. If businesses along a riverside are overturned by economic change, the river will soon be cleansed when they stop allowing dirty substances to flow into it. So too does the economy have recuperative and self-protective powers. As people come to see the dangers in a certain type of industrial development, so through democratic processes they will impose controls and the marketplace will see new opportunities in accommodating those controls. When people became aware of the rate of attrition of the Brazilian rainforests, those selling wood products in Britain realized that many of their customers were not prepared to buy beautiful looking hardwoods if they thought they had been felled from a forest in Brazil that would not be renewed. They had to adjust their market strategies, substituting other hardwoods for those from the Brazilian rainforest, or taking an interest in the Brazilian rainforest itself to be able to reassure their customers that their products had come from woods that were to be replanted.

Whole businesses developed on the back of green consciousness.

The phenomenal success in the 1980s and early 1990s of the Body Shop was based upon the entrepreneurial perception that green policies sold products and that buyers of cosmetics and body lotions needed reassuring that they had not been tested on animals and that they were produced in a way that was friendly to the environment. Once the competitive market was let loose in the electricity industry the industry immediately improved its environmental performance. The nationalized monopoly had insisted on building coal-burning power stations which were fuel inefficient and produced a large volume of carbon dioxide in relation to the energy generated. The new, more competitive privatized industry chooses to produce power through much more efficient combined cycle gas turbines, which reduce the carbon dioxide emissions substantially for each unit of power generated. The more competitive industry began to look at wind and tidal power and combined heat and power that had all been rejected by the nationalized monopoly.

The contrast between the competitive market response and nationalized planning underlies the difference we have already seen between former East and West Germany and their respective approaches to ecology. The imperatives in East Germany throughout the post-war period were to produce more and more steel product, the heavy industrial base that underlies weapons production. In West Germany the accent was upon more consumer-oriented products and processes with much more beneficial consequences for the emission rate to water and air. In the competitive marketplace people are driven to experiment with new technology and to cut down their resource use. They are also driven to take into account sensitivities and worries people have about the consequences of headlong industrial exploitation with no thought for the environment. It has been demonstrated yet again, in green matters as in others, that a combination of democracy and free enterprise capitalism is more benign than a combination of monopoly and state control.

The central arguments of the 1990s and into the millennium will be about whether the global market can live happily alongside local roots and loyalties, and within the confines of our unique but sometimes fragile planet. It is true that as mankind improves his powers to control the physical environment and marshal resources for technological and industrial purposes, so he must have a greater sense of his responsibility towards the capacity of the planet to renew itself and to future generations. The ally in this argument for those who wish to ensure that global capitalism does not damage the planet and does not trample too heavily on local loyalties and any sense of identity is the common sense of people themselves. People eventually rose up and threw off the trammels of state communism in eastern and central Europe. In vibrant democracies they are constantly making their feelings felt that local issues and local concerns are most important and that the quality of life is not merely a question of prosperity. If you are hungry the most important thing is a field of corn and the construction of a bakery. If your society has passed that point of scarcity then other things become important too: it becomes important that the neighbourhood in which you live has a balance between building and greenery, it becomes important that the water you drink and the air you breathe are relatively pure, and it becomes important that you have something to pass on to your children. It is vital that where you live is not just a green and prosperous land, but also gives a sense of who you are, where you came from, and to which place you belong. These senses of community and of nature become even more important with the coming of the global market and with the unleashing of such huge technological power which lies in the hands of relatively few people.

FOUR·

Towards World Government?

Does the development of global capitalism require new policies
from the governments of the world? As business transactions
occur more and more across frontiers, as goods, services, people,
and capital move freely around the world, as technology speeds
the process, are national governments and regional blocs fleet
of foot enough to deal with the problems it produces? Are
there already signs of evolution towards world government?
When world leaders frequently meet in economic summits, the
G7 meetings, through the GATT and at environment summits,
they seem to be recognizing intuitively and sometimes explicitly
the need to coordinate and develop action between governments
across frontiers. The world has expressed itself forcefully with a
number of centripetal as well as centrifugal forces. At the very same
time that the western European countries are trying to harmonize
some of their regulations to facilitate cross-border trading, the
large Comecon (Council for Mutual Economic Aid) bloc of the
USSR and Eastern Europe has fallen apart: national and local
sentiment has taken over as people have realized the failure of
totalitarianism to delivery prosperity. Whilst there has been a
notable increase in the strength and importance of the United
Nations, there has been a move to civil war in several central
and eastern European territories. Where before there were two
super powers with nuclear weapons now there is only one and
a number of other smaller states. The world picture has altered
fundamentally. The change in the balance of power has given
more potential clout to international organizations supported by
the United States, but simultaneously it has created a host of new
problems as the Soviet empire breaks up and new countries jostle
for position.

One of the strongest arguments for a world government is that it might be able to catch the new breed of global criminal. Financial crime and fraud often know no frontiers. The expert financial criminal may need to use the markets of the large and better policed countries, like the United States of America, Japan and the United Kingdom, but he will be adept at laundering his money in such a way that it is difficult to track. Typical financial frauds and scandals use pyramids of companies which spread themselves through a number of different territories, making it difficult for investigators to pursue questioning. Sometimes discovery of what is going on only reveals how difficult it is to make charges rest in a jurisdiction with a strong legal system. The separation of the individual criminal from the laundered money and bank accounts creates numerous jurisdictional problems in trying to pin him down or bring him to justice. International money laundering has been high on the agenda for discussion between financial jurisdictions for a number of years, as countries painstakingly piece together a number of measures to co-operate with each other in the relentless search for the criminal and his money. It requires great effort to bring such criminals to trial successfully in a country with the jurisdiction and power to tackle the problem.

It is not just fraud that can run across frontiers. Recent financial collapses have demonstrated that the development of international capitalism makes simultaneous crashes in different centres much more likely if a large company or group falls apart with interests spread around the world. If a bank has overlent in the United States of America and has branches in Tokyo and London there will be a knock-on effect throughout the three major financial centres of the world. The interlocking assets and liabilities mean that each of the three major banking jurisdictions may have to take action. They may need to co-ordinate their enquiries. It is much more difficult for the banking regulators to be sure of the stability and the asset and liability position of any individual bank under their watch, given the complexity of the holding company structures and given the difficulty of aggregating the assets and liabilities around the world. A number of recent banking problems have demonstrated the need for the leading financial regulators of the world to work together. First, they need to understand the complexity of the groups they are monitoring and second, if necessary, they need to co-ordinate their action to prevent over-lending or to wind up a business in a timely and orderly fashion.

An individual subsidiary or main bank in one regulated territory may look fine on its own. It may be making all the proper returns demonstrating that it has enough cash to deal with any surge in requests for money. It may have assets and liabilities in reasonable balance. The problem may be in another territory which in turn may be relying upon the alleged strength of the bank in the major financial market. This second territory may have a more precarious relationship between assets and liabilities and the home bank may have underestimated the possible losses that its overseas subsidiary could make. It is this kind of calculation which is leading financial regulators to work more and more closely together. It is also leading the world inexorably towards more global regulations and common definitions of capital and prudence.

Frauds, company collapses and scandals know no boundaries. The recent simultaneous collapse of the property markets in New York, London and Tokyo had a dramatic effect upon a number of large property companies. The financial difficulties of the O & Y Company, which had begun its property acquisitions in Canada, spread them through New York and then finally taken on a massive development in London's Docklands, illustrates how the combined impact of market declines in more than one territory can be very severe on the balance sheet of an international company. Whilst its activities in any one centre may well have been containable and financiable even through a property recession, the combination of the obligations in three different centres along with the complexity of the borrowings arranged by international syndications and banks across frontiers made it harder for the company to survive without financial restructuring.

The global criminal is an even more serious problem than global financial distress. He may be involved in peddling drugs across frontiers or in armament trading, surreptitiously supplying the parts, the technology and the weapons that tyrants of emerging Third World authoritarian regimes think they require. Saddam Hussein in Iraq was only able to get as close as he did to building a nuclear bomb thanks to the complicated network of companies and arms traders that were able to supply him. Choosing to supply different parts from different companies and countries around the western world made it more difficult for the authorities to work out what was going on or to see the overall impact of the individual permits to supply individual pieces. Drugs have become a mighty industry, providing a ready source of revenue for those capable of growing the products and more especially for those dealing in them, who often amass huge fortunes from the large margins they charge.

The international community is keen to clamp down on criminal actions in these areas. Much work has gone into seeing if the police and detection activities of the different states can be brought together to increase the success rate in striking against such people. Often money laundering, drugs and international armament trading go together and if the authorities are able to detect the money they can detect the criminal and vice versa. The nearer the world can come to global government in these areas, the quicker these problems could be resolved. Part of the problem is undoubtedly the clash of jurisdictions, the difficulty of following the trail for evidence into every territory and through the complexity of the company, banking and dealing systems across frontiers. Governments as a whole are stretched when dealing with people who are well financed, well resourced and capable of taking extreme action. Terrorists and some drugs and arms dealers have powers and weaponry which enable them to take on the authorities of the smaller states.

The world is attempting to deal with these problems by co-operation and some harmonization. Law codes are being examined territory by territory to see if they need strengthening. The flow of extradition cases is increasing and a number of leading countries are signing agreements between each other to improve the pursuit of crimes and misdeeds across frontiers. Some also claim that this work needs to go further, towards the establishment of world regulation for global industries. If, they argue, it makes sense to bring criminal codes and detection work closer together to catch the global criminal surely it also makes sense to bring regulators and regulatory codes closer together to control global industries more effectively. The case can be made in a wide range of areas and has already been made strongly in the banking industry. As we have seen, the banking industry is particularly prone to difficulties with cross-border regulation. Effective regulators nationally may be stretched beyond their competence if the problems lie between companies in different countries or within the holding structure of a sophisticated international group. Each national regulator is tempted to give the benefit of the doubt to important banks in its own territory. No individual regulator may feel totally to blame or responsible for the combined impact of the whole group.

In the Basle group and other fora these problems are being sorted out. Regulators believe that there needs to be a common definition of capital with an international system measuring it so that regulators around the world can control their banks with similar standards. They also believe that there have to be common codes of practice about how banking should be conducted and more regular exchanges of information so that the regulators can be aware of what is going on territory by territory. Some people wish to see the establishment of a lead regulator for each bank, usually the regulator in the territory of the head office or main branch. Others favour the college of regulators approach where the leading regulators meet together across borders to discuss the banks that span their jurisdictions.

There is also a need for regulators to spread the word to one another about banks that concern them. If a regulator in one territory is getting worried about the capital adequacy or the financial propriety of an institution in his territory he should be able to draw on the doubts, fears, information and skills of the regulators in other territories. The collapse of BCCI demonstrated the need for cross-border co-operation and surveillance in difficult cases.

A similar case has been made out in the more general financial services area. The advent of global financial markets with many investors trading shares across frontiers means many see the Japanese, American, British, German and French markets as all part of one global equity marketplace. In these circumstances there is an increasing need for world regulators to recognize the snares and problems that can arise with vigorous cross-border trading. Through the International Conference of Securities regulators they do meet together like their banking counterparts to see if they can agree common standards of prudence, fair dealing and capital adequacy for the firms under their aegis. Progress has been made in hammering out definitions for different types of trading, in reaching agreement on sensible rules of conduct for financial service business and moving towards a common financial framework for the conduct of such business.

It is never easy getting agreement between the different jurisdictions, given the variety of practices that have developed. What makes sense in one type of marketplace may not make sense in another. If a stock market is based upon a number of traders taking risks on their own accounts it is difficult for them to publish the price and volume of each lot of stock they are purchasing, as it exposes their position. A market maker will become reluctant to take on such a position, thus damaging the liquidity of the market. Conversely, in a market where the traders simply match final buyers and sellers and do not take a risk themselves there is every reason for the volume and price of transaction to be published at the time it is undertaken. In this type of market it is much more difficult for customers to be given firm quotes of the price and size at which they could deal. World regulators are learning that they will not be able to harmonize everything and that some differences are legitimate differences of competitive practice which may be in the customer's interest to protect. Instead the financial regulators have to find ways of making sure the customers in all types of market have access to reasonable quantities of information, that information is accurate and that the market remains open and competitive enough to satisfy its prime tasks.

In many product markets there is a demand for global standards or global regulation as well. The largest consumer product of them all, the motor car, is emerging as a worldwide product. This is leading people to ask whether there should be global emission standards, global safety standards, and whether many of the product differences should be eroded further by modifying or removing specific national and regional regulations. If it makes sense to specify a certain kind of headlamp or to demand a certain resistance to impact in the Japanese market, could it not make sense to demand similar standards in the American or European? If it makes sense to demand the fitting of a certain kind of catalytic converter or exhaust emission control in Los Angeles should it not also be required in London and Lisbon?

As with financial regulation, there are here interesting problems about the intersection between competition policy and the search for world regulatory harmony. If there is no common regulation, but a welter of different national regulations affecting the specification of product, this can stand in the way of the large international companies gaining the full benefits of the economies of scale by exploiting a global market. If a motor manufacturer has to produce an entirely different type of car to sell in Britain from that which is sold in Japan it is to some extent a restraint on trade against manufacturers in either country exploiting each other's marketplace. If, on the other hand, the global car is so precisely defined by the regulators that there is little scope for national or local product differentiation the multitude of existing companies producing to different standards could find themselves in danger. More importantly this could in the medium term be damaging to the creativity of the industry itself. Herein lies the regulators' dilemma. With no regulation there may be less inducement to produce the global product, but with too much regulation the global product could ossify and the drive to find better styles and standards be impeded.

When video recorders were first developed there was a battle between several different standards. In the United Kingdom some bought Betamax machines and some bought VHS. Over a period of years and after much struggle VHS gained the upper hand and is now the effective dominant standard in the market. Should the regulators have stepped in earlier and insisted that everyone built to one standard or was it right to allow innovation and competition to have its head? There is certainly a danger in the regulators moving too far too fast as competition is the main engine of progress.

In the case of motor cars where there are national or regional standards it must make sense to see if they can be harmonized across frontiers, but there also needs to be a patient examination to see just how many standards there ought to be and how many areas of car manufacture and design can be left more open to encourage creativity. Transport generally poses special cross-border international and global problems. Both the shipping and the aviation industries have long seen the reasons for some cross-border and international regulation. Aviation has proceeded primarily by a series of bilateral deals between nation states, which have bartered routes with one another in order to promote or protect their national carriers. They have done this in the names of safety and economic regulation of the business. The states have come together through the international air traffic body, IATA, to provide some minimum standards of common carriage provision, guaranteeing people compensation and safety to a specified limit. The mixture of both economic and safety regulation is being attacked in the more liberalizing regimes. In the United States there was massive deregulation of the price, route and service licensing controls for national carriers some years ago, leading to an increase in the number of services run, to cuts in prices and then to an over-expansion of capacity in the industry followed by financial difficulties for some of the carriers. It was wholly beneficial to the customer, but made the operating environment more bracing for the businesses within it. The European Community has been debating for a number of years, making similar deregulatory moves, but the presence of several large subsidized and nationalized concerns on the continent of Europe has made progress more difficult to achieve.

Again it is true that if it makes sense to regulate these things it makes sense to regulate them globally rather than nationally or bilaterally or in regional groupings. The issue is the extent to which they need regulating at all. Of course the travelling public wants safety regulation but it does not necessarily want price regulation into the bargain. In the shipping field the ship owner or manager has a choice of territories where he can flag his ship, operating under different conditions concerning crewing and operating standards. None the less, there is an international framework and code of conduct governing the passage of shipping from territory to territory and governing the use of the sea lanes in international waters. There are safety and trade policy issues which need policing. Jurisdictions also try to place controls on things like tank washing at sea which can pollute the water.

The food industry also perceives the need for supra-national standards. As the global market emerges, and as packets of biscuits, pots of shrimps and tins of salmon make their way around the world, the regulators demand that proper standards be enforced by all in the chain who may be handling the food. Infection and disease need to be controlled and when something goes wrong a product needs to be chased quickly and the source of it cleansed. National inspectorates working closely with customs are perceiving the need to co-operate more fully with jurisdictions in other countries.

The pharmaceutical industry is one of the most highly regulated of all. Before a new drug can be sold to the public or offered on prescription by doctors it has to go through a vigorous set of tests, as we saw in the first chapter. These tests have to be monitored carefully by a drug agency before the drug is licensed. To date most of this work has been carried out by national authorities, with the American drug agency leading the field in its reputation for rigour and with drug agencies like that in the UK also being widely respected and commanding authority elsewhere. Some countries accept product which has been through regulatory testing approval in a well-respected territory abroad: others demand the right to national testing before sale. Within the European Community there has been progress towards the development of a European pharmacopoeia as the Community counties have attempted to bring together their standards for drug testing and approval. Given the globalization of the drug market there is an increasing need for further collaboration and co-operation between the drug testing agencies around the world with further exchange of results and the bringing together of standards. In the area of drug approval economic and safety regulation are strongly bound up together. A product cannot be sold without the safety certificate and so the drug agencies have within their power the ability to license or restrict new competitors in a given health area. Many other industries would also claim that they need global regulation. The aviation industry would point to the need to bring together air traffic control systems of adjacent countries. Trying to fly across Europe means passing from national control to national control over air space with great rapidity. It is important with so many different jurisdictions, control systems and languages to have more co-operation between them. English has become the accepted language of aviation, but the computer languages of the French, British and Spanish systems also need to make sense as the volume of traffic flying from London to Barcelona over French airspace intensifies. Similar problems arise in the congested skies over the rapidly growing Pacific rim and even over the less congested Atlantic. Who is to own and control these systems? Do we see the emerging need here for a new layer of government?

Similar issues arise in satellites and telecommunications. All the time that telephone traffic was primarily national the sensible regulatory area was the nation state. International traffic was a luxury for a few rich individuals and companies and represented a tiny fraction of total telecommunications activities. The 1990s will see a huge surge in international telephone fax and data traffic, stretching the current organizations providing satellite and cable links and international controls. The emergence of global telephone companies led by the likes of Cable and Wireless in the UK and the Bell companies in the States makes sensible liberalization of different national jurisdictions that much more important to power the growth more rapidly. The task ahead is mainly a deregulatory one. Over-tight national regulations using safety and system development as arguments to bolster national monopolies will need to be relaxed in order to allow market entry to the new competitors taking a global view. As new companies wish to drive a digital highway around the world they will encounter national restrictions from regulators. Countries wishing to exploit the benefits of the new technology will need to find a way of letting them in.

Some see the need for global government in the management of the economies of the world. A welter of international organizations has grown up in the post-war world. The International Monetary Fund has become the lender of last resort or in many cases the lender of first resort to a host of struggling developing countries. The World Bank has undertaken a number of development projects worldwide whilst the framework of Bretton Woods followed by economic summits has provided a forum for finance ministers to hammer out agreements on currency markets, the management of interest rates, and similar issues.

It is commonplace now to say that an individual country, unless its one of the big three – Japan, United States or Germany – has little direct influence over its own currency and interest rates strategy. If rates go up in Frankfurt they go up in Milan, Paris and Madrid as well. If rates go up in America they can have an impact upon London and Tokyo. International finance ministers have attempted over a number of years to provide some framework within which the yen, dollar and deutschmark can trade one against the other to offer businessmen some degree of stability in a turbulent financial world. Whilst there are many sceptics who feel these stabilization policies are destabilizing, and market forces will have out in the end, a great deal of energy has been devoted to currency management by governments.

The large international institutions certainly need managing with aims in view. Should the World Bank finance government-owned projects thereby extending the powers of nationalized industries and governments within the recipient countries, or should it lend to the private sector to strengthen freer or competitive marketplaces? Should the IMF impose austerity packages and restrictions on the host economies receiving the money it lends to countries under pressure or should it be more permissive when it comes to growth and inflation? These are big issues for the international community to decide on and its decisions will always be in part based on the current economic fashion. Money is very footloose around the world. With the globalization of the banking system it becomes more difficult for an individual national authority to control the process. Decisions taken in Tokyo may have a direct impact on the degree of liquidity and competitiveness in the British banking system. If the Japanese banks decide to rein back, or if the regulators decide that they need to rebuild their asset base, then the growth of lending in sterling to British businesses in the London market may be directly reduced. Conversely, if the Japanese banks are asset rich and in a period of expansion then their actions become an important part of the domestic British monetary scene.

Those against the development of too much world government would argue either that these things do not need controlling or that it is undesirable they should be controlled at a global level. Free marketeers would argue that governments do not need to intervene in the currency and interest rate process unduly. They would argue that finance ministers in countries that are not linked or converging are never going to be able to control the markets, however grand the scale of their operations. The tidal waves of speculative money will defeat even the most concerted central bank intervention if the intervention is against the mood of the times. All the time there are national currencies there need to be national central banks following a domestic policy, guided by whatever means they see fit. Some would be guided by domestic monetary aggregates, some by reference to other currencies and some pragmatically by a range of indicators. Interventionists would say that the globalization of credit necessitates the globalization of government to control currencies and interest rates.

The case has also been made out recently for strengthened world arrangements in the environmental field. If it makes sense for the UK to clean up its rivers and sewerage treatment systems to limit the amount of waste being passed into the North Sea so it must make sense for the Dutch, the Germans and the Scandinavians to take similar action. The improvement in the North Sea is not going to be that great if only one country bounding it enforces the necessary higher standards. There is not much use in one country taking action against fluoro-carbons to limit the damage to the ozone layer unless every other country in the world takes similar action. Cleaning up the planet is an important task which does require patient international negotiation and some agreement over the duties and obligations of individual countries to make their contribution to improving the environment.

Since the Second World War it has been recognized that international agreements are required for the proper conduct of trade. Successive rounds of the GATT have lowered tariffs and removed other barriers to trade across frontiers. It is a process which needs to continue if the prosperity machine is to remain in gear. Many countries still do not accept the fundamental proposition behind the GATT that they will be richer and the world will be too if they pull down tariff and non-tariff barriers to trade. There is always the lurking danger that countries will resume the idea that they can steal a march on the rest of the world if they retain a barrier when others do not. One of the things they usually seek is the reassurance that if they do open frontiers to trade others will also do so and penalties will be enforced if anything should go wrong.

Some believe there is an even bigger role for world co-operation or government in the defence and foreign affairs area. The abolition of war is a noble aim. The human condition has been punctuated by endless brutal civil and international wars. The twentieth century has had a particularly bad attack of the war virus and after each of the two major conflagrations new arrangements were put in place to try to create a framework of international co-operation backed up by the international police force. The League of Nations was soon overturned by the rise of fascism and autocracy on the continent of Europe and in Japan. The United Nations for much of the post-war period has found its effectiveness limited by the presence of two highly armed superpowers. If the superpowers did not agree on how to handle the conflict in the world it was difficult for the United Nations to do anything as both the superpowers had a blocking vote on the Security Council. The collapse of communism has changed all that. There is now much greater opportunity for the United Nations to take a role as a peacemaker and law enforcement agent in many parts of the world. The states that made up the former Soviet Union are more willing to co-operate with the United States of America and more willing to argue the case for peace in the world's trouble spots. As a result, the United Nations has taken the lead both in the Middle East and in Central Europe.

The United Nations provides a model of how international co-operation can develop. Every country has a vote and those that are most important have a veto over the United Nations' action. Countries only send troops to a United Nations peacekeeping force if they are willing to do so and support the action that the UN is taking. The UN tries to proceed by negotiation and peacemaking, but, if necessary, it can call on the reserves of the armies of many countries in the world or it can allow armies to concentrate their actions to enforce a UN resolution. Whilst the UN does not cramp nation states unduly, and allows them full rein to their views and their votes, it can decide to take action in cases where there is considerable agreement between countries around the world.

We have seen that there are many developments in international co-operation. Some would argue that there are many requirements which need world government to solve problems. A large number of them arise out of the growing internationalization of companies, trade and commerce. The question is how far should this go and how far do we want it to go?

FIVE

The Rush to Democracy

Democracy has been through a rebirth worldwide. The conception of its renaissance came from the mass protest movements that have felled or wobbled many regimes in Asia, eastern Europe and the Third World. The pattern of peaceful protest they have generated has brought the streets to life and has made governments aware of how difficult it is to exercise power when they have lost people's consent. Freedom has flown proudly on the banners of protesters from Bucharest to Manila. Once a regime topples there is an immediate difficulty in transmuting an opposition protest movement into a method of government. Constitution-building proves problematic and the search for precedents and for new styles of government begins.

Everyone agrees that the central question in remodelling torn and battered constitutions is how to exercise the power of the vote. In the British and the American models each person receives one vote, as many candidates as wish to can put up for election, and the candidate who secures the most votes on the day is declared the winner. This system has several advantages. Firstly, if constituencies are of equal size or if, as in the case of the American presidential election, the whole nation is eligible to vote, each vote has equal weight. A decisive result is usually arrived at. In the case of United Kingdom parliamentary elections it is exceptionally rare in twentieth-century experience for one party to fail to gain a majority of seats needed to be able to form a majority administration. Similarly, only one president can be elected in the US.

The establishment of a majority party in government, coupled with collective responsibility, ensures that electors know who to blame. Voters have a genuine opportunity every four or five years to throw out the government if they think its performance is unsatisfactory, or if they think the alternative party can do better. In the United States, 'first-past-the-post' voting has been used in a constitution with segregated powers to deliberately limit the power of individual groups of politicians and an individual party to shape policy. It was quite common for the nation to vote Republican for the presidency and Democrat for the Congress and Senate. Now a Democrat president has been elected we may see a subsequent swing to the Republicans in House and Senate elections. Segregation of powers in the American constitution has many strengths when it comes to represent differing viewpoints or to expose wrong policies. It is, however, passing through a period when it is failing to deliver strong domestic government. The segregation of powers has left the president with considerable scope to pursue an independent foreign policy, but with little scope to pursue an independent domestic policy free of the trammels of budgetary procedures and the views of the Congress and Senate. Conversely, the hostile Democrat Congress and Senate found it difficult to persuade the president to accept many of the legislative measures they would like to see, so, on crucial issues like trade policy and social policy, policy formation can become log-jammed.

The American model shows that it is not just the voting system which matters. There are Americans who admire the British system, believing that the advantage of a strong majority government is not totally outweighed by some of the disadvantages of concentration of power. For whilst there is no legislature capable of checking the British executive as the legislature and executive are combined, there are other measures in the British system which are missing from the American one. For example, the United Kingdom has an independent civil service whose loyalties are to the system and the nation and not to an individual party, whereas in the American system the executive bolsters its own position by the recruitment of senior officials from amongst its own party supporters. This makes even more important in the American constitution exposure of the executive by the legislature and the free press, to avoid any drift to corruption or malpractice. Any similar deviation can and should be arrested in the British system since the civil service remains independent and the departmental accounting officers are civil servants rather than the political masters of each department. In addition, the British system has the added strength of the ability to cross-examine the head of the government twice weekly in free questions in the House of Commons. There is nothing to compare with Prime Minister's Question Time in the American system. A president can choose when to hold a press conference and when not to hold one and usually operates at arm's length through his press officers rather than directly. He rarely has to answer to Congress and is never subjected to the kind of rough cross-questioning on a variety of issues that a British prime minister faces weekly.

The Anglo-Saxon systems based on the 'one man, one vote' principle have been transmuted particularly on the continent of Europe by the introduction of proportional representation. Exponents of proportional representation believe it is a fairer system as they claim that their system alone gives each vote equal weight. There are three systems that are worth examining to evaluate this claim.

The purest form of proportional representation is the multiple transferable vote. Faced with a ballot list of several candidates each elector is required to list his order of preferences, numbering them against each candidate. When it comes to counting the votes, if no candidate has a clear majority of first preference votes, then second preference votes will be transferred. The candidate with the largest number of first and second preference votes combined can then be declared the winner.

This system is designed to deal with the apparent injustice of the 'first-past-the-post' system that a candidate can be elected on a minority of the votes. It does so at the expense of the other principle that each vote should have equal weight. For what it means is that those who vote for the more popular candidates as their first choice get less value from their second transferable vote than those who choose to vote for minority candidates for their first choice. The re-partitioning of the votes of the least popular candidates by allocating instead the second preference vote from those electors to the other candidates means that the electors choosing minority candidates effectively vote twice in the election, whereas those choosing the mainstream candidates only vote once.

In a typical British election the adoption of such a system would completely change the outcome. Recent British election results have been around Conservative 45 per cent, Labour 35 per cent, and Liberal 20 per cent. In a multiple transferable vote system the Liberal second preferences would be redistributed to decide who had won the election. As most Liberal second preferences are likely to go to Labour rather than to Conservative, the one-fifth of the electorate who had decided to vote for neither major party would then vote effectively for a second time, and decide that the least popular major party should win the election. It is difficult to see the justice in this system of 'two votes for the price of one'.

A weakened variant of this is the two-round election. This has been adopted in France as a compromise following flirtation with thoroughgoing proportional representation. In this system a first round ballot is held between as many parties and individuals as wish to run. A second ballot or run-off is then held at a later date where only the main candidates are allowed to run again. This system has many obvious disadvantages. It prolongs the agony of the election before a result is known. It adds to the administrative cost and complexity of running the election, meaning that two elections have to be run instead of one. But above all it replicates some of the drawbacks of the multiple transferable vote system, again meaning that those who choose to vote for minority parties in the first round have disproportionate influence on the outcome of the election in the second. It is less unfair than the multiple transferable vote as there are only single preferences on the ballot paper, and it also gives the opportunity to those voting for the major parties to switch their allegiance, should they choose to do so in the light of the tactical information they have gleaned about the result from the first round ballot. In practice, however, this method still gives greater choice and greater influence on the election to those who chose on the first round to vote for minority parties, than it does to solid supporters of the major candidates who would be unlikely to change their vote between the first and second rounds.

The third system, the one most commonly imagined by those discussing proportional representation, is the system of allocating the number of seats in relation to the percentage of the popular vote taken by each party. The purest form of this system would be to elect everyone by a national or regional list. The election would be conducted between the main protagonists of each party, and people would vote simply for a given party in their own locality. The aggregate results of their voting intentions across the country would then be reflected in the distribution of a certain number of seats to each party, awarding seats to those on the approved party list in the order of preference of the party. Thus were a British election to be held on these principles, 45 per cent of the seats would be awarded to the Conservative Party, 35 per cent to the Labour Party and 20 per cent to the Liberal Party, assuming people voted in a similar way to recent patterns.

This would mean that voters would have no direct influence or control over their representatives in Parliament. The names of the individuals would be selected for them by the party, and whether they were re-elected or not would be determined by their position on their own party's list, rather than by their own relationship with the electors. It is very difficult to see how such representatives could be made accountable to the electorate in general or to groups of electors in particular. One of the crucial features of the United Kingdom system which has proved popular and has survived the test of time is the link between the individual Member of Parliament and his constituency. It is because the individual has to stand for re-election before the same group of electors at periodic intervals that he is likely to be particularly attentive to their wishes and needs. It is because he has to go to his constituency regularly that he learns more about popular opinion on the issues of the day. He is likely to run surgeries, seek redress for people in trouble and stand up for people against malpractice or the misdeeds of the government because his actions are scrutinized closely by his local press, his local party association and by his local electors. All this is lost under the pure proportional representational system based upon national or regional lists.

There is another larger problem with this kind of proportional representation. It provides an incentive for every lobby group, special interest group and protest group to form its own party, and to campaign for a share of the national vote, as a very modest share of the national vote can translate into seats. In the case of the United Kingdom Parliament with 650 members, securing 0.15 per cent of the popular vote only would be sufficient to secure one Member of Parliament elected. It is much easier to secure 0.15 per cent of the national vote for a particular protest or cause than to secure 40 or 50 per cent of the vote in an individual constituency, which the single subject campaigner currently needs to do in order to get representation in Parliament.

Some would argue that parliamentary democracy would be strengthened if there were more parties and more single subject campaigners elected to Parliament. Others would argue strongly that it would make government much more difficult. The evidence is there on the continent of Europe to illustrate what happens if you move close to this paragon of proportional representational virtues.

A typical system on the continent is to combine single member constituencies with regional and national lists to top up the number of members. In these hybrid systems some element of local accountability is maintained for some of the elected representatives, but others are chosen by regional and national lists to top up the representation of the minor parties who would otherwise not secure much or any representation in Parliament. As a result such countries find that they never elect majority governments. The Italians have had fifty different governments since the war, more than one a year, and often have periods with no administration being formed at all. The Germans have experienced permanent coalition government, with Free Democrats nearly always forming part of the administration, even though they rarely collect more than one in ten of the votes.

In the United Kingdom debate there has been an assumption that the introduction of some variant of this type of proportional representational system would serve to strengthen the centre ground of politics. This has often been erroneously identified with the fortunes of the Liberal Party, even though they are becoming a left-wing, green-campaigning organization. Little credence has been given to the warnings of others who point out that proportional representation is just as likely to strengthen extremes as it is to strengthen the centre. The continent again shows the dangers. In Austria, in Germany and in France their different electoral systems have given platforms to the National Front and neo-Fascist groups who have now secured the election of many members to their different levels of elected assembly. No Fascist has been elected to the United Kingdom Parliament since the Second World War because our electoral system makes it inconceivable that anyone would get the necessary support in any given constituency to be returned. In many elections, however, the National Front have secured sufficient votes to qualify for Members of Parliament under a proportional representation system. The same is true of the other end of the political spectrum, where Communists have regularly been elected to P R-based assemblies on the continent, but have never been elected since the war to the British Parliament.

In much proportional representational thinking there is confusion between the different roles of an elected representative and a protest movement. Protest movements are an integral part of a thriving and lively democracy. They do not, however, require representation in the Parliament to be effective. British politics illustrates how far a strongly organized protest movement can get, and how it is often better for it not to be compromised by power or place. It is the job of the elected representative to assess the mood of his electors or the nation and to take into account the intensity of a protest movement's actions and whether they speak for a wider element of the electorate or not. This balance in judgement would be removed if all the major protest movements had their statutory number of Members of Parliament based upon their small minority share of the popular vote.

There is no evidence that, for example, green campaigning is made impossible because the Green Party cannot gain representation in the House of Commons. The British public think green issues are important, but they do not think they are sufficiently important to warrant the return of single subject campaigners as Members of Parliament. The public recognize that the green movement has a number of other ways of making its point, and that it has been extremely influential in recent years in encouraging debate of green issues on their terms. They have done so by their access to a free press, by their intervention in elections in a number of constituencies, by their influence upon public opinion, and by their influence upon elected representatives from the main parties. Were the Green Party to develop a wider ranging and more balanced view of politics it might attract more general support. Conversely, all the time it remains a single subject campaign it is likely to be more effective not in the ballot box but through its influence on events by lobbying by researching, by drawing public attention to the issues that matter to it.

In recent British political debate Liberal Democrats have argued that 'balanced parliaments', as they like to call them, would be fairer than parliaments dominated by a majority party. Their opponents call them 'hung' parliaments.

A hung parliament completely changes the relationship between the electors and the elected representatives. A majority party is elected on a manifesto which sets out the general principles that underlie that party's conduct of public affairs, and usually sets out a series of specific pledges which the party will try to fulfil over its term of office. A major opposition party will also have a manifesto setting out their principles which they will use to oppose the government, and a set of specific promises which they will lobby and campaign to persuade the government to adopt. The majority party would be unwise to deviate far from the principles it had laid before the electors, as the electors would expect consistency and fair-mindedness from the government, reflecting its prospectus to them. The public would expect the opposition to remain true to their basic principles and to put up a vigorous fight against government proposals that are least popular or most hazardous.

In a hung parliament there is no way that the individual parties can deliver their manifestos. Power shifts from the accountable politicians, answering directly to the electorate, to less accountable politicians dealing behind closed doors to try to find a way to form majorities on individual issues, or trying to piece together a coalition to fill all the jobs available in government. The balance of power switches from majority parties that have won most votes and most seats to the minor parties who could be crucial in controlling the balance of power.

Let us imagine a British hung parliament with 300 Labour seats, 300 Conservative, 25 Liberal and 25 Nationalist. This is an over-simplification as the Nationalist groupings will not usually vote as a block, Ulster members inclining towards the Conservatives and the Scottish and Welsh Nationalists traditionally of a socialist disposition. The introduction of the idea of two simple minority blocks is for the purposes of illustration only.

This hung parliament could result in a Lib./Lab. coalition governing the country, relying upon some support or abstention on the part of the Nationalists to ensure majorities. It might rely upon a Lib./Lab./Nationalist coalition which would have a clear majority. In the early days after the election, both the Liberal and Nationalist groupings would set their price for their support for a Labour administration. Whatever had been said beforehand, the price would be tailored to the circumstances of the post-election position. The electors would have no direct influence on which policies Labour, Liberal and the Nationalists were prepared to broker with each other as they jostled for ministerial jobs and individual policies. The Liberal Party might think it more important to secure two or three major cabinet posts than to stay true to any particular principle or policy they had identified in the election campaign. The Nationalists might understandably want to concentrate on one or two policies of direct relevance to Wales and Scotland, but not be unduly worried about the policies being adopted for the nation as a whole. These are all decisions that the electorate would be unable to influence directly. Negotiations would clearly entail substantial compromises of principle compared with the positions set out in the election campaign.

The difficulties do not end with the creation of a coalition. Coalitions are notoriously more difficult than majority party governments. There is always the risk, if circumstances go against the government, that the minor parties would decide to leave in the interests of disassociating themselves from the fortunes of the administration and in the quest of more votes at the ensuing election. Their departure might also hasten the election if they think that would be of benefit to them. The Liberal Party was prepared to keep the Labour Party in office in the 1970s, but broke from it well before the general election of 1979 in order to give itself time to distance itself from some of the policies of the administration which it had supported. Fortunes of governments and administrations in a coalition are more likely to be controlled by the whims and ambitions of one or two people than in a majority party system. Recently in a hung county council in England, one single member defecting from the Labour Party to the Conservative Party was sufficient to give the Conservatives control of the council, but then the offer to him of the vice-chairmanship of the council on the condition that he would be independent and support a Lib./Lab.

coalition was sufficient to change the composition of the council's governing parties yet again. Neither of these moves was endorsed or recommended by the electorate. In a national government the high offices of state become bargaining counters, goods up for auction, as principles are broken and policies swapped in the interests of keeping people in office.

Cynical commentators believe that proportional representation is favoured entirely by those who do not believe they can amass enough votes to win by the 'first-past-the-post' system. It is notable that when the Liberal Party was a majority party in government, it resisted proportional representation very strongly. When the Liberal Party wins outright control of county or district councils it behaves just like any other majority party and does not seem unduly concerned about the concentration of power or about the fact that it is often elected on a minority of the votes. Its consistent campaign for proportional representation above all else seems to be a recognition that, as the third party in a strong two party system, its only hope of making a breakthrough in representation is to change the basis of what a vote is worth.

Reviewing the evidence on proportional representation leads to the following conclusions. There is no reason why proportional representation should strengthen the middle or the sensible forces in politics: it is just as likely to strengthen the extremes and the irrational forces. There is no evidence to support the contention that proportional representation systems are fairer in the way they give each vote: on the contrary most of these systems strengthen the importance of voters for the minor parties at the expense of the majority of the votes cast. There is a great deal of evidence to support the contention that proportional representation leads to weak and coalition government and makes decisive outcomes in elections more difficult. Proportional representation certainly reduces the responsibility and accountability of politicians, by allowing them to say that they have changed their minds or compromised their principles in the interests of reaching agreement, and that the policies that are being pursued do not reflect their chosen preferences but are the result of the inconclusive election.

As we have seen in the American example, democracy is about more than the casting of votes, central though these are to choice and to the democratic process. The institutions of a free society range more widely than the elected representatives. Modern socialist thinking in Britain has begun to worry about the citizens' right of redress against the public sector. Bryan Gould has been the most outspoken critic, acknowledging in his writings that for years British socialists have seen the public sector as the answer to injustice, the problems of poverty, inequality, bad housing and lack of access to good services, but they are now having to ask the question whether the citizen perhaps needs some protection against the public services themselves. His formulation is an extreme one, but he is belatedly catching up with Conservative thinking developed through the Citizens' Charter. When a government comes to spend more than four-tenths of all the income in the country it wields massive power. In all advanced western societies people are working for almost half the year, or in some cases for longer than half the year, for the government before they start earning any money for themselves. The quality of children's education, the quality of health care, the quality of provision for old age, the quality of most of the transport system and access to much rented housing depends mainly or wholly upon the provision made by the public sector.

The traditional socialist response to any problems of public provision has been that there is nothing wrong with it which more money would not put right. Indeed, in the United Kingdom debate this has been largely a bi-partisan response, with successive administrations, whether Conservative- or Labour-voting, increasing sums of money for the crucial services like health and education. There has been an implicit assumption in much of the thinking that quality can only improve if productivity declines. Success in raising the quality of teaching is measured by the reduction in the number of pupils taught by any given teacher. Improvements in quality of medicine have traditionally been assessed by increasing the number of doctors and nurses relative to the number of patients.

Like many unchallenged principles there is an element of truth in it and an element of falsehood. Clearly it is likely that a child will be better educated in a class of twenty-five than in a class of fifty. He or she is more likely to get noticed and to get a greater degree of individual attention in the smaller class. It would also be the case that to have three teachers to one pupil would not provide a better quality of education but would clearly result in a massive waste of resources. Somewhere between the three teachers to one pupil and thirty pupils to one teacher lies an optimum level of teaching commitment. Similarly, in hospitals there must be enough consultants and nurses to make sure that operating theatres can be manned and operations carried out in a reasonable space of time for those in need of treatment. But over-recruitment of nurses and doctors would result in greater difficulty in delivering a high-quality service as they would begin to get in each other's way. Three theatre nurses may well be better than one, but thirty-three theatre nurses would be impossible.

These extreme propositions illustrate that as with most things in life there is a delicate balance to be struck between the interests in improving productivity and quality, and that there is not always a simple linear relationship between more people and a higher quality of service. Trying to get this accepted in the British debate has been a hazardous and difficult task which is none the less a necessary one.

There has been a fixation in analysing service provision by measuring inputs rather than outputs. So often we are told that the service must be better because £X00 million is being spent on it. So often we are told that the health service must be better because there are more doctors and nurses, or that the education service is improved because there are more teachers. Part of the revolution of the Citizens' Charter is to redirect analysis away from inputs and the mechanics of provision, to measuring outputs – whether the customers or the clients of the service are satisfied, and whether the medical treatment has worked and the education has been of high quality. If we need medical treatment, there are two quality variables above all else which matter to us. The first is how long will it take us to get access to the treatment, and the second is whether the treatment was effective. In education what matters to parents and pupils is whether at the end of the process the children pass the exams they need for their future career, and whether they have developed their talents and matured as individuals so they can fit in well with the society around them. Measuring outputs is an important part of fuelling a revolution in our approach to public services.

The question then arises about what redress the citizen has if he doesn't like his own individual experiences with the service, or if he feels the quality of the service overall is falling short of that which the public should expect. In a democratic society it is not sufficient to say that he has enough redress through his elected representatives and that they will be able to wave the magic wand and put everything right. Of course the elected representatives are there to see that the health and education services are set suitable quality targets and that they are well administered. Parliament is there to expose malpractice, incompetence or a failure to provide the resources necessary to deliver the quality required. But there needs as well to be redress, choice and opportunity at the local level, more directly responsive to the individual needs.

Democratic societies rest upon freedom of information and upon the capacity to make choices. In the case of the great public services, the publication of information about the quality and range of service on offer is important to giving individuals power. People should know what are the achievements of the local schools in their area, and it is helpful when the local schools set out in individual prospectuses the style and quality of education they offer. This enables the parents to make informed choices about the school to which they wish their child to go. The power to choose begins to influence the style of provision made in the local area. If a large number of parents in a given area decide they prefer a primary school based upon traditional methods of instruction in English and arithmetic, then that school will receive a large number of applications, whilst the schools offering different methods will discover their number of applications falling. In a system which tends to give everyone their first choice place wherever possible, this will lead to expansion for the successful school, and to the pressures of decline on the less popular schools. This in turn should lead their boards of governors and their head teacher to reconsider the style and quality of education they are offering in an attempt to attract more pupils.

A system based upon publication of information and choice at a local level also begins to undermine the intimidating monopoly exercised in the traditional public services. People have felt their democratic rights damaged because they have found themselves powerless to influence or affect the outcome in the services that matter most to them. Under a system where all the schools are comprehensive and where the only form of redress is to write to a Councillor or Member of Parliament, most people would feel they have very little influence over the style or type of education their children were to receive. In a system where power has been devolved to individual schools in the locality, and where those individual schools are differentiating their product, people begin to have some power through choice. They may wish to extend their power by sitting as parent governors on their chosen school board, thereby having a direct role in choosing the new head teacher when a vacancy becomes available. This is the single most important thing that anyone can do in moulding and developing the future of an individual school. The system can be and is backed up by appeal mechanisms to try and improve people's chances of getting their first choice school, and by the ebb and flow of place provision at schools depending on whether the school is in a popular or unpopular phase of its recruitment. The creation of different types of school ranging through technology colleges, comprehensives, magnet and grammar schools also extends the range of choice for parents.

Individual rights can be bolstered by ombudsman procedures to investigate maladministration, by parent-teacher meetings, by strengthening non-executive and parent representation on governing boards, and by independent inspectorates responsible for checking up on the quality and on the figures being presented to the parents. In these ways democratic accountability is strengthened in the locality in addition to the overall right of redress through the elected representative and through Parliament.

Pressure group politics also has a role to play. In the case of education it is possible for a pressure group to emerge to campaign, for example, for more traditional techniques in teaching. Pressure groups have become adept at winning media time and influencing people. Opinion surveys, surveys of existing styles and results, informed articles, and arguments about how things can be better, create news opportunities which in turn can exert pressure within a democratic society upon elected politicians in county and national government responsible for the education service. They also have an influence upon the profession. Much of what Mr Gould means about the difficulties for citizens from an overwhelming public sector comes from making senior officials and professionals accountable to the users of the services. If I do not like the way a solicitor or a private accountant behaves when working for me I can always go down the road to another one and may get a better service. If I do not like the way the local head teacher or the consultant at the hospital does his job, it has until recently been more difficult to do anything about it. Owning something does not always give the government control over it and providing all the money does not always purchase the leverage which people would like.

Challenging professional orthodoxies is one of the hardest things to do in a democracy, but often one of the most important. There is a danger in even the most active democracies that the politicians are carried along upon the wave of other people's opinion. Fashions in public sector management illustrate this point vividly. In the early 1970s it was popular management wisdom that big was good and biggest was best. In the United Kingdom local government was reorganized to create bigger county administrative units capable of planning on a wider scale. The health service was reorganized to create health regions and move towards more centralized control in many areas. It became accepted in both the education and the health services that units needed to be larger. In place of the 300-or 400-pupil school the 1200–1500-pupil school became the ideal or even the norm in many areas. In place of the 50–100-bed cottage hospital and the 300-or 400-bed local hospital, the 1,000–2,000-bed mega-hospital was willingly planned and often constructed. Politicians and individual people were swept along by this tide of managerial enthusiasm for scale. They accepted the idea that you needed larger schools in order to spread overheads and to provide a wider range of specialist teaching. They accepted the case for the large centralized hospital on the grounds that it would provide a better quality of care, allowing people to concentrate resources and buy the sophisticated new equipment which medical technology is developing.

In both health and education a limited number of people were rich enough to exercise their own choice in the private sector. What was curious was that at the very time the public sector had decided that scale mattered above all else, those choosing to spend their money as private providers and those choosing to spend their own money as private patients or parents of private sector pupils, chose very often to spend the money on smaller units. Private hospitals were constructed with tens or hundreds, rather than thousands, of beds. Many private sector schools flourished with well under 1,000 pupils on the roll. Planners had forgotten to ask people what they preferred. In local government people found it difficult to associate with some of the large new counties and districts created by the 1973/4 reforms, preferring instead to associate themselves still with the older, smaller counties and urban and rural districts and towns that had pre-dated the boundary changes.

Successful government offers a challenge to conventional wisdom and a rigorous scrutiny of professional advice. Politicians who too readily accept that they are slaves to some defunct economist soon discover they have little impact upon the conduct of policy. Politicians need good professional advice and usually have access to the best that money can buy. They also need to apply their scepticism and their understanding of the commonsense view so that they are not hijacked by errant or unfortunate professional misconceptions.

In all mature democracies there is a constant tension between, on the one hand, the wish to preserve a free society and, on the other, to make governments more and more accountable for more and more elements of life. Combative democracies naturally encourage the idea that the government is to blame for anything that goes wrong in the country. An alert opposition will exploit any weakness, any social problem, any economic malaise, whether it is the fault of government action or inaction, or the fault of some other cause. They will naturally wish to ascribe it to government error as part of the competitive jostle between parties seeking advantage.

Governments are then placed in a dilemma. They can claim that it is no responsibility of theirs and that they do not control that aspect of life. Oppositions will claim that this is an abnegation of responsibility and will attempt to force the government into accepting some responsibility or adopting a policy that tries to tackle the underlying problem. Governments may be reluctant to make a heroic stand on the grounds that they are not competent or powerful enough to influence the problem. They will then willingly suggest a policy that they think will improve or moderate the problem and are caught on the hook of competence and the need to exercise power. By these means free liberal democracies have given government more and more powers and more and more claims of responsibility for large areas of life.

Carried to extremes, this can be dangerous. Freedom needs defending every day, and a free society rests upon the independent actions and choices of individuals, families and companies, in addition to the actions of government and its intervention in some aspects of life. Whilst it may be right for the government to assume responsibilities to improve the incomes of the poorest members of society, and whilst this may do little damage to the freedom of the community overall, if the government extends its intervention right up the income scale, so it becomes responsible for settling the effective incomes of most or all people in the community, then clearly freedom has been gravely damaged. Similarly, it may make sense for the government to take responsibility for controlling the quality and safety of certain sensitive products like children's toys or electrical appliances, but it would represent a serious incursion into economic freedom if the government moved from this to laying down blueprints and designs for every type of manufactured product.

The erosion of freedom can easily come about through the best of intentions. What begins as a desirable process with the government intervening to achieve a specific social and economic goal, could end as a complete raft of controls and interventions across the society limiting freedom and making government too powerful. In this situation democracy can approve the means of its own undoing, with the free democratic process leading to unreasonable levels of government control. It then often proves to be self-correcting, with parties, policies and programmes forming to resist further incursions of government power and to act as a brake or check upon the expansion of the over-mighty state. In this lies the origins of many of the freedom, privatization and liberalization movements now common in western democracies.

Money can prove the force that both advances the strength of government and in due course turns out to be its limitation. Government power is often expressed in the form of offering grants, subsidies, inducements, tax rebates. Government action may take the threatening form of levying special taxes, duties, licence fees and imposts upon the conduct of commerce. People are attracted by the lure of what they think is easy money and so they readily queue up to apply for grants, subsidies and tax inducements and are willing to enter negotiations and accede to restrictions and stipulations in order to qualify. As the government becomes more powerful and dispenses more money from its system, so it becomes more important to devote considerable business and individual resources to gain access to the ear of government and to analyse the opportunities for taking money from government. Some companies in certain lines of business particularly susceptible to government orders, grants and subsidies, may start to devote their better or best managerial talent to dealing with government to try and maximize their take from the government account, rather than to handling design, production management and their private sector customers. This can be seen at its most obvious in the cases of nationalized industries in large western countries where a prime aim of nationalized industry management is to have good relationships with government to ensure the smooth passage of cash and subsidy, or high-profile disputes with government where they can appeal over the heads of government to demand more money for their purposes.

At a certain point the debate becomes crude and oversimplified. A nationalized trading concern will constantly say that what impedes a higher quality of service to its customers is a shortage of government support and funding. The private sector too might join in at an advanced stage in this process, by alleging that the tax system or the failure to make adequate grants was the cause of the problem. It is difficult to find a voice for the consumer and a voice for the tax-payer in a debate like this. Government will be crowded out by the arguments of the vested interests. An easy line for the journalist to take is that the only thing that is wrong is an absence of public money, and this will be reinforced by opposition arguments and by all of the so-called professional opinion.

In these conditions the government needs to be especially firm in speaking up for those who have to pay the bills, and in challenging the professional advice that is being offered.

The Danish referendum on the provisions of the Maastricht Treaty illustrates what can go wrong when an elite combines to force a view upon a country against the wishes of the people. In Denmark there were always popular worries about the loss of national and community identity within a larger European Community. There was always a fear of German power and influence and a reluctance to see Denmark swallowed by her larger and more powerful neighbours. Danish politicians, business interests, civil servants and intellectuals combined to argue that Denmark only had an economic future within an enlarged economic community, and that this economic future would be jeopardized if Denmark failed to go along with the move towards greater political union in western Europe. So confident were they that they would carry the country that they campaigned in what seemed to critics an off-handed, even arrogant manner, suggesting to the Danish people that there was no alternative, and that there was nothing wrong with the provisions of the Treaty. They were overwhelmed by the popular demand to see the Treaty itself and read its provisions, by the strength of the 'No' protest movement, and by the passion of the arguments in public meetings, open air concerts and through the press. The end result, with a little over half of the Danish people saying 'No' to the Maastricht Treaty, shocked the establishment. They had felt that people should have taken their professional advice, that 'No' meant that jobs would be lost, that business would be set back, that Denmark would be sidelined.

These professional experts failed to explain to the Danish people why more trade, commerce and prosperity requires common institutions and centralized government from Brussels. The Danish 'No' voters could see that higher tax demands might be needed in order to pay the transfer payments to the southern members of the community, that there might be higher tax demands in order to pay for enlarged institutions and greater bureaucracy; they could also see that, far from gaining influence over their own affairs, they might lose it as they became subsumed within a much larger political framework.

The Danish 'No' vote in the Maastricht referendum was the first time for several years in which the peoples of an individual nation were allowed to express their own view on what the politicians and bureaucrats were doing to create a more united Europe. It sent shockwaves through the political establishment, reminding them that in democracies their proposals have to be saleable and that they can only go at the pace which people in the country will accept.

Had the Danes negotiated an opt-out from the social arrangements and special protection over the Single Currency in the way that the United Kingdom had negotiated them, the outcome of the referendum in Denmark may have been different. Had Denmark had a more extensive public debate before the Maastricht terms had been finally agreed in the way the United Kingdom had done, they may have gained more consent from their people for the proposals. The fact that they did not and the fact that the Commission during the course of the Danish referendum campaign was pressing on with yet further plans for centralizing bureaucracy showed that the political establishments had grown out of touch with the people in a very dramatic way.

In many parts of the world people are suspicious of experts. Experts try to insulate themselves from the public by speaking their own special language, by stamping too many documents 'secret' and by conducting debates behind closed doors. The purpose of the democratic debating chambers is to bring into the open the decisions and the arguments that lie behind public policy and to translate those policies into a language which people can grasp. Where professional groups and elites fail to put enough matters to democratic challenge and test, they run the risk of the overthrow of their policy or even of themselves.

The dilemma of democracy used to be expressed by the professionals. How, they asked, could the public, ill-informed as they are about the theory and practice of public policy, make sensible decisions about the wide range of issues coming before government? History has shown that the public are often more sensible than the experts, and that the strength of democracy comes when the people challenge the experts and when their elected representatives stand up to them in the interests of common sense. The weakness of democracy from the point of view of the individual is knowing how he can be sure that there will not be a conspiracy against him by professionals with vested interests in misdirecting the country or keeping him in the dark.

The most likely way the individual's interests will be affronted is by interested parties and the government machinery taking more money in taxation from him to spend on their joint purposes. Politicians can easily believe in the Dutch auction approach: they come to conclude that the business of politics is in offering more and more apparently free goods and services from the centre, in the hope and belief that people will enjoy the free services without recognizing the additional costs and taxes they impose.

Northcote Parkinson many years ago set out a thesis which said that there was a limit to the taxable capacity of any given country. When tax reaches a certain level of income, he argued, it becomes worthwhile for people to emigrate or to evade or even avoid paying tax altogether. Black economies spring into action, tax accountants earn bigger and bigger fees and government has to become cleverer at trying to block loopholes. He did not consider the counter proposition that when government reaches a certain size and complexity it has within it its own in-built momentum which makes it very difficult for the public to arrest its growth. His own work on the expansion of bureaucracies demonstrated that there could be an ineluctable logic to the appointment of ever more people, but he did not recognize that this could be reinforced by the competitive bidding of the Dutch auction political process. Government advisors would encourage government ministers to believe that they had to give way to the 'political' pressure for more spending and for the assumption of more activity and responsibility by government. This in turn would lead to strong demands from the bureaucracy for more staffing in ever more offices to meet these unavoidable demands.

Recent years have shown that there are ways for the public to hit back. In extreme situations where the public sector has taken over 90 per cent or more of the activity of the country, the eclipse of freedom has become so final that it has led to the eventual overthrow of the whole government system. In democracies protest and political action have at times perpetuated in the face of the ever-increasing expansion of state bureaucracy and taxation. In the United Kingdom in 1992 election a comparatively moderate programme of expanded public sector activity and taxation was decisively rejected by the electorate, despite the economy being in recession and despite the electorate having some reservations about the record of the government in power. In many local elections rate-payer or tax-payer candidates are returned and start to exercise some influence upon the spending patterns of their local council. In the United States propositions on the ballot paper in favour of capping or reducing taxation can have a powerful effect upon the spending plans of State governments, and on the continent of Europe, especially towards the South, the black economy is very pronounced where tax levels are high.

The whole privatization movement is an answer worldwide to the worry about the ever-growing tentacles of a state and the ever-increasing tax demands for subsidy and other payments. Although these policies and programmes are fiercely opposed by many of the interest groups most affected, the persistence and success of many of these programmes illustrates that there are strong counter pressures that can be harnessed to place some limitation upon the growth of the state.

In the United Kingdom there is vigorous debate about two kinds of freedom. The Conservative Party lays especial stress upon the freedom of individuals to choose to do things, to raise their own money and to choose their own spending pattern, relatively free of state intervention and free of penal taxation. The Labour Party tends to emphasize the freedoms which it believes state intervention can give to those who would otherwise be less well off. It believes freedom comprises benefit transfers to the poor and the granting of rights of access to 'free' public services.

Although the debate accentuates the difference in practice both major parties agree that both types of freedom are an important part of a free society. The Conservative Party in power has often increased the range and eligibility to benefits and their value, recognizing that people who are incapacitated through old age, sickness, ill-health and disability do need transfer incomes from taxes on others to give them some spending power and choice in their lives. The Conservative Party also recognizes the need to provide free health and education services to all those who require them, to ensure adequate provision whatever a person's means. For its part, the Labour Party accepts that there has to be some limit upon the amount of tax imposed upon individuals, otherwise the wealth-creating process is damaged, incentive and choice are removed. The debate is increasingly about the margins. Recent political events have shown that at the current level of government intervention in the economy, people are very sensitive even to proposed marginal changes to increase tax and the provision of apparently free services.

True democracy rests upon getting this balance right. There

does have to be some income transfer so that all people have basic choices available to them in their lives, but there has to be a clear limit upon the degree of intervention and the amount of regulation and the level of taxation imposed, or else freedom perishes. Some continental countries during the 1990s may discover that proportional representation gives too easy a task to the neo-Fascist and nationalist movements likely to breed against a background of religious disputes, civil wars and mass migrations of peoples.

The democratic traditions of western Europe also have to adjust to the evolution of European Community law-making, which is having a growing impact on constitutional developments.

SIX

The European Community: We Must Have an Agreement

The evolution of the European Community is interwoven with debates about accountability and democracy. The EC is organized as a law-making body. The Commission is always seeking to regulate more areas of our lives on a cross-border basis from Brussels. The emphasis all the time is on getting agreement to another law rather than on the terms of that law and what it might achieve. Every directive that passes, every regulation that goes through gives to the Commission new powers to intervene across the member states. It means that cases under those regulations and directives can be taken to the European Court. It means that the European Commissioners have powers to represent the member states in other countries on those subjects. It means that the Commission staff have rights to investigate what is going on in the member states and if necessary to insist on changes to bring them in line with the growing corpus of European law. Only the Commission can draft a new proposal: only the Council of Ministers can decide whether to pursue it.

A major Commission legislative programme was linked to the British idea of a Single Market. A large group of directives and regulations totalling 282, thought to be important to the achievement of a truly common market, was brought forward. Subsequently the Commission discussed with the socialist and Christian Democrat states the need for a social dimension. This resulted in a new programme of sixty-five directives being proposed to cover everything from pensions and welfare through to employee relations and trade unions. One of the ideas behind the Commission's negotiation was to identify new areas in which community competence could be developed, leading on to more directives and regulations extending Commission power. The United Kingdom argued for clauses which set out the areas outside EC competence and introduced the concept of leaving to national authorities those things that did not have cross-border dimensions. It is within the European Community itself that one of the most important global battles between free trade and protection is being fought out.

The Community's legislature is the Council of Ministers who act on the advice of the Commission and discuss drafts from the Commission. Most measures these days go through under a system of qualified majority voting. Around the table the twelve member states are seated with 76 votes in total. For a measure to go through 54 votes are required in support. A member state wishing to block a directive, or part of a directive, needs to assemble at least 23 votes against the proposal in order to prevent it. The four big member states – France, Germany, Italy and the United Kingdom – have 10 votes each. Spain has 8; Greece, Portugal, the Netherlands and Belgium have 5 each; Ireland and Denmark have 3 and Luxembourg has 2.

There are no in-built majorities within the Council of Ministers. There is a loose English-speaking group comprising the United Kingdom, Ireland, Denmark, the Netherlands and sometimes extending to Greece and Italy. There is a slightly stronger French-speaking group comprising France, Belgium, Luxembourg, Spain and Portugal and sometimes extending to Italy depending upon the Minister or representative present. There is a free trade group centred around the United Kingdom, Germany, Denmark, the Netherlands and sometimes including Ireland and Luxembourg, balanced by a protectionist interventionist group led by France and supported by Spain, Portugal and Belgium, and sometimes encompassing Greece and Italy. There is a Code Napoléon group based upon French systems which comprises France, Belgium, Luxembourg, Spain, Portugal, and often extends to Germany and the Netherlands, against a smaller parliamentary and common law tradition comprising the United Kingdom, Ireland and Denmark.

As these lists demonstrate, there can never be a majority in the Community for a pure free trade measure or for an entirely socialist protectionist measure. This is why the Community has never passed a privatization directive, even though privatization is now a common policy amongst governments around the world, and why it would be impossible in the current political configuration for the Community to back, say, a French proposal for a nationalization directive. Each directive or regulation takes the form of a compromise between the different systems and different views of the world. To succeed a directive must have a genuflection to free trade and something for the interventionists. It must be able to accommodate part of the Anglo-Saxon common law system whilst being largely rooted in the Napoleonic tradition. In order to meet these tough requirements directives are often loosely worded leaving the ultimate meaning to be determined by the member states and in turn by the European Court of Justice sitting in judgement over them.

When negotiating a directive under qualified majority procedures a member state is well aware of the limitations of its power in trying to protect its own system from fundamental change as a side-effect of the directive. Most are only too aware that it is difficult to impose a coherent world view upon a group of directives because of the compromises necessary. Some examples will show how negotiations work out in practice.

The Commission, subjected to strong lobbying from Philips and Thompson on the continent concerning satellite television broadcasting systems, decided through Commissioner Pandolfi, an Italian, to put forward a High-Definition Television Directive. The original draft directive was designed to force all community satellite providers to use the Philips/Thompson HDTV D2MAC technology, and for all television sets to contain D2MAC decoders in them so that simulcasting, the joint broadcasting in conventional television signals and D2MAC, would spread more widely. It was a typical example of a move to create a European national champion industrial strategy by the back door. The ostensible intention to further the use of high-definition TV combined with the purpose to prefer one way of creating HDTV at the expense of others.

The United Kingdom took the lead in pointing out the dangers of this proposal. Firstly, it meant that existing satellite services, like BSB/Sky in the United Kingdom, and Astra in Luxembourg, could be forced to change all their equipment from their traditional PAL transmission system into D2MAC at considerable cost. It could, indeed, have had the perverse effect of closing down the two largest and most successful satellite services in the European Community, faced as they would have been with the very large expense of completely changing all their technology and the equipment of their service recipients. Secondly, the UK opposed the imposition of a £50–£200 additional cost on every purchase of a television set in order to have a D2MAC decoder. Thirdly, it seemed dangerous to restrict European Community industry by law to a single form of technology which had not been proven in the field and which to date has not been popular. At the same time as some European Community companies on the continent were developing D2MAC the Americans were close to achieving a completely digital system, an area of development which was also of considerable interest to the Japanese. When the UK first set out these arguments only Spain was known to be concerned about the issue, with the possibility that Luxembourg would also take exception to the impact the directive would have on Astra. This would create a 20 votes minority, short of the 23 needed to block all or part of the proposed measure.

There was, however, a weakness in the other position. Those member states like France and the Netherlands that were keenest to see the directive through wished it to be joined by two other measures. The first was to be an agreement between the participating companies to develop this particular HDTV technology, and the second was to be substantial Community funding of the research and development necessary to get D2MAC into a shape where it could be a commercial reality. Commissioner Pandolfi had promised anywhere between £660 million and £1300 million for this task but had no budget approval. He required the support of all member states on a unanimous vote to approve such a large increase in Community expenditure.

It was the turn of the Dutch presidency to hold the debate on this particular directive. The presidency chairs Community meetings and is held by each of the twelve member states for six months on a rota system. The presidency has certain powers to work with the Commission in fixing the agenda for the Council meetings and in deciding how much negotiating time and priority should be accorded to particular proposals. The Dutch decided to make this matter a priority for their presidency and allocated substantial negotiating time in the

Telecommunications Council and in informal sessions outside the Council to see if an agreement could be reached. The United Kingdom took a vigorous line on the arguments of principle, setting them out in public, to the House of Commons and to the international press. At the same time those member states most likely to be sympathetic to the UK case were lobbied.

The United Kingdom made it clear during the negotiations that there could be no question of approving any funding for this project if the directive went forward in a largely unamended form. The UK also made it clear that there could be no consideration of funding until a proper business proposal was put forward explaining what the money was going to be purchasing, what controls there were going to be over the costs of the programme and what the likelihood of success would be. Some other member states and the Commission were happy to discuss the funding of up to £1300 million without any such prospectus before them.

In the early negotiating sessions the important concession that existing satellite service providers should be able to continue running with their existing equipment and not forced to change was granted. The UK added to this the important proviso that those existing services should be able to invest and reinvest in the expansion and development of their system without shifting technologies at the same time. This allayed the fears of Luxembourg and Astra and dealt with the BSB/Sky problem. The Community also began to make progress on the question of a decoder in every television set, although the Germans were particularly strong in wishing to support simulcasting.

The final negotiating session was a long one. It lasted from 4 p.m. until 2 a.m. and was followed by a hectic morning of comings and goings and a further two hours to completion of the directive. During the course of this negotiating session the United Kingdom held firm to its principles and discovered that it had wide-ranging support from other member states despite the original fear that there would be little support beyond Spain and Luxembourg. Towards the end of the negotiation it became clear that ten member states including the United Kingdom agreed that no extra imposition should be made upon the cost of the ordinary television set in people's homes; they agreed that existing satellite providers must be protected, and that digital technology should be exempted from the directive so that it could be separately developed by companies within the European Community in competition with the Americans and Japanese if they saw fit.

In return the United Kingdom accepted that there should be some kind of directive (the UK had felt for a long time it would have been better without one at all) and accepted that it would consider a suitable business plan to see if there was a case that could be made out for any funding of the R&D necessary for the development of D2MAC. Unfortunately the two member states that were in disagreement with the common position were France and Germany. France led the attack, seeing this as an opportunity to develop an indigenous European technology distinct from the Japanese and American and to seal the European market from competitive forces from overseas. They saw it as a test-case for the kind of industrial policy that their socialist government favoured but had been thwarted domestically to some extent by Treaty of Rome competition rules. They were supported by the Germans, largely because the Germans traditionally in the pre- and post-Maastricht era support the French on a wide range of issues.

The Community could have overridden France and Germany as they only have 20 votes between them, 3 short of a blocking minority. However, the Commission was unprepared to amend the draft directive it had tabled despite the views of the ten member states seeking substantial changes. Without Commission consent to amend the proposal under Community rules the member states need to reach unanimity before they can force upon the Commission a draft other than that which the Commission has tabled. The long negotiating sessions allowed breaks for the French minister to telephone Paris for higher instructions. Eventually the news came that France would rather have the slimmed down directive that the ten states had designed than no directive at all, and with the change of France, Germany changed her position creating unanimity. The Commission was then obliged to accept the amended directive.

This lengthy example has many of the elements of a normal Community negotiation. The original idea put forward by the Commission is based upon a narrow range of opinion. It contains many impracticalities which need to be ironed out during the negotiating and consultation process. The fact that the United Kingdom and some other member states are prepared to distribute these draft directives widely and to seek a broad range of views from industry and individuals greatly strengthens the task of law-making. It means that if amendments are accepted the laws are more practical and their harmful effects less pronounced and damaging. It also demonstrates the important role played by qualified majority voting and by the fairly loose procedure in the Community. Negotiations are behind closed doors and are relatively free of procedural constraints. Amendments do not have to be tabled in advance and may not even be written down. If, however, an amendment catches the mood of the meeting it may then be written into the draft and either accepted by the Commission or imposed if all the member states so decide.

It is very unlike parliamentary passage of laws. In Parliament there is a clearly defined procedure. A formal first reading is followed by a second reading debate of the principles. The committee stage deals with the line by line commentary, providing the opportunity for opposition and back-bench members to bring to bear the views and opinions and voices of all those likely to be affected by the legislation, and to comment or amend line by line. The third reading provides another formal debating opportunity to discuss the major issues and the report stage provides further opportunity for amendment by the government in the light of criticisms and comments or by the opposition if they can marshal enough supporters.

In the Community legislating does not have the same benefit of formal procedure and formal opposition. No one around the table of Ministers is charged with the task of exposing the follies and inadequacies of the draft. Member states only expose them if it is against their own national interest for the draft to go through in its existing form. The opposition is not public unless the member state chooses to make it public in press briefings or press releases before or after the meeting. There is no statutory formal consultation procedure for the Commission to follow and the range of consultees responding may often be random as people and companies in many member states are still not used to the need to lobby the Commission and the European institutions.

The negotiation of the Merger Regulation demonstrates how much easier it is to maintain a national position against the background of a proposal requiring unanimity. The Commission had long held the ambition of wanting direct powers to regulate mergers between European companies on a continental scale. They had strong allies in the form of the smaller member states and Italy. These states either did not have a strongly developed competition and merger strategy of their own at home, or they felt by virtue of their size that they were unable to enforce remedies against very large corporations acting across borders. Countries the size of Luxembourg, Belgium and the Netherlands find that practically all deals involving large companies entail big cross-border issues as the companies are much larger in their geographical spread than the confines of their own market. Conversely, in France, Germany and the United Kingdom there is a greater incidence of national companies entering deals that pose questions for the competition authorities that do not cross national borders.

This difference of background and national sentiment created the dividing line over the Merger Regulation. The principal issues were what size of transaction and company should be covered by European rather than by domestic competition regulation, what should the criteria be for settling merger issues, and how much power should there be for a member state to call the matter back into national jurisdiction despite the existence of European Community competence?

France, Germany and Britain were united in agreeing that the Community's action should be limited only to those very large mergers likely to entail big cross-border deals from large member states. France, Germany and the United Kingdom dug in over the issue of thresholds and said that the combined turnover of the merging parties should be at least 5,000 million ECU where the Commission and the smaller member states wanted a figure of 1,000 or 2,000 million ECU. The presence of national vetoes and the existence of a 30-vote block amongst the large member states meant that if the smaller states wanted any kind of Merger Regulation they had ultimately to accept the fact that the large member states were going to insist upon a higher threshold.

The issue of criteria split the Community in a different way. The French led their socialist protectionist block arguing strongly for a Merger Regulation based upon industrial policy as well as competition. They felt that the European Commission should have rights to decide what was in the general industrial interest of Europe, however vaguely defined, with the inclination that some large cross-border mergers which might be anti-competitive should none the less be allowed on the grounds that they would create Euro-champions capable of taking on large Japanese and American competitors. The United Kingdom and Germany argued strongly against this, with some help from some of the smaller states of a free trade disposition. The UK believed that the whole system should be competition based, on the grounds that preserving a competitive market is the best way to strengthen the competitiveness of companies within the European Community, making it more likely that it could resist the attack of American and Japanese groups. On this occasion the French were in the chair. They therefore became very keen on an agreement despite their clear national interest in industrial policy clauses. They were ultimately prepared to accept the competition-only regime with very vague and loose words about industrial policy that had no real impact upon the way the Commission should proceed.

The third issue of exits to national jurisdiction isolated Germany. Germany has a strong competition-driven system and was very worried that the European Community version would be weak compared with the German Bundeskartellamt. Consequently Germany sought the right to parallel consideration of transactions with a view to them being blocked by either competition authority that thought them anti-competitive. The United Kingdom and many other member states resisted this particular proposal and it was agreed that the national exits would be quite limited with a view to trying to create for merging parties the maximum certainty about which jurisdiction they would face.

Because it turned out that each member state did, however, have some national interest or other that needed protection, exits did have to be provided through the regulation to permit separate consideration of other issues. For example, the United Kingdom was keen that its system of prudential regulation of financial businesses, its defence and security interests and its special handling of media transactions should not be jeopardized. France was worried about her banking industry and Germany was worried about industry in general. These particular problems were picked up in the national exits that were allowed.

With unanimity it is possible to dig in and to drive a regulatory directive in a more minimalist direction. As member states do this the Presidency and the Commission become keener for agreement at any price and are prepared to delete matters from such a directive or regulation in order to get agreement. With qualified majority voting there is no such natural tendency towards the minimalist solution. Instead there is a tendency towards log-rolling of proposals, however inappropriate they may be for some members, in the interests of finding that solution which the majority of states can go along with whatever impact they may have elsewhere.

A proposal under simple majority voting can go through with very little member-state involvement. It is extremely difficult to find six member states agreeing in order to block a proposal going through under simple majority. The Commission is well aware of its strength and on these issues discussion is normally perfunctory. It is unlikely for the draft to be amended substantially in the negotiating session as it is very easy for the Commission to get the required votes.

The issue western Europe has to face is whether this is a good way of legislating for 340 million people. The first issue commonly discussed is the so-called democratic deficit. Those who argue that there is a democratic deficit in the European Community are arguing the case for a much stronger European Parliament. This is to misconceive the current nature of the Community and its legislative process. Its method of passing directives is based upon intergovernmental discussion and negotiation. For that reason the Council of Ministers is sovereign. Whilst the Commission has enormous power to propose and to amend proposals, if the member states are agreed that they do not want a particular proposal or they do want another kind of proposal, then they have the ultimate right to insist upon it. The Commission has been very skilful at strengthening its power by finding common ground between member states and by shifting the voting rules in a way which favours more compromise and agreement. For the European Parliament to be a successful legislature it would need to have the right to propose laws, which it does not have, the right to amend and the right to approve final legislation. At the moment the European Parliament has the right to offer its advice and amendments on proposals in certain defined areas, but even these amendments and advice can be overturned if the Council of Ministers is unanimous. Under the Maastricht proposals the European Parliament also has the right to block a proposal which the European Council of Ministers has agreed. This negative power could mean less legislation in the Community, or it could mean that some members' votes around the Council table start to reflect the arguments and fears of the European Parliament in the interests of reaching an agreement which sticks and is not vetoed by the Parliament when it comes to consider it.

Those who believe that the process has to be inter-governmental in the main do not believe in the so-called democratic deficit. Whenever a proposal comes to the United Kingdom it is sent straight to the Parliament at Westminster, to the House of Commons and the House of Lords Scrutiny Committees for their consideration. A consultation document is usually sent out to the press and public, with individual copies sent to those associations and companies that will be most affected by the proposal to seek their views. Often ministers and officials hold meetings with the most important parties to begin the task of hammering out a common United Kingdom view on the proposal. This common United Kingdom view is formed as a result of the consultation replies and parliamentary debate, and is agreed if necessary with Cabinet. It is then made public. The press, public and Parliament are usually kept up to date with progress in a negotiation. If the proposals change materially or if it seems likely that the UK will not be able to achieve its minimum negotiating objectives then a further memorandum is sent to the Scrutiny Committees of each House. This process is extremely democratic.

The one problem with the process lies in the meetings in Brussels, where press and public are excluded from the final negotiating sessions which replace the committee stage in House of Commons legislation. Some say that if people could see their legislators at work around the Council of Ministers' table through the eyes and ears of the press and the camera, it would make the process that much more democratic. Many member states and commentators argue that this would be unreasonable as negotiating sessions have by nature to be private. Any change would heighten the distinction between, on the one hand, the informal sessions over lunch and in private rooms, and, on the other, the more formal statements of position and negotiating sessions around the full Council table. In practice, deals and agreements are often hammered out outside the Council chamber already.

A typical process is for the Commission and the Presidency to amend its proposals in the light of a discussion in the Council of Ministers and then to take the amended proposals to the two or three member states most critical to winning a qualified majority, or most critical to removing a blocking minority, with a view to trying to change the votes on the table. If 23 votes are blocking a particular proposal and, for example, a small member state with 3 votes as part of that block has a slightly different negotiating objective from the two main states in the 23-vote coalition, the Commission and the Presidency will often try offering the small member state something which is of no use to the other two member states with a view to dislodging it from the blocking minority. If part of a blocking minority is one of the southern states very often the Commission suggests that more money might be available for southern purposes, or that they could get a derogation from the coming into effect of the proposal for a period of years, making it easier for them to sell it back home. These private negotiating sessions would obviously be strengthened were the Council itself to be subject to full public scrutiny.

Proponents of openness say all would not be lost as a result. It would be more difficult for some member states' ministers to intimate by their language or by their mannerisms that they are happy to be outvoted on a particular proposal as they sometimes do in the closed sessions of Council. Some ministers are arguing a case other than the one they really believe in for the sake of public consumption back home, and are quite delighted when the Council of Ministers vetoes them and makes them do the right thing against their will. It would also make it more difficult for some member states to be treacherous in their support of particular causes. The eleventh-hour ditching of strongly held principles or important commercial interests would be very apparent under the light of the camera and might make some member states more hesitant about agreeing to inappropriate legislation.

The Community is a legislative machine rather than a government. Its executive powers and rights are quite circumscribed by natural caution on the part of member states about the creation of a European police force within their own territories. Given the composite nature of the regulations negotiated in Brussels there is a danger that Community practice could degenerate into the over-regulation of every facet of our daily lives and the creation of a large black economy that is outside the regulations.

We can already see this happening in areas like food retailing and processing. The strong rules of the Community for health and safety reasons are already being ignored in hundreds upon hundreds of small shops and street markets around the Community. Regulations about hand basins, special lighting to control flies and storage conditions for food are not appropriate to many a street market and are simply ignored. It creates another kind of problem in Britain, where many businesses feel that in our law-abiding culture they have to incur the extra costs and responsibility of implementing every part of Community legislation, whereas their competitors and comparators on the continent are often exempt with a shrug of the shoulders. It is difficult to see how many of these measures are designed to stimulate more Community friendship and inter-member state trade. There is no reason why the Single Market should be a free market. Many of its exponents on the continent think it should be the opposite: a protected area closed to the outside world by reciprocity clauses, tariffs and other restrictions, and tightly controlled on the inside against the radical competitive challenge of the innovators and small businesses.

The United Kingdom is worried that too much regulation will create an area of low or no growth and stagnation. For this reason the UK introduced into the Commission measures and resources to look after small businesses and deregulation. Regulation is not an end in itself. There are certain things that it is important for government to regulate. Basic common standards in health and safety can make a useful contribution to employees' lifestyles and to the safety of products in the shops. Basic rules about fair trading to ensure that everyone's goods can freely circulate have to be upheld by a strong central authority and competition itself has to be policed through a common mergers, cartels and restrictive practices policy. But it does not require Community legislators to invent standards, designs and blueprints for every type of good and service to be supplied throughout the Community. To do so could cut the Community off from the most innovative developments in the world market and could make it much more difficult for Community companies to remain competitive and at the forefront of modern technology.

The evolution of the European Community in British debate has been different from that in the central continental countries of the EC. The United Kingdom in the early 1970s thought it was entering a kind of free trade arrangement. It was seen as a natural successor to and replacement for the European Free Trade Area. The main arguments about entry and in the referendum campaign in 1975 on whether to stay in the Common Market or not, were based on the economic pros and cons of belonging to a larger trade grouping. Reassurances were given to the British Parliament and people that there would be no major incursion into our sovereignty and capacity for self-government. The record in the House of Commons debates contained promises from government ministers that Britain would retain the right of veto over all important areas, that the Luxembourg compromise was in being, which meant that, even in those areas where majority voting was common, the government could in extremis demand Britain's right to veto. There was a reassurance that the main purpose of the agreement was to increase prosperity and trade across the borders. The Single Market programme was designed with a similar aim in view as far as the British government was concerned. Disturbed by belonging to a trading club for almost a decade and discovering that there were many barriers and obstacles in the way of trade, a British Commissioner, Lord Cockfield, put forward in the 1980s a programme for building a genuinely Single Market.

Others always saw it differently, seeing the clauses of the Treaty of Rome signed by the United Kingdom in 1972 as being the prelude to a political union and seeing the Single European act as a further step in that progress. During the course of the 1980s the phrase 'Economic Community' became more established in British debate to replace the 'European Economic Community' or, the more common form, of the 'Common Market' which was the phrase used at the time of seeking membership and joining. The debate about Maastricht and the phrases 'political and monetary union' first brought to public attention the fact that some people in continental countries had always been embarking upon a move towards the creation of a western European superstate. Maastricht, the Treaty of European Union, presented the United Kingdom with several challenges. Other member states wished to sign us up to the concept of full monetary and economic union rather than growing *rapprochement* between our economies and more co-ordination and co-operation over policy. Some wished to sign up all member states to the notion that political union was the ultimate goal and that further major steps could be taken by creating more common policies and by reducing the capacity of any single member state to block particular proposals.

The British Prime Minister used the presence of a British veto over treaty amendments with great skill to ensure a final shape to the negotiations much more in keeping with British character, temperament and ambitions. He was unable to accept the social chapter in the draft Treaty. As a result the other eleven member states had to sign up to that as an independent document to be held outside the framework of the European Community itself. On monetary union the Prime Minister made it clear, with German support, that convergence of economies was vital before considering whether and when to join a single currency area. Some of the other member states with their usual eye upon the general political acceptability in their country of wider European union, and with little attention being passed to the detail of the proposals, were much more in favour of signing up for a monetary union immediately.

The British contribution to the debate exposed the difficulties of moving rapidly or immediately to a single currency area. It was surprising that other member states needed persuading to look more carefully at the small print, given the example of the German currency union which had been conducted as if in a laboratory experiment for the western countries to observe. The decision to convert the ostmark at one or two deutschmarks depending on the type of account being transferred as a grand gesture for political union between the two Germanys created massive transitional and dislocation problems in Eastern Germany. The five Eastern länder soon recorded a 50 per cent unemployment rate as they discovered that practically all their industry was uncompetitive and uncommercial at the fixed exchange rate of two ostmarks to one deutschmark which could then never be changed. They had lost one of their most powerful weapons – the ability to regulate their competitiveness through changes in the external value of their currency.

The United Kingdom pointed out in the monetary talks that convergence of interest rates, inflation rates, growth performance, productivity levels, real wages and the other crucial economic variables is essential before countries could think about entering a single currency area with little risk of major transitional pain. In the western European Community, with inflation rates ranging from 2 to 20 per cent and unemployment rates ranging over a similarly wide area, there is little chance of an immediate move to a single currency by all of the twelve. On the continent there is much more growing convergence between the French, Belgians, Luxembourgeois, Dutch and Germans, although only one of these more closely allied countries would currently meet the convergence criteria set down in the Draft Treaty on Monetary Union.

There are many issues which have to be sorted out before planning any possible currency issue. The exact composition and details of the Central Bank and monetary policy machinery require precise definition. Is there to be any political control at all over the Central Bank? If there is, what voting system is going to be used by the member states to have this influence? In the United Kingdom the Labour Party believes that there should be a European currency and monetary policy, but that it should be subject to the control of the Council of Ministers meeting in closed session and presumably proceeding by qualified majority vote. The United Kingdom would therefore have one share in 7.6 in determining this common European monetary framework.

Other exponents of a non-inflationary policy favour the creation of an independent Central Bank. Such a bank would not be subject to Council of Ministers or Parliamentary scrutiny. However, these exponents have to explain a little more about how independence can be guaranteed. Someone – presumably politicians – has to choose who is going to sit on the Central Bank Board of Governors. They have to decide how long a term the Governors enjoy, the basis on which they can be removed from office, and the nature of their contracts. Someone also has to set up the constitution of the Central Bank and specify its aims. Those who set it up could presumably amend or change its nature. What blocks, if any, could be imposed upon constitutional experimentation with the bank if its governors were carrying out a policy the politicians did not like? How can we be sure that people would be chosen for the Central Bank who share these particular theorists' view that inflation is the main evil? Is it right that this should be the only criterion by which the Central Bank should be judged? Isn't there also a role in monetary policy for considering the impact such policy has upon growth and other important economic variables? It is one of those ironies of history that at exactly the point where the independent Central Bank was at its most popular in western Europe the one practical example of such a bank said to be fine testimony to its efficacy should be discovering that it was not independent at all.

The German Central Bank under Herr Otto Poehl had a long post-war tradition of regarding inflation as the main evil and running a tight monetary policy for Germany, even at the expense of a slower rate of growth in Germany in recent years than in some competitor economies. This had not caused any problems, because all the major political parties in West Germany agreed that inflation was the main evil, based upon the traumatic German experience of hyperinflation in the 1920s and the wish to avoid any such problem again. When Herr Otto Poehl started to express views both about western European monetary union and about the acceptable rate to peg the deutschmark to the ostmark in a single currency area, he found that he was not as independent as he had hoped. The German Chancellor disagreed strongly with the Central Bank Governor and it was only a matter of a few weeks of disagreement before the Central Bank Governor had resigned. A more suitable man was appointed to the post who seemed to be happy about the ostmark/deutschmark decision and who took a lower profile during the important debates on monetary union which were handled primarily by the Chancellor and his office. The large rise in the money supply caused by the ostmark/deutschmark merger caused considerable monetary difficulties.

A third issue which monetary reformers are going to have to examine is the handling of foreign exchange intervention and foreign currency reserves. The creation of a common currency means the pooling of every member state's foreign currency reserves in central hands. The foreign exchange convertible reserves held by the United Kingdom and other countries would have to pass to the

European Central Bank or monetary authority or be used under its guidance. It would not be possible in a western European system to have the different member states of that Central Bank intervening on their own. They could only intervene as agents of the European Central Bank and it would be more sensible for the whole operation to be controlled from the Centre, including the pool of reserves.

The question then arises whether or not this central monetary authority should pursue a heavily interventionist policy to try to control the value of the ECU against the major world trading currencies, especially the yen and the dollar. Evidence with the Gold Standard and with the Bretton Woods Agreement has shown that it is extremely difficult to control currency rates satisfactorily on a global basis. The danger is always present that misaligned currencies will cause other tensions and pressures to build up within host economies until such a point that the pressures blow the parity apart, however much intervention the leading central banks are inclined to indulge in, and however far a central bank may be prepared to go in raising interest rates and taking tough fiscal measures to strengthen its currency. When the United Kingdom came off the Gold Standard in 1931 it followed a period of great austerity enforced both by the Labour Government and then briefly by the National Government. Even substantial cuts in public sector wages, cuts in the government deficit and high interest rates were insufficient to sustain the pound at its then value against gold. Coming off the Gold Standard immediately allowed the pound to find a more realistic level and then, in due course, allowed the economy to start growing again following the very bad slump of 1929–31. It is important that these lessons are learned so that any future European Central Bank does not embark upon trying to stabilize all major world currencies in keeping the ECU at some rigid rate against both the yen and the dollar.

Western European businessmen may ask governments to do no less. All businessmen dislike uncertainties and they worry a great deal about changes in currency rates. The costs of not allowing currencies to realign one against the other are more diffused and their causes less well understood. Ask a businessman if the government should keep a currency stable and he will immediately tell you 'Yes'. Ask a businessman if he wishes to see reduced public expenditure on industry, or higher taxes or higher interest rates and he will undoubtedly tell you 'No'. Yet the preservation of a given rate or a given currency against other international currencies may well require the latter group of policies in order to sustain it. As in all things there needs to be a balance of objectives. Throwing caution to the winds and allowing the currency to devalue rapidly often triggers worse economic performance and higher inflation. Insisting upon inflexible currency rates between such very divergent economies as Germany, Japan and America, on the other hand, could well cause enormous tensions in particular economies leading to unemployment, high interest rates and other problems.

The huge pressures that built up in the ERM in September 1992 showed just how difficult and dangerous controlled currencies can be. The Norwegian krone, the Swedish crown, the British pound and the Italian lira all came out of the DM system. The Spanish peseta and the Portuguese escudo were devalued, and Spain, Ireland and Portugal imposed exchange controls. High German interest rates, necessitated by German political and monetary union, dealt a body-blow to premature plans for western European monetary union.

There are two arguments put forward for the economic benefits of a single currency. The first is reduced transaction costs. Some journalists point out that if you start off in London with £1 and you convert it into the respective currencies of the twelve member states as you travel through them you will end back in London with only 60p, the other 40p having been absorbed in foreign exchange transaction costs. It is difficult to imagine anyone other than a journalist doing this: most of us travel with pounds or dollars and we only convert them as and when we need to spend them in a specific local currency. Businesses similarly indulge in bilateral currency transactions between the exporting and the importing country. There is therefore only one commission, say 1 per cent of the transaction value, rather than the 40 per cent recorded in the journalists' example.

Of course it would be good if we could save this 1 per cent transaction cost, but we have to consider what the price of so doing might be. If it were a series of expensive economic policies to stabilize one currency against another in a divergent group of twelve countries, meaning much higher interest rates and other costs, business might not benefit but could face a worse condition. Similarly we have to look at the cost of social cohesion payments to southern poorer member states in the currency union. The southern states will only join the currency union if they believe substantial transfer payments will be made available. Business has to ask itself how large a series of transfer payments it is prepared to countenance from the richer northern countries to the poorer southern ones in order to complete the union. Unless inflation, living standards, interest rates and debt have been brought closely together first, a union could be very problematic. The case for greater convergence between, say, Portugal or Greece and Germany before narrow band membership of the ERM has been accepted in those countries is very strong.

The second argument put in favour of currency union is that it would simplify trading enormously. It is true that it is sometimes advantageous to trade in a single currency rather than several. This is why many of London's markets are dollar-based. Commodities like oil, gold, metals and agricultural products are usually dollar-denominated and many of the transactions are carried out in dollars. This would not be altered were Europe to move to the ECU given the importance of dollar-based trade in the world trading system. The fact that London makes such liberal use of the dollar for many purposes shows it is quite possible to enjoy the benefits of a common store of value in a common currency without having to have a single currency. No one has said that because America is our main trading partner and because British business has invested so much money in the United States, we now ought to have a single currency with the dollar. It would be as logical as saying we ought to have a single currency with the Germans because our trade with Germany has built up to comparable levels with that of the US in recent years and because some German companies are now making modest investments in the UK.

The UK was right to reserve its position on currency union. It is too soon to say how easy it will be to bring the different economies into line to make it feasible, too soon to assess all the costs and benefits. Recent experience with the ERM shows much more has to be done to bring western European economies closer together before anyone thinks of a single currency.

The trend towards global markets is the most important business trend of the 1990s, as we have already observed. The danger for the western European Community is that the protectionists and interventionists will gain too strong a position within the Councils of the Community, thereby cutting the Community and its businesses off from the most important developments of the global market. It will not help western Europe if telecommunication standards set here are incompatible with America and Japan, because the essence of modern telephony will be the creation of global networks. It will not help television, satellite and other communication services if we set exclusive standards in western Europe that are not used anywhere else in the world. Far from helping our industry it will mean they would be unable to export product to all those parts of the world primarily influenced by America and Japan, and they will find the domestic market is damaged by concentration and restriction on the technologies that are less than optimal. It will not help us if western Europe holds out against further progress in the General Agreement on Tariffs and Trade. The reluctance of some members of the European Community to make a decent offer on agriculture did damage to the Uruguay round of the GATT. Earlier acceptance of the need for agricultural reform and a preparedness to take up the American challenge for a major reduction of agricultural subsidy and support would have sped and improved the chances of a rapid upturn in world trade. Any hints and signs that western European industrial policy and protectionism is going to have a greater sway in Brussels' decision making will be a bad signal to the world and could well mean that the tight money policies of the early 1990s are the background to a deterioration in trading conditions brought about by protectionism. Economists and economic advisors would be well advised to read the economic history of the late 1920s and early 1930s. Protection and tariff was then the cry and the result, combined with extremely tight monetary policies, was a major recession which turned into a slump. The 1930s too were a time of enormous structural change and opportunity. Whole new industries based on new materials like Bakelite and early plastics, new products for mass consumption like the motor car and the radio, and new styles of clothing, housing and house refurbishment, all provided plenty of opportunity for exciting growth. It was politicians and the political economists who messed it up with their espousal of tariffs, the Gold Standard and protection.

What then is the future of the European Community in the new political world of the 1990s? Its economic future is delicately poised. The Cecchini Report suggested that the Single Market programme would add 3 per cent to western European GDP growth. That would be a startling figure, but it looks as if as the programme reaches maturity the results are going to fall short of that. The early 1990s have seen recession in most of the western European economies. Only Germany kept going for a bit longer, but Germany herself entered recession in 1991 and took extremely tough action to curb incipient inflation, causing its growth to remain restrained for the foreseeable future.

The Single Market programme has sometimes disappointed where measures have been unsatisfactory compromises between the principles of free trade and the principles of industrial intervention. The magnitude of gain is likely to fall well short of what Cecchini argued. Part of the magic of the 1992 programme was the hype. It was designed to make Europe an attractive place in which to invest. It was designed to raise the animal spirits of entrepreneurs to gear up for a bigger market, to develop new products and to sell them more widely across western Europe. If the background for their doing this is a constrained western European economy with inadequate bank finances available in the continental countries and with France, Italy and Spain following a policy of higher interest rates at a time of recession in their own economies, the likelihood of the hype working is greatly reduced. As Douglas Hurd, the British Foreign Secretary, has said, some of the Community's work has become an essay in intruding into the nooks and crannies of everyday life instead of being a truly market-opening programme.

It all began so well. The Cassis de Dijon Judgement established the principle in western European law that one product being satisfactorily controlled and marketed in country A could be sold without further restriction in country B or country C within the European Community. It does not require a great deal more than that judgement to create a truly open, independent western European market. Instead a whole series of directives has been imposed upon western European industry forcing producers around the Community to change their style of production and their design of product. Forty-four directives have been put in place to specify the European type of motor car. Individual directives deal with the details of, for examples, permitted tyres and permitted glass. Some manufacturers say this is important in harmonizing and standardizing. Others point out that it makes it very difficult to experiment and innovate because the manufacturer may well come up against a type restriction built into European legislation and discover that getting an amendment or changing that legislation is extremely difficult. In order to prevent the Single Market ossifying it will be necessary to revisit the directives approved so far with a view to seeing whether they need altering in the light of experience and entrepreneurship. If they cannot be demonstrated to be making a positive beneficial impact on western European growth and enterprise then they should be abandoned or reformed.

The European Community has not yet started to play its full part in the world trading system. The European Community, if it is to be successful, should be offering leadership based around the principles of free trade and the wish to extend those principles to the Third World countries who so desperately need them to help lift themselves out of poverty.

It is the Common Agricultural Policy itself which some think does damage. The decision to suspend the laws of supply and demand and to fix a price at a level convenient to continental farmers rather than to their customers has created substantial surpluses in various products that are heavily supported. This has led to the difficult problem of deciding what to do with these surpluses as their release onto the western European market would lower prices and undermine the carefully contrived price structure established by Community legislators. Very often these surpluses are released abroad outside the European Community, allowing customers in countries like Russia to buy food at a fraction of the cost to western consumers within the European market. This in turn undermines their own agricultural industries and represents a direct transfer of resources from western European consumers and tax-payers on the one hand to Russian ones on the other. In the process the Third World countries capable of producing food at cheaper prices than the western European Community are denied access

139

to two different groups of markets. They find they cannot sell into the western European market as they are kept out by quotas and controls so that they do not disrupt the high prices charged by European suppliers, and they are also kept out by commercial pressures from those markets where the European surplus is being dumped at uneconomic prices. The Third World desperately needs trade to improve its living standards. Long periods of western European governments giving aid have not succeeded in buying prosperity for the countries that receive the donations. All too often the aid is spent on large and grand projects that do not work properly or are not plugged in to real consumer demand. All too often the aid has gone to governments that lead privileged lives and has not filtered down to those in poverty and hunger beneath. The aim must be to open markets in the rich part of the world so that the poorer countries can sell the things they are best at producing and take advantage of their relative opportunities, be they the result of cheap labour or more productive land.

Attempts to reform the Common Agricultural Policy have had to deal with the vested interests of the farmers in continental countries, led by France. The United Kingdom has argued for reform as many of its farmers are farming larger units more successfully with higher yields per acre than their continental compatriots. The subsidy machine often rewards the small marginal inefficient farmer, the famous Bavarian farmer who farms at weekends and makes BMWs during the week, or the small French farm which is the result of the partition of inheritances over the ages. If only the prices charged in the marketplace could be brought closer to the price which would balance supply and demand, the customer would benefit from lower prices, the tax-payer would benefit from less subsidy needed to buy up the intervention stocks and the Third World would benefit from fairer competition into our market. It has been computed that in the United Kingdom the average family is paying £15 a week more for its food than it need do if we were able to buy food at world market prices. This is a large extra tax upon the average family. The Common Agricultural Policy has to balance the interests of farmers with the interests of consumers.

Reform of this structure will be slow and difficult. Many on the continent see the Common Agricultural Policy as the one example of a clear, centralized European Community policy that is good news since it brings, as they see it, essential support to their farming communities who, they believe, would be wiped out if they had to face true competitive pressures. That they have not carried the logic through into industrial policy is just a sign of how the balance of the Community has shifted now it is twelve rather than six. For there are around the table those present who might well countenance the idea of subsidized prices for industrial products based upon a company's contribution to R&D and the development of Euro-champions. They might even countenance intervention stocks of motor cars or steel or high-definition television sets in the event of the planners getting it wrong and producing quantities of these goods that the market didn't want to buy. That, after all, is the system they adopt for wheat and meat, and logic would suggest that true industrial policy exponents should extend it into high technology and industrial goods.

The decision to widen the market area to include the EFTA countries in the European Economic Area is an important one. The EFTAns bring greater interest in free trade and more suspicion of centralized power and institutions. To this extent they are natural allies of the United Kingdom. The United Kingdom has argued long and hard for their inclusion in this wider group and would like to see this extend in due course eastward to the Urals or beyond. The logic of the Single Market is a market based on free trade and open access where customers can buy the best goods at the keenest prices whoever may make them. If that logic works within the twelve it must work within eighteen, twenty-four or any larger number you care to think of. The twelve is an important first step if *and* when a true open market can be completed. The European Economic Area is a very welcome addition and the Association and Trade Agreements now being structured with eastern Europe are signs of the way policy must move.

It does not require a common government to have an open trading system. That must be our insistent message to our European partners. Trade and commerce breed friendship and mutual support. No one wishes to interrupt a prosperous commerce with wars or political divisions. Go further and try to create a political grouping or a superstate, and then the tensions can become acute as people fear that their national characteristics and local requirements are going to be overridden by a remote central power. The history of empires is not an attractive one and Europe should avoid trying to recreate a centralized one that may be bad for trade and bad for friendship as well.

Moving too quickly to monetary union, or even to fixed exchange rates, could cause financial tensions and a deeper recession. Countries and currencies need some room to breathe.

SEVEN

The Defeat of Communism

Whilst western Europe has been debating the Single Market as a response to global capitalism, elsewhere more fundamental issues have been at stake.

Over the skies of Iraq during the brief Gulf War in the winter of 1989–90 communism met its Waterloo. A devastating display of military pyrotechnics from the West underscored the enormous technical superiority of western capitalist democracies. What Gorbachev had feared for so long, and what the hard-liners in the Kremlin had written in their secret memoranda, was now being demonstrated for all the world to watch. On prime-time television around the world newsreels pushed out the message that some of the best Soviet hardware could not compete with the overwhelming fire power of the western allies. The Iraqi airforce, using some of the best Soviet planes with pilots trained by Soviet instructors, put up little resistance during the campaign. In the early days the Iraqis and their Soviet advisors discovered that their planes could be blown out of the air by missile attacks from American planes before they could even see the western attackers on their radar screens. The Soviet planes were out-ranged, out-gunned, out-manoeuvred. They were blind where the Americans could see. Their weaponry lacked the sophistication, penetration and accuracy of the western fire power.

On the ground amongst the sands of Operation Desert Storm the message was the same. A mighty host of an Iraqi army, well armed with Soviet-built tanks, missiles, guns and heavy artillery, was bombed, strafed and out-manoeuvred into submission. Scarcely an allied life was lost. It was possibly the biggest military victory ever achieved in world history. An army of half a million men or more was put to rout or surrender with scarcely a death amongst the attacking forces. A large number of Iraqi troops died. During the course of the campaign the Americans had demonstrated their ability to send missiles to street addresses many hundreds of miles away from the launch site. Western audiences could watch it happening night by night on their television screens. It was as if the western allies had so much confidence they were treating it as a training exercise to make military promotional videos. They were able to display in wartime conditions their remarkable arsenal in operation.

The message was not lost on the Soviet regime. Some western commentators, particularly in the United States of America, felt that the whole rationale for Gorbachev's *perestroika* and *glasnost* reforms was to try to get from the West the technology the Soviet Union desperately needed to maintain and advance its status as a first-class power. On this interpretation the hard-liners were permitting Gorbachev as front man to offer a friendly image to the West in an effort to buy the Soviet system time. If serious arms reductions talks could stall the West their scientists could desperately try to catch up. There was evidence around to match this interpretation. Soviet trade delegations of the new style in the *glasnost* era arrived to tell the West that the Soviets had a great deal of interesting technology which they would like to exchange. They suggested joint exhibitions and had in mind western government-funded schemes. Those who looked at the idea decided that the Soviets had little interesting technology that the West would want to buy, whereas the Soviet shopping list, ostensibly for civil purposes, concentrated on technologies which could also have military applications. The constant refrain of the Soviet regime and of the eastern European satellites was that the COCOM list system for controlling the export-sensitive goods and materials to the Communist bloc needed relaxation to oil the wheels of trade.

There was another explanation of the Gorbachev era. The more optimistic felt that it was a genuine attempt at reform, driven in part by the ideals and wishes of the ground swell of opinion in favour of a more liberal, democratic, western-style regime. There is nothing incompatible between these two interpretations. A complex revolution is driven by many forces and individuals and the power of ideas can become overwhelming. To some it came as no surprise. It was only the pace and dramatic dynamism of events that impressed.

In 1987 I wrote a book called *Popular Capitalism* which showed how wide-ranging a movement of ideas popular capitalism had become and looked at the way in which private enterprise and democratic systems could meet the aspirations of their peoples far better than state-controlled, nationalized Communist systems. It looked at the forerunners and precursors of the movement and explained how the ideas of privatization, market liberalization and democracy were spreading worldwide. It examined the beginning of a period of democratic revolutions. My conclusion was that

> Popular capitalism is a large movement whose time has come. The present evidence is that in every country in the world politicians and civil servants will have to react one way or another to these powerful ideas. All are beginning to see that the world is in a mood for more political freedom through the ballot box and through a free press. It is also seeking more economic liberty through privatization, deregulation and getting out of debt into equity. Popular capitalism is nothing short of a major world revolution. The politicians who try to resist it will be tossed aside like trees in a hurricane.

The hurricane had already started to blow through Asia. A democratic revolution had overturned the dictatorship of Marcos in the Philippines. Cory Aquino, the brave Philippines leader, had with her supporters pioneered many of the techniques for the democratic revolutions that were to come. They were, in the main, to be non-violent, characterized by mass protests on the streets and incredible bravery against armies, machine guns, and the command posts of state power. The hurricane had blown into Pakistan and Burma; it was threatening corrupt tyrannies in other parts of the Asian Pacific area. It was not long before it started to hit across eastern and central Europe.

Why should these ideas have suddenly become so powerful? Why should people who had for years been cowed into submission by the strength of state power, take up the cause now and succeed? As historians come to examine causes behind the substance and seek progenitors of the democratic revolutions, they will see a powerful conjunction of events by the late 1980s. The history of eastern European communism had been characterized by localized revolts in single countries which were brutally squashed by strong expressions of imperial military power. The Hungarian uprising of 1956 was dealt with summarily. The Czechoslovak uprising in 1968 lasted little longer, with tanks soon stationed on every street corner in Prague. The Polish revolt of 1980 ended up in similar tribulation. In the 1950s and 1960s the condition of the peoples in eastern Europe in comparison to the West was not as bad as it subsequently became. The regime had a much tighter grip on events, led by determined men keen to exploit every vestige of state power through intelligence networks and military force. There was no lack of political will to control the people and still a sufficiently powerful patronage system to reward the more able, the more intelligent, those prepared to be collaborators. Ambition could be channelled into Communist ways and the few who refused were treated as dissenters and sent off to labour camps or psychiatric prisons.

In the 1960s many people in the West still felt that the Communist system had much to offer and might well turn out to be technologically superior. It is one of those ironies of history that Harold Wilson, a former British Labour Prime Minister, is best remembered for his speech which included the phrase 'the white hot heat of technological revolution'. He campaigned the country on this slogan, implying that Labour and its state planning methods would inject into Britain the kind of technological vitality that only state control and state planning would produce. Most people have forgotten or never read the context in which the phrase occurred. It was nothing less than a eulogy to the Soviet state planning system, warning that unless we copied some parts of their system we would be left behind and they would be the technical masters.

That an intelligent man like Harold Wilson could make such a large error in his forecast and in his understanding of the rival merits of the two systems shows just how pervasive the idea that state planning had a lot to recommend it was. In the 1950s and 1960s intellectuals could believe that communism was perhaps the vital doctrine of the future. Socialists in western Europe looked admiringly to the Soviet system for its emphasis on new technology and industrial might. The sensible democratic ones like Harold Wilson were aware that they had to reconcile this with a lack of personal liberty, and made suitable genuflections about the undesirability of limiting people's right to choose which was inherent in the Soviet system. Others were less cautious and seemed to think that the lack of personal choice in the Soviet system was more than repaid by what they took to be a greater equality of living standards and more likelihood of economic progress.

By the late 1980s many of these circumstances had changed. The Soviet empire was stretched to the limits. The ruinous war in Afghanistan had placed a great strain on the Soviet military machine. Many Soviet citizens saw loved ones going to Afghanistan suffering privations, wounds or even death in rugged and hostile terrain. The Soviet military machine was being tested by the resumption of the arms race in the West. The Soviets gradually came to realize that President Reagan's dream of Star Wars Defence might turn into reality, given the great success of western scientists. If something was not done about it, the Soviet Union would no longer rank alongside the United States as one of the two world superpowers. Despite spending a much heavier proportion of their gross domestic product on weapons procurement, the Soviets fell further and further behind. Two prime factors lay behind this. The first was the growing relative impoverishment of the Soviet economy so that weapons took a bigger proportion of a much smaller GDP per head. The second was the inferiority of a planned state-run system to generate the ideas and the technology required. The technology of the 1980s and 1990s is the technology of ideas and individual enterprise. It is the technology of smart computer programmes and software, the technology of open systems and individually designed computer and communication and data links. The command system found it more and more difficult to force the pace and encourage the imagination required.

It had not always been thus. The Soviets had been successful in targeted areas in the beginnings of the space race in the 1950s and 1960s. They had beaten America to the first unmanned Sputniks. They had beaten America to the first man in space. They had beaten America in the early days of the orbiting laboratory programme. Many took seriously the possibility that they might be the first with men on the moon. The first big public humiliation of the Soviet technological drive definitely came in the failure to put men on the moon at all. Evidence is now emerging to remind us how seriously they took this race. We can only guess at how devastating a blow it must have been to realize that they were not able to complete the necessary equipment, even after they had seen the American system succeed. Soviet space technology became frozen in early 1960s shapes. They were unable to develop new types of rocketry, and their control and command systems fell way behind the growing sophistication of American computer-based ones.

To this technical failure and the overstretching of the state must be added the crack in the political will to maintain a vice-like grip across the outflung stretches of empire. President Gorbachev was a pivotal figure. We shall never know whether he was at heart a reformer, or at heart someone who felt that the system could be saved with a little more democracy and openness added in. He tried to balance the forces. He equivocated. His statements were ambiguous, containing both the full red meat of radical popular capitalism and cautionary notes about the need to preserve some or all of the old system. It understandably took him time to move from being a Communist to agreeing to the end of the Communist Party. It took him time to agree to move from a central command economy to embark upon a more liberal pattern of economic reform.

It took him less time to decide that he could allow the western empire to go. His early decision to withdraw from Afghanistan was forced by the logic of events. The army was exhausted and the resources of empire overstretched. It was a much bigger decision to allow the eastern and central European states to establish their independence. Mr Gorbachev was caught by his own dilemma. Had he taken strong action and reinforced the army, using it to face up to and break down the street revolts, he might have succeeded in individual countries for a period of time. It would have ruined his international reputation, brought the process of arms control limitation talks to a halt, and exposed the Soviet military machine at a time of its considerable weakness to the full brunt of western anger. If he was buying time he needed to let eastern and central Europe go. If he was a genuine liberal he needed to let them go to establish his credentials. For once the ambiguities pointed in the same direction and so the will cracked and central and eastern Europe was allowed to find its own future.

These things did not rest in the balance for very long. In

a period of a few months the principal eastern and central European countries were freed. It quickly became apparent that Germany would want to reunite and that West Germany would take a paternal view of East. Czechoslovakia, a historical accident waiting to happen, already contained talented and brave leaders ready to take up the task of government. Out of dissent was forged a protest movement and then an alternative government. Hungary, with westward leanings and memories of the Austro-Hungarian empire, had never been fully integrated into the Soviet system. For many years it had been experimenting with some modest degree of economic liberalism. They merely carried on at a faster pace. The brave Poles, whose protest occurred some twenty years after the Hungarian uprising, had seen the Solidarity movement grow even under the last days of communism, and turned naturally to Solidarity for freedom from the Soviet army of occupation. Yugoslavia edged itself away from the Soviet system. Bulgaria followed. Only Rumania plummeted itself into bloodshed in order to overthrow the hated extreme Communist dictator, Ceauşescu.

One month after the revolution, the atmosphere in Rumania was still fevered. A caretaker Communist government remained in power and it had no authority and no respect. Everyone was looking forward to the elections. The problem arose as to how many parties there were going to be and whether they could find leaders that had not in their turn been discredited by collaboration under the rule of the dictator. The wreckage everywhere to be seen on the ground showed just how monumental had been the failure of communism.

Ceauşescu had attempted to bulldoze whole villages in order to force people off the land and into urban blocks of flats. In the cities they would take up paid jobs under Communist Party control. He had arranged shops in such a way that a few in the centre of the major cities had a range of goods for display for the foreigners to see and buy, but the ordinary Rumanians were unable to shop as they could only shop adjacent to their homes: before buying anything Rumanians had to show their identity passes which contained their addresses. The Rumanians were used to electricity being cut off for many hours of the day and night as there was insufficient energy to meet all the requirements of industry and residential consumers. They were used to food shopping being a long expedition with many hours in many queues at different shops to try and piece together the requirements for a Sunday lunch. They were used to spies from behind the net curtains, to informers and to the secret police, the ubiquitous secret police trying to control not only their every deed but also their every word and thought.

The complete failure of communism was dramatic both for its final speed and for the realization on the part of its subject peoples of just what they had missed through the tyranny of their system. The power of television should not be underestimated. The ability of people in eastern and central Europe to see on covert television screens or to hear on radio sets tuned in to the British and American world services what they were missing was an important element in the strands that make up the revolution. It was said that many people in East Germany knew the West German commercials better than the West Germans themselves, as they tuned in to watch this fairyland of the West with the lifestyles of the affluent there on their television screens before them every night. It was an unattainable ideal, a nirvana to visit, a Utopia that was beyond their grasp.

All those of us who lived through those events will remember the looks on the faces of the East Germans as they poured through the early breaks in the Berlin Wall to see for themselves the fabulous riches in the stores of West Berlin. I remember well an early Soviet group visiting Wokingham. They were young people, amongst the brightest and best educated of the Soviet system, speaking reasonable English, but they had never been to the West before. When I asked them what they most noticed about the West their replies were revealing. One young man said that he was amazed at the range of styles and the quality of the cars on the streets. He had never seen choice and wealth like it. One young lady explained that what was surprising was that people in the shops and on the streets smiled a lot. I asked her if people didn't do that in her country. She said no, they didn't. When I asked her why, she said, 'We don't have anything to smile about.'

The heads of Soviet and eastern European peoples were definitely turned by images and visions of the West. In those early days few perhaps realized how difficult it would be to emulate the West and how much had to change in order to earn the West's prosperity and lifestyle. So many habits of western capitalism had been lost or never gained. In the case of the Soviet Union there was no tradition of individual enterprise or commercial success. Ever since 1917 the Soviet system had been locked under Communist rule. Before that it was largely a peasant culture with just a few brief experiments in westernization. Russia had not introduced or built a large middle class in the way England, France and Germany had. Peter the Great had tried to force the pace of change and modernization by copying western styles. He had run into difficulties with the Orthodox Church and with his aversion to beards, just as Mr Gorbachev met resistance from orthodox Communists.

It was different in central Europe. Czechoslovakia had once been one of the richest countries in western Europe and there are people alive today in Czechoslovakia who can remember being part of that economic success in the 1930s. In Hungary there is a commercial folk memory and a more recent tradition of stronger links with Vienna, and with the whole of Austria, a far more economically prosperous country. Poland had contact with a large expatriate community of Poles in France, Britain, the United States and other rich western countries. There are strong traditions linking Poland and the West through contacts made during the Second World War and more recent exchanges.

Popular capitalism during this period of heady expansion also had its reverses. The most brutal took place in Tiananmen Square in Peking. Catching the mood of the times the Chinese liberals took to the streets and felt that it was only a question of raising enough people and keeping them in the square for long enough and the Chinese regime would fall as well. At one point it looked as if they might be right, as the army's loyalty was in doubt and it seemed likely that large numbers of army units would be unprepared to fire on the people or to mow them down under the tank tracks. In China, unlike the Soviet Union, the political will at the centre did not break and the old men with memories of Mao, original revolutionaries, decided that they would not let their revolutionary legacy perish under the weight of popular protest. They found army units that were loyal. They forced them into Tiananmen Square. The fragile bodies of the protesters proved no match to the weight of the army and metal of the tanks. Most of us will remember the poignant image on our television screens of a single young man trying to hold up a tank in the centre of

Tiananmen Square. He did not succeed in holding it up for very long. Western journalists who, inexplicably, were allowed to stay during the early days of the clamp-down, were able to send back lurid and awful accounts of the way in which tanks trampled over people, the way in which arrests were made and the liberals were bundled off to the dungeons.

Why then, did the movement fail in China at that juncture and not elsewhere? The Chinese empire was not as overstretched as the Soviet one. China had not followed international ambitions and had avoided reopening its old conflicts with the Soviet Union and with Japan. An inward-looking Communist culture, it had been more successful than the Soviet regime in keeping contacts with the West at arm's length and in avoiding people within China becoming too aware of the growing gulf between the two cultures. China did not have the same great technological ambitions as the Soviet Union and was not trying to keep up with the Americans in the arms race. Above all, the political will of the leaders of China – first generation revolutionaries rather than third or fourth generation as in the Soviet Union – endured at the most critical time. They showed they were quite prepared to use brute force to repress *freedom* movements and did so with ghastly effect.

Other brutal regimes have found that the pressures from emulation and from the force of ideas and popular protests were too great to withstand. The Albanian regime held out for much longer than others in eastern and central Europe, but it too bowed to the inevitable as it discovered that the tide of opinion within Europe in favour of democracy and economic freedom was so great that it was bound to be engulfed by it. The Baltic states put up a magnificent and heroic stand against the Soviet Union in demanding their independence. Resting their claims on the pre-Second World War position when they were independent with their own governments and their own currencies, they tried to restore their past. They had the belief that they would be more prosperous and freer if they were part of the Baltic trading system looking towards the Scandinavians in the West rather than part of the Soviet empire. This struggle with David pitted against Goliath reminded us that it was possible for David to win. In the West in Cuba there were rumblings but for the time being the Cuban regime continued, assisted by the strong willpower of its leader and by its insular position protected from some of the pressures that were flowing across the borders in Europe.

In four brief years the democratic revolutions achieved remarkable results. A long list of countries in Europe and Asia had turned from tyranny to democracy. Everywhere there was discussion, the noise was the same. There was an outbreak of constitution building. There was a clambering through old records to discover past precedents for new structures and a re-examination of old borders. People were going back to their roots; they were trying to re-establish their links with their old religions, cultures, languages and histories. Far from history being abolished with the demolition of the Berlin Wall, it was as if history had broken out again across the European continent. For some forty-five years European history had been on ice, with all complex disagreements and tensions subsumed beneath the much grander ideological glacial clash between the USA and the Soviet Union. Once that glacier began to melt it was possible to re-examine all the old problems and troubles that had not been resolved post-1945, troubles that had been calmed down by the creation of the two massive blocs facing each other across the gates of Berlin and the East–West border that ran like an iron curtain across the continent.

The triumph of popular capitalism and democracy shows that the human spirit can be stronger than any amount of armament. Post-Second World War history demonstrated that strongly entrenched feelings, powerful resistance movements and Communist subversives could make surprising headway against even the most sophisticated technology and the most overwhelming of odds. Those dedicated subversives, the Vietcong, had held up and finally seen off the whole might of the American military machine in Vietnam. The poorly armed Afghans had pinned down a vast number of Soviet troops over many long years in the Afghan war. They too were ultimately successful. The difference between the two systems and the two conflicts was that the Afghan army was fighting for the Afghan people, whereas the Vietcong were a small band of fanatics whose system in turn would be swept away along with the violence that had perpetrated it as soon as the idea developed that people could be democratic and free. The 1990s will probably see the collapse of North Vietnam and its Communist system and the reunification of the Vietnams as a single country. It will certainly see something similar in Korea, another angry border in the 1960s and 1970s likely to be pulled down by the logic of democratic capitalism. The contrast in living standards between North and South Korea is enormous. The South Korean economy is developing rapidly, driven by an urge to work and to become more prosperous. The North Korean economy has been held back by state intervention and control and by the great military burdens imposed upon it through the Communist system. As more trade and diplomatic missions explore across their border along the 52nd parallel, so the inevitability of reunification and change becomes much greater.

When I wrote the postscript of *Popular Capitalism* at the end of 1988 it was clear that the centrifugal forces pulling the Soviet Union apart were becoming very strong. The uncertainties surrounding Europe, I wrote, were greater than at any time since 1939 with the outbreak of nationalism and the return to the old conflicts becoming very apparent. In that postscript I underestimated the weakness of the Soviet regime, thinking that the Soviet Union would wish to prevent the growth of German power at the heart of Europe and would have some more diplomatic cards to play to put off the complete loss of empire. The pace of events since 1988 will be explained by historians as demonstrating just how fundamentally weak the Soviet system had become. Commentators enjoy the benefit of hindsight. In 1988 looking down the barrel of the Soviet gun, looking at the vast panoply of atomic weapons and missiles still owned by the central Soviet system, western observers were understandably cautious. Never has a great empire fallen as rapidly as the Soviet one. It took many decades for the Roman empire to teeter and fall. It took many years for the Dutch overseas empire, the Holy Roman empire and more recently, the British and French empires to pass into the sunset. The Soviet empire has completely collapsed in five years, leaving only Russia.

Watching the process has been like seeing somebody peeling an onion. He is constantly looking for the centre, but each layer he takes off just leaves another layer damaged and ready to unravel. Christmas Day 1991 marked the formal end of the Soviet Union. After many days of indecision President Gorbachev announced on television that he was resigning as the last President of the Soviet Union. He used satellite to the West with translation in a symbolic gesture of his western orientation. We saw the red flag being pulled down from above the Kremlin building. President Yeltsin of the Russian Federation had triumphed. The Russian tricolour flew again at the heart of Moscow. Now the question is whether Russia can remain united, or whether that too will split under pressure.

The role of Yeltsin in the final downfall of the Soviet empire is an important one. It was he who distanced himself from communism earlier than the other leaders including Gorbachev. It was he who showed resolve in persistently opposing the Gorbachev reforms and saying that he would go much further were he in control. It was he who managed to speak for the popular dissent on the streets. As Gorbachev's early reforms were timorous and produced less, not more, bread in the shops, more inflation, less employment, so Yeltsin was there campaigning against him. It was Yeltsin who had the courage to stand for popular election and won a large mandate in the ballot box. Gorbachev dithered and never himself held elected office. Yeltsin's combination of populist politician, elected mandate, and the ability to avoid all blame for the things that were going wrong during the crucial years of opposition meant that he was well placed to take advantage as soon as his lucky break arrived. It came in one of the strangest forms, with a coup against Gorbachev from the hard-liners trying to restore the former glories of Communist Party control over the Soviet arsenal. Many in the Soviet Union felt that this was a put-up job by Gorbachev to show that without him the Soviet Union would return to its old ways and that he was the bastion of liberty and freedom. Others who were less cynical pointed to the obvious distress of his wife during the events and to the fact that far from delivering the kingdom to Gorbachev it delivered it to Yeltsin.

Yeltsin behaved magnificently. He rose to the occasion. He stood in the Parliament building as the symbol of liberty and choice. The people rallied to him, the plotters turned out to be drunken, worried men, and the coup was soon defeated. From that moment on President Gorbachev was President Yeltsin's puppet.

Yeltsin had all the hunger for power that a campaigning politician sometimes attains. He set about demolishing the last vestiges of Soviet control, undermining the tax revenues passing from the

Russian Federation to the Soviet Union, taking away many of the officials and ministries from Soviet control into Russian control, and making sure that legitimacy and power flowed from the head of Russia and not from the head of the Union. He was able to work with the leaders of other republics who had had enough of the Union and were building their own campaigns based upon Ukrainian or Baltic nationalism. As Leningrad was renamed St Petersburg it was only a matter of time before the Soviet Union within its shrunken borders would be renamed Russia.

The new Russian Federation has taken the seat of the USSR at the Security Council and has taken over control of many of the nuclear weapons that made up Soviet power. The borders of the Soviet empire have shrunk mightily. The whole of the Balkans has been lost. The whole of the eastern and central European plain of East Germany, Poland and Czechoslovakia has been lost. Afghanistan has been surrendered and there is doubt about the loyalty of the Muslim-oriented republics to the south between the Caspian and Tibet. The Baltic provinces have been lost and only an act of political will and diplomacy kept some semblance of co-operation between the Ukraine, Russia and Belorussia in a loose federation. Everyone's atlases need remodelling as new countries emerge and borders shift.

Much of this began as a movement for economic liberalism. It has now been engulfed in nationalism, religion and history. In its origins it was the failure of an economic system. The Marxist system was based essentially on an economic theory. Marx took pride in denying the role of spirituality, the afterlife, historical tradition and culture in the lives of peoples and nations. The new brave world of Soviet communism set about destroying the old associations and links with the past. I remember a Soviet visitor coming to see the Palace of Westminster. He remarked how amazing and delightful it was to see a nation living at ease with its past. We have not had to spend years tearing up street signs and names and christening everything anew after some modern hero of the revolution. We have not had to convert all our cathedrals into art galleries and palaces into government offices. The Palace of Westminster has evolved. It is still a royal palace. The most magnificent rooms are still those where the Queen robes and through which she processes to open Parliament.

Parliament remains the centre of the nation's life but its balance of power has shifted as monarchical rule has given way to rule by elected representatives. Things have been different under Communist systems. Whilst some of the greatest treasures have survived like the Kremlin itself, entirely new traditions have been imposed upon it. The May Day Parades, demonstrations of military power, the severing of all links with the tsars, the layout of new streets and squares, and the renaming of everything in a vain effort to erase all thoughts of the past: all signs of a country at war with itself.

What Marx failed to realize was that peoples are in no small measure the product of their histories and geographies. The Soviet Union by the end of Soviet rule faced exactly the same problem that Russia faced at the beginning of Peter the Great's reign. The technologically backward country needed to look west and ape western manners and mores in order to try to catch up. Its subjects, many of whom were serfs to the tsars and then to the Soviets, finally rebelled in a sullen Russian sort of way and demanded something better.

The contradictions and conflicts in Marxist theory had long been apparent to western critics. The army of such critics has grown. It was always clear that Marxist revolution had taken place in the wrong country. Far from happening in an advanced westernized, industrialized country, it occurred in backward, peasant-dominated Russia. It was also evident from a fairly early stage that the revolution had created a new class and class structure based upon membership of the Communist Party. As the Soviet system developed it became clearer that more and more privilege was dispensed through the Party apparatus. The only way to gain access to the better housing, the motor cars, holidays and even decent food was via Party membership. Party members had special privileges: they shopped in special shops, they could obtain goods and services that others could not acquire for love nor money. Segregated education was developed for the bright children of Party members, who also had the privilege of travelling abroad and were generally better informed than the rest of the people. A small elite of a few millions ruled a mighty empire.

The Marxist system was based upon liberating the whole of the proletariat and seeing class pass away as everyone developed proletarian virtues and values. In the Soviet Union this was taken literally with the mass murder of the kulaks, the one group of successful entrepreneurial farmers who had started the process of capital accumulation before the revolution and were attacked out of a fit of jealousy and fear in the Stalin era. The state began to put down all its enemies. Mass graves have subsequently been discovered illustrating the range and duration of the purges and the terror.

Western critics and observers were all too willing to turn a blind eye to the human rights violations, to the impoverishment of the working people, and the balance of terror needed to maintain the Soviet state. Many in the West felt they had to do business with the Soviet Union because of its power and status. Others wanted to do business with it because they were trying to exploit weaknesses and political opportunities within their own countries and found it inconvenient to admit that there was anything wrong with the Communist system.

Pulling down the red flag from the Kremlin and the resignation of President Gorbachev marked the end of the vestiges of state Communist planning in Europe. Communist parties in western Europe, which over many years have survived and adapted through the democratic process, are now left with the need to find a new, different programme, and to become even more careful in espousing the cause of democracy and eschewing the Soviet model.

The Chinese students at Tiananmen Square sought to replace the Marxist class struggle with a toleration of other views, discussion and debate. They set up their own Statue of Liberty; they sought a democracy. Their first aim was

> to establish legitimate, autonomous and unofficial organizations gradually to form a non-official political force as a check to government decision making: that is the essence of democracy. Rather ten devils to check each other than one mandarin with absolute power.

This moving manifesto of popular capitalist democratic action on the streets understood in its words that the American model required more than the vote, that even mighty China needed to learn from the mistakes of the past, and that China had fallen a long way behind the West technically and in terms of its prosperity.

In the summer of 1989 I wrote the *Popular Capitalist Manifesto,* just before the mass movements in eastern Europe were to overwhelm the Soviet Empire. It was designed as an antidote to the Marxist manifesto and the restrictive straight-jacket of Marxist economics. In place of the Marxist wish to nationalize land and take over all land for the state, popular capitalism substituted the broadening of ownership of land with the vision of every man as a property owner. Where Marx and the Marxists sought very high and penal taxes to prevent anyone excelling or saving and investing, popular capitalism depends on tax reform, concentrating on lowering the rates of income tax, delivering incentives to those who strive. Where Marxist land reform depended upon taking land and property away from families and putting it into the hands of the state, popular capitalist reform depends upon breaking up the large public estates and encouraging privatization, thereby creating family ownership which can be passed on from generation to generation. Where Marxism set about imposing ever stricter controls upon economic life, especially exchange controls, with a view to the eventual abolition of money – something which Lenin tried and which failed dramatically – popular capitalism rests upon the free exchange of goods and money and the conduct of a prudent monetary policy. Where Marxism thrived on taking into state ownership the sinews of commerce and industry, popular capitalism returns them to owners through denationalization and privatization. Where Marxism attempted to control the supply and demand for every product, fixing prices and removing markets, popular capitalism reintroduces the market, allowing supply and demand to come into balance through competition and free exchange. Where Marxist states were happy to see more and more money taken over by the state and more and more debt incurred, popular capitalism depends upon the reduction of international debt and the reduction of state debt. The intention is not to burden future generations with the sins and errors of past generations who have borrowed too much.

Popular capitalism believes that there is a role for the state. The state should be able to guarantee a basic standard of pension and national insurance to give protection to all, and it has a vital role in defending the country and in maintaining law and order. Finally, popular capitalism depends upon the success of small enterprise and entrepreneurship and needs a series of policies to encourage them. Marxism rested upon an equal requirement of all to labour through the establishment of industrial armies. Where capitalism encourages people through incentive and choice, Marxism told them what to do and made them do it. Marxism rested upon the centralization of means of communication and transport and the centralization of credit through a monopoly nationalized bank. It enjoined the confiscation of property of all immigrants and rebels, the abolition of the right of inheritance and the forced movement of peoples to ensure a more equable distribution of population between town and country.

The Marxist programme arose out of the writings of Marx and Engels as a response to what they took to be half-hearted and lukewarm socialism of the socialist parties of contemporary Europe. They believed in going the whole way, centralizing as much power as possible in the hands of the proletarian state and assuming that those who wielded the power would be like themselves. They wanted them to be visionary and benign and to improve the lot of everyone. The arrogance was overwhelming. It was remarkable that anyone should attempt such a programme and even more remarkable that they should get away with it for so long and in so many parts of the world.

It did not take long to discover that centralized power corrupts. No one was allowed to criticize or put the people at the top under pressure. There was no way to force them to retire or resign, so they stayed on well into their old age. They lost the capacity to embrace change. The more they stifled criticism the more stifling their ideas and views became. Soviet society died from the top downwards. People only worked hard when they were put under pressure or under firm labour discipline. It was threat rather than encouragement that worked the system, fear rather than greed that was a predominant emotion, sullenness rather than agreement the most likely response.

The Marxist cloud occluded so much light from the firmament. Religion was banished or driven underground. Those churches that remained, those worshippers that insisted on still going were a mere shadow of their former selves. It was dangerous to be too openly associated with them and the Church had to avoid taking a radical course against the regime. Never had so many groups, aspirations and ideas been suppressed for so long by so single minded a state.

The collapse of the idea was sudden. Once the power behind it was taken away, no one could be found to defend it. Chaos erupted as different groups and parties emerged into the sunlight to challenge for power. Each had different ideas about how to begin to piece their societies together again. They collected under the different coloured banners of the old nations of Europe which had predated the Soviet empire. Language, religion and origin became important again.

Soon the Balkans were ablaze, as Yugoslavia fell apart. Muslim and Christian, Catholic and Orthodox, Croat and Bosnian, Macedonian and Serbian demanded self-government. Civil war followed, as the idea of 'ethnic cleansing' was reinvented, people saying that they wished their neighbours to share their religion, language and background. Europe entered an era of mass migration, as the dispossessed took to the roads and joined the economic migrants moving west in search of work and riches. Germany, at the crossroads of Europe, became the melting-pot, with Poles, Magyars, Rumanians, Croats and Bosnians arriving in their thousands. Simultaneously, many East Germans head west in pursuit of riches. The Yugoslavia civil war illustrates how easy it is to discover injustice and wrong in the old system of government, but how difficult to unite disparate people in struggling for something new. Religion, race and history are more important than the unity of Yugoslavia. Serbia is on the march, and the other territories want their independence.

People were discovering that Communist order had repressed old conflicts as well as standing in the way of economic progress. Their quest for the elixir of capitalist success is what we must now follow.

EIGHT

Economic Reform in Eastern Europe

Touring the eastern European countries as a western visitor interested in trade and the economy was a depressing experience under
communism. The typical pattern of meetings in down-at-heel and
tatty ministries was for a series of officials ranged on the other
side of the table to the visiting delegation to read at great length
a huge volume of statistics about production and output plans
for their particular sectors of the economy. The performance was
hierarchical, with the leaders speaking first and for longest. These
meetings were tedious because the officials spoke in abstract and
technical language, and because there was barely a flicker of
understanding between the two sides, or any of the usual human
asides or courtesies that characterize diplomacy or the transaction
of business.

These presentations were a just reflection of the style of government. Everything had to be planned from the centre. A large
army of officials was required to collect statistics and information
about what was going on in the state-owned farms, factories and
collectives. Another army of officials was required to set out the
details of the plan in a comprehensive document and to send
instructions to the different factories and economic units around
the country asking them to meet certain targets. They rarely
did, but a ready industry developed in misleading the officials
about the true levels of production. The whole system rested
upon misinformation. It was based on the Mussolini principle of
government, that as long as people at the top believed things were
alright they could go on living in a world where they were alright.
The underlying reality was not allowed to intrude too often.

The planners were never very good at discerning new trends
and developing new technological ideas, save in a limited number
of areas related to weapons and defence. As the 1970s and 1980s

advanced the discrepancies between the economic performance of eastern and western Europe became more and more marked. The economies of eastern Europe were planned to rely on heavy industry rather than light industry. They were planned to depend upon industry rather than services. They were planned to be oriented towards defence goods, steel and basic food supply, rather than based upon consumer electronics, tourism or leisure. Labour was organized in vast armies which were under a crude and not always effective labour discipline. There were no incentives, little differentials by way of pay, few rewards for hard work, and no rewards at all for entrepreneurial success which was positively discouraged in many areas.

In Czechoslovakia they were proud of the large amount of steel they produced. It was difficult to see what they could do with it all given the limited number of outlets in steel-using industries and the lack of spendable income in Czechoslovak homes to afford wanted steel goods like motor cars, dishwashers or washing machines. In many eastern European countries they were proud of their nuclear power station programmes, but inspection has shown many of them to be unsafe, and in several countries there was a shortage of electrical power for domestic consumers. In Rumania the typical experience for the average consumer was electric power for only a few hours of the day, as the highest priority was accorded to the aluminium factories which were very inefficient and used large quantities of electrical power – more than was available without rationing.

At the end of Communist rule the extent of backwardness and economic dislocation was very pronounced. Practically no one had a telephone in their home and waiting times ranged from eight years in the more efficient countries to twenty years in the least efficient ones before you could get one, unless you were a party member who could pull special strings. Cars were in very short supply and the few cars that were available were of low grade, dirty, noisy and heavy users of fuel for their relatively small engine size. Whilst many of the countries of eastern Europe and the western Soviet Union are rich agricultural territories, and whilst they were still able to grow substantial quantities of food, the distribution system was so chronically inefficient that there were still enormous shortages in the shops. It is estimated that one-third of all the food harvested in the Soviet Union in the latter days of the Soviet empire was wasted before it could reach a customer owing to the inability of the transport system to take it around the country and the lack of refrigeration and freezing capacity to look after it during its long transit and storage times. There is an absence of good roads throughout eastern Europe. The housing stock is of very low quality, mainly high-rise flats built in the 1960s era of concrete buildings, many of them now decaying. Most of the industrial plant and equipment is of 1940s, 1950s and 1960s vintage, heavily outdated and very uncompetitive compared with the best in the West.

The task facing the economic reformers in 1989 when they seized power from the ailing Communist regimes was therefore a formidable, even an impossible, one. Everything needed changing. Nothing worked properly. The difficulty was to know where to begin and how much reform people would stomach.

The first issue that many bravely addressed was price control. Inflation had been avoided and large price increases ruled out by political action: the simple expedient of rationing and queues was instituted. Governments decreed the prices of goods and services. Many people found factories unwilling and unable to supply them at the approved price, and so a black market sprung up to meet the real demands for services and goods at a more realistic price. For the rest, people just had to wait in long queues and accept lower quantities as the prices became too unrealistic. As the regimes weakened, so the problem increased. The only way the circle could be squared at the height of the Communist regime was by establishing a very severe labour discipline which enforced work and demanded a certain amount of production from the factories, however uneconomic the price they could charge in the market place. As the discipline began to crack in the later years, and as the regime weakened in its intent, so the scarcity of goods in shops and on the black market became more acute. In Rumania, despite a very brutal work discipline imposed from above, people were so disinclined to work other than when they were being directly supervised and chastised, that the shortages became chronic. A severe form of rationing was introduced where people could only go to a shop if it was close to their home. People were compulsorily transferred from rural villages to the new vertical villages of urban high-rise blocks, designed to house the swollen armies of the industrial work-force.

Freeing prices was an essential requirement to get the economies on the move again. Unless the right price signals are sent through the system people will not produce enough of the goods and services that others wish to buy. Early experiments with price decontrol in countries like Hungary were very successful in so far as the shops quickly filled up with western goods offering much more choice. The problem was that whilst they were imported it meant that the incomes to afford them were not being generated domestically by enough people. Food shortages were replaced by the scarcity of price rationing, which meant that many Hungarians were unable to afford the excellent goods being imported into their shops.

Price decontrol has been attempted in all of the eastern European countries and now in Russia and the Ukraine themselves. In each case it brings with it considerable problems. Communist training teaches that a great deal of capitalist activity is akin to criminality, based upon speculation and unreasonable profiteering. In the early days of price decontrol, when there is a shortage of producers and a shortage of goods, conditions are very favourable to those who wish to profiteer. It is easy to make a fortune in such conditions by buying large quantities of sought-after goods as quickly as possible, putting them into store and releasing them only as and when the prices are sufficiently high to make a very large profit. It takes many months or even years for the proper competitive response to emerge from higher prices, namely indigenous production of enough goods and services to bring the prices down to a realistic level.

The presence of profiteering and sky-high prices in the early days of price decontrol in several countries has undoubtedly caused substantial political difficulties. It has given new ammunition to the Communists, now a beleaguered and dwindling number in opposition, strengthening their claims that little good will come of economic reform and that the evils of capitalism will be rampant and obvious. These attitudes are worse in Russia and the Ukraine where communism was entrenched for that much longer and where communism was the embodiment of imperial success for the Greater Russia. Even under the Gorbachev reforms, speculators were still regarded as criminal and were usually blamed for all the evils of the Russian system, even though most of the evils were those of communism laced with the difficulties of partial liberalization and the weakening of the Communist work discipline.

A related problem was the reformers' attitude towards money and monetary policy. In the latter days of the rouble empire the money supply had been allowed to grow quite substantially. A bankrupt Imperial system and government needed ever more money for its weapons procurement. Because the economy was failing to generate the true wealth the government needed to raise in tax in order to make its weapons, the government resorted more and more to printing banknotes in order to pay for its heavy defence expenditures. The result was a massive overhang of roubles circulating in the economy. These did not cause direct inflation for the goods and services that made up the bulk of the meagre average standard of living of the typical Soviet family, as these services were controlled by the planners and sold at controlled prices. In consequence, the large rouble overhang was primarily saved. Massive numbers of roubles were stashed away in people's bank accounts, hoping that one day the economy might perform better so that they would be able to spend them. They were led to believe that one rouble was worth one dollar or, as *glasnost* began to filter through, that maybe a rouble was worth somewhere between twenty and fifty cents. They lived on in the hope that one day they might be able to convert their roubles into something worth having, either goods or someone else's currency.

The only other thing that could happen to roubles was that they could be used to bid up the prices on the black market for goods and services there, and help line the pockets of the speculators with yet more roubles. This was a minority use of the large rouble overhang, as speculators tended to have more sense than to want large rouble bank accounts. They specialized in hard currency transactions, and encouraged a growing clandestine economy denominated in dollars or deutchsmarks.

With price relaxation, with the removal of political controls over many prices, the rouble overhang was bound to cause a price explosion. At last people were told that their money would have some worth and that they could spend it and would thereby bring forth more goods and services under normal capitalist rules.

Unfortunately, the overhang was so immense that all it was ever going to do was to trigger a great inflation. As the government dithered over whether it should allow convertibility of the rouble, a flourishing black market in trading roubles for dollars grew up. By the end of 1991 the going exchange rate on the black market was 150–200 roubles to the dollar. People who had been told that their rouble was worth a dollar were shocked to discover that in practice on an open market of sorts a rouble was worth one half of a cent.

More direct attacks upon the rouble overhang were undertaken in the Gorbachev era. Realizing that there would be a massive inflation as a result of too many roubles chasing too few goods, he simply announced one day that all holders of certain large denomination notes would lose all value for those notes as they ceased to be legal tender and could not be exchanged into other notes. None the less, draconian though this was, it was not sufficiently draconian to take enough roubles out of circulation to give the remaining roubles any real value. In such conditions in western Europe in the past, the only answer was to announce the end of that particular currency and to start again with a new currency to build people's confidence and to restrict its supply so that it had value. The introduction of the rentenmark in the 1920s was a singular success, taking Germany out of the mark hyperinflation into a period of relatively stable prices and economic advance.

Other countries that were part of the Soviet empire are keen to establish their own independent currencies. It is a sign of nationhood, sovereignty and independence. The first thing a monarch always does is to impose his image upon the coin and the banknotes. Estonia, Latvia and Lithuania have all made it clear that they wish to establish their own independent currencies. To do so they need to gain the confidence of people at home and overseas. They decided that the most natural way to do this was to go back to a gold base for their coinage. They were owed substantial sums of money in gold that had been taken elsewhere during the upheavals of the Second World War. Agreement by France and the United Kingdom to return gold to the Baltic republics was important in beginning the programme that will lead to separate currencies with gold reserve backing.

All of the central and eastern European economies have experienced grave problems with hyperinflation and high inflation following price decontrol. Poland experienced inflation that reached 700 per cent in 1990 although it subsequently came down to a more realistic level. Territories that made up the Soviet Union hit 400 per cent in 1992 whilst Czechoslovakia went over 50 per cent in 1991. Hungary was the most successful, with its inflation rate as publicly stated not rising much above 30 per cent and back below 20 per cent in 1992. This reflected the greater degree of success of the Hungarians at maintaining monetary control, and the absence of large saved balances in Hungary, reflecting the closer contacts between Hungary and the West, and the greater extent of illicit trade in hard currencies that had been going on in the country in the latter days of the Communist empire.

A third problem confronting the economic reformers was the question of inherited debt. Only Rumania amongst the eastern European countries had no problem. The fanatical Ceaușescu had imposed substantial privations on his peoples in the latter years of his power in order, in part, to repay all of Rumania's foreign debt. He succeeded in doing so, thus placing Rumania in a rather better position than the other eastern European countries, to borrow abroad, free of the burden of historic debt, if western leaders accept the political risk. Conversely, the Commonwealth of Independent States that was the Soviet Union has a massive debt overhang of some 50,000,000,000 dollars, and Poland an overhang of 40,000,000,000 dollars. Hungary's at 20,000,000,000 dollars is also substantial in relation to the size of the country, whilst Czechoslovakia's at $5,000,000,000 is a bit more manageable.

These dollar debts, whilst not large in relation to the dollar debts incurred by western states, are very large in relation to the number of people in the countries concerned and in relation to their productive potential and their foreign currency earning power. For many years the Soviet Union was a good credit risk as far as the West was concerned. It had borrowed substantial sums of money from the West, but it had a long tradition of paying its interest and capital repayments on time, and of obeying the rules of international banking. The collapse of Communist discipline and the end of Communist government changed all that. The successor regimes did not feel that they necessarily had to take over the whole burden incurred by the Communists whom they had fought and opposed in the latter months. They also recognized that the burden was now very large in relation to the productive potential of the former Soviet Union. In the latter years of communism when they had been building up the foreign debt, the economy had actually been contracting and its capacity to earn hard currency revenues reduced.

One of the former Soviet Union's main revenue earning activities was the production of oil. In the latter years of the 1980s the oil producing regions of the Soviet Union fell into decay. Pipelines were ruptured and not repaired, wells fell into disrepair, oil spurted out over hundreds of square miles of Soviet territory and no one seemed to know what to do about it or no one cared. The productive capacity of the Soviet oil industry was gravely damaged by a lack of new technology and a chronic lack of maintenance of the old. The Soviets did not encourage until recently the substantial western investment that might have put the matters right. Similarly, the substantial Russian exports of gold, which had done well in periods of great international tension and a high gold price, did rather less well in the later 1980s as the gold price was stable at relatively low levels and interest in the gold market greatly reduced. Conversely, the Soviet Union needed ever increasing quantities of hard currency to import the grain and meat it needed to feed its people, and to import many of the consumer and industrial products that the people increasingly craved but were unable to afford.

There are three ways to reduce the burden of debt in a country. The first is to renounce the debt, to tear up the obligations and to cock a snook at the international community. This is the course that many in the former Soviet Union are now advocating and the Russians are now around the negotiating table with western bankers talking about non-payment of interest and phased payments of capital. If you owe enough and threaten enough it may be possible to get some reduction in the terms or some stay of execution. It is, however, an extremely high-risk and damaging strategy for a country to follow. Why should people in the future lend you more money if you fail to repay the money you borrowed in the past? What happens if enough countries renege on the whole of the western banking system, threatening it by their action? Could there be a danger that the goose that lays the golden egg is itself gravely damaged? No one is saying at the moment that it is going to go that far. The Latin American debt situation has been calmed, whilst the Russian debt situation on its own is containable. Other eastern European countries have wisely avoided this course, recognizing that they could say goodbye to western aid and western technical support if they took too hard a line on the debt issue.

The second way to deal with the burden of debt is to convert into equity or encourage more equity investment. A country, like a company, can borrow too much and get into difficulties as a result. Like a company, the way that a country can get out of the difficulties is to raise more equity money from willing partners. One technique which was most useful in the Third World was the technique of debt/equity conversion. An overseas investor with hard currency wishes to make an investment in the country. He agrees to purchase a certain amount of the country's overseas debt and redeem it. In turn the host country then grants him enough local currency to carry out his investment. The terms of the deal could be made advantageous to the overseas investor – an inducement for him to enter a debt equity swap, and for him to invest in the country in the first place, reducing the risk somewhat by the extent of the discount offered. In countries like Chile which pioneered the debt equity swap the discount was related to the market value of the debt.

Such a programme will have to be tried in those eastern European countries and former Soviet territories that are heavily indebted. At the same time the development of investment pro-grammes, especially from overseas investors, must serve to raise the total stock of wealth in the country in relation to its debt, if new borrowing is strictly controlled. Failure to control new borrowing sufficiently will jeopardize any chances of recovery. It is very easy to get into the Third World syndrome where a country feels it needs to borrow in order to invest, but discovers that the investment projects always fall short of the ambitions for them, and as a result the debt burden becomes greater relative to national income rather than smaller. Many Third World countries have discovered that it is easy to borrow for large projects but difficult to make money out of them. They have discovered that it is all too easy to get to the position where interest on debt absorbs an extremely large proportion of the hard currency earnings of their country, making their economies more fragile and recovery that more remote.

Success lies in ring-fencing the risks of given investment projects and in choosing suitable financing techniques for such projects. If a project is entirely equity financed, then the providers of the capital are only rewarded if the project is a success. If the project is financed by a mixture of debt and equity specific to that project, then it is possible for it to be a success without the debt cost of capital over-encumbering it. Even if a project is entirely debt financed, but the debt is pledged only against the project, there is some hope for the economy as a whole. If the project fails, then the provider of capital loses his money and it does not remain as an obligation permanently against the state. Complete debt financing of projects, however, makes it less likely that they will succeed as the costs of the interest charges in the early years can be very difficult to meet out of the early revenues of the project.

The question of foreign investment is never an easy one for newly-emerging nations seeking economic recovery. Many people in the countries will be apprehensive about allowing the foreigners to buy into their assets and run many of their major businesses. This will be especially so in the former Soviet Union, proud of its past and used to being in sole control of its own destiny. In the capitalist West people have got used to the idea that foreign companies own a substantial proportion of the economic wealth in any given country. In western Europe we have experienced the tidal wave of American investors in the 1950s and 1960s and now in the 1990s are beginning to experience a similarly powerful movement from Japan. The former Soviet territories have experienced none of this for a period of more than seventy years.

The development of myopic nationalism could be one of the reasons why the former Soviet Union remains in economic difficulties. Foreign capital brings a number of positive adjuncts with it. The foreign investor often possesses a technology which the host economy needs. He often has superior management and organization skills which could be deployed to good effect in the host economy. He nearly always has a strong brand and product design of a kind that consumers desire. He also usually has the financial resources necessary, either investing the ploughed-back profits from his ventures elsewhere or having the balance-sheet strength to borrow and raise the necessary equity finance to invest in the new territory.

The eastern European countries soon discovered after 1989 that they were in competition for the world's footloose capital. It became clear to them that there was a limited amount of foreign investment capital for eastern Europe and that that capital would go to those territories offering the most auspicious conditions for it. The overseas investor seeks freedom from dividend control, so that he can remit a proportion of the profits he earns if his venture is successful. He seeks political stability as he does not wish to see his investment disrupted by violence on the streets, by civil war or by political intervention in prices, business planning and related areas. He seeks a low and stable inflation environment as hyperinflation can be very disruptive for his business; and seeks good infrastructure since he needs to be able to transport his goods to market and wants a reasonable lifestyle for those of his executives that have to be seconded to the new territory. Eastern Europe does not have a large enough territory in terms of the number of people and their disposable wealth to warrant the establishment of investments in each of the countries. The main overseas investor, if he is considering building a car plant or a domestic appliances manufacturing facility, will be looking for a maximum of two or three factories in the whole of eastern and central Europe, strategically located in countries that are friendliest to him.

The countries of central Europe soon responded, announcing reasonable regimes for the taxation and repatriation of dividends, and trying to create an impression that they would deliver a stable political and legal framework favourable to free enterprise. Much of the argument centred on the crucial issue of exchange rates.

The overseas investor is not very attracted to the idea of earning mountains of roubles or zlotys unless those currencies are stabilized and can be converted into hard currencies. Currency has value if it gives you direct command over resources or if it is freely exchangeable into other people's currencies that have such control over resources. The eastern European currencies left by the Communist regimes had no such advantages. None of them were freely translatable into dollars or pounds, and none of them had control over sufficient real economic resources to have great intrinsic value. A great deal of trade was conducted with the eastern European countries on a barter basis, and all of them had very small foreign trade sectors, especially with respect to their trade with the hard currency areas.

Each country takes pride in having its own currency and each country has attempted some programme of monetary stringency to limit or control the amount of inflation in its domestic economy. It would take longer for the Baltic republics and the emerging independent republics in the former Soviet territory to establish their new currencies, but those too need to gain and retain the confidence of overseas investors.

Moves towards currency liberalization have been evolutionary. A typical pattern is for a country to permit the conversion and repatriation of capital where an overseas investor has in the beginning brought in hard currency to the host economy. The second phase is to allow people living in the country to earn and repay hard currency. In practice, many were doing this long before the fall of the Communists. One of the most notable things in Hungary was the number of people who already had Austrian schillings, American dollars and German deutschmarks as a result of their illicit contacts with the West over several years. People in eastern Europe have also been receiving hard currency from their friends and relatives who migrated many years ago to western democracies. In Poland a successful dollar economy has been created as people have often found it better to trade with each other for dollars than for their own domestic currency.

Money provides the sinews of trade. The Communist system was based upon rigged prices, planned quantities and an orderly system of exchange between the different economies of eastern Europe. Each one of them had a distorted industrial structure based on the needs of the empire as a whole. Each one of them was required to exchange their surplus production in their chosen areas with the surpluses in the others under the Comecon system. Their major trade was often with the Soviet Union itself. A typical pattern was for an eastern European country to receive its primary materials, especially oil and energy, from the Soviet Union in return for the supply of industrial components and goods back to the imperial economy. As the economic system started to collapse the Soviet

Union's planners realized that they needed hard currency for their gas and oil exports. It was one of the few things that they possessed which had a clear value in hard currency in western markets. Yet, it was vital to the success of the poor performing economies of eastern Europe who were entirely dependent upon Soviet oil and gas for their energy requirements.

As a result the Soviet Union itself provided a substantial part of the impetus towards the ending of the Comecon system. It demanded dollars from Czechoslovakia and Poland and Hungary and the other countries dependent upon its energy. In turn the satellite economies started demanding hard currency for the industrial goods they had traditionally sent to the Soviet Union.

The result was a major contraction in Comecon trade. The Soviet Union did not want as many of its industrial goods at the new hard currency prices as it had wanted at the old rigged exchange rates and prices of the planned system. In its turn the eastern European countries found they could not afford, or did not need, as much Soviet energy as they had needed at the height of the Comecon system. Everyone was desperately keen to trade with the West, the source of hard currency receipts that they so badly needed. In the rush to trade with the West people were negligent of the trade they were doing with each other in the East. A process of inexorable decline had set in.

It was not easy to reorient their trade towards the West. Most of the goods they made were unsaleable in western markets. There was no demand in western Europe for the Trabant car of East Germany, and little demand for the Lada. These vehicles were some twenty years out of date compared with the technology and designs of the West. There was certainly no demand in the West for basic materials like steel which eastern Europe made in superabundance, as the West's own steel-producing industries were in the grip of a steel recession and there were plans to close western plants.

There was more opportunity for the export of food and drink products from the better agricultural lands of eastern Europe, particularly the South. Even in this area however, the differences in style and quality between the East and West were enormous, making sizeable exports extremely difficult. Packaging in eastern Europe was extremely rudimentary. The poor quality of packaging and of presentation made it very unlikely that the goods as then produced could be sold on western supermarket shelves. Quality was often disappointing, as food manufacturing processes were based upon out-of-date technology and very old equipment. In addition eastern Europe has to contend with the protectionist pressures of the Common Agricultural Policy designed to ensure that western Europe should be self-sufficient in food, and should be difficult to penetrate as a market from the outside. When Poland began to produce meat that was saleable in the West, the French immediately took to the streets to protest about it being allowed in. Something similar may happen to Rumanian wine as they solve their quality, labelling and bottling problems.

The clothing industry of eastern Europe has had some success. Polish-sewn suits and separates are now apparent in many British stores. It is possible that the Czechoslovak glass and shoe-making industries will be revived and that they too will be successful exporters to the West. Tourism will undoubtedly grow as eastern Europe solves a chronic lack of good hotels and invests money in tourist routes and other facilities. A town like Prague is breathtakingly beautiful, unspoilt at its heart by the developments of the 1950s, 1960s and 1970s and capable of sensitive restoration to make it one of the finest towns in Europe. To do so would be good business sense given the tourist commercial potential it would then have.

Modest progress has been made in creating a trading framework for East to meet West. The United Kingdom took a lead within the European Economic Community by insisting upon trade and association agreements between the Community and the emerging democracies. These agreements commenced the process of reducing tariff barriers on eastern European goods and act as an incentive to eastern European countries. Some eastern European countries like Hungary and Czechoslovakia believe that they should move rapidly towards full membership of the European Community. Whilst the British government is much keener on a wider community than some of its partners, it has to be acknowledged that the economies of eastern Europe are in no shape for immediate membership. In order to meet the myriad of regulations and directives now laid down as part of the Single Market programme, there needs to be a major revolution in production, transport and management in the eastern European countries themselves. The right way ahead is to build on the trade and association agreements, lowering the tariff barriers gradually and giving eastern European economies time to bring themselves up to the standards of western Europe. If they wished, the eastern European countries could make the task easier by adopting areas of European Community law directly into their own new law codes, facilitating the process of transition.

One of the crucial areas for immediate progress in eastern Europe is the environmental one. Early opinion polls in Hungary and Czechoslovakia showed that far more important in the popular mind than the relative poverty was the dirt and degradation of the environment around them. There is a realization that life expectancy is much lower in eastern Europe than in western Europe, primarily because of air and water pollution from factories. People are aware of how unsafe many of their nuclear installations are and of the substantial threat they pose. In the post-Chernobyl age people living near nuclear plants are only too conscious of what can happen should something go wrong. Energy ministers in all these countries are faced with an impossible problem. Heavily dependent upon unsafe nuclear capacity, they would dearly love to close it. The result of so doing would be to leave their country short of energy, shorter even than they are already, and to increase their reliance upon the coal-burning stations which are far filthier than the ones in the West. The incidence of bronchitis, bronchial pneumonia and other lung disorders is very high in many of these countries, reflecting the degree of pollution from coal-burning power stations and from other factories.

The rivers that drain the north European plain are heavy with dangerous metals, sewage and industrial pollutants. Chemical works, steel works and engineering factories use the Elbe and the Vistula as waste disposal routes. Those cars that were available under communism had dirty exhausts. The atmosphere of many towns in eastern Europe is sulphurous and heavy on the breathing. The conditions inside the factories were often shocking. Little attention was paid to health and safety at work, industrial accidents were all too rife and many workers suffered from the impact of extremes of temperature, noise and atmospheres heavily charged with pollutants.

The provision of clean water to individual homes, with cleansing of the rivers and the reduction of airborne pollutants, are high priorities in all eastern European countries. The West's expertise and investment capital is desperately sought. It will require billions of dollars to provide the necessary filtration and cleansing in all of the industrial installations.

The creation of a free enterprise economy will not be achieved merely by trying to strengthen the foreign trade sector, by currency reform and the freeing of prices. All of the reformers immediately understood that it would require a massive privatization programme. Typically, 90 per cent of all economic activity in these eastern European countries was in the hands of the state. As important, most of the economic activity was in the hands of very large organizations which tend to be less flexible and less creative in contrast to the successful western economies where a lot of the dynamism, growth and new jobs come from a myriad of small firms. Eighty per cent of all Japanese work for small enterprises, fiercely competitive one with another, supplying a few large assembly and foreign trade companies. In the United Kingdom following the successful 1980s, more than 3,000,000 people work for themselves and there are over 1,000,000 live companies.

The Soviet system was the complete opposite. In order to give the planners a bit more control over what they were planning it was necessary to organize production in very large units. The whole was based upon 1950s and 1960s premises: the idea was rife that there were economies of scale which could be maximized if production was concentrated in a few very large units. Soviet planners never understood the diseconomies of scale: the greater difficulty in organizing labour and providing incentives, the inability to be creative and to develop new ideas, the lack of challenge which a lack of competition generates.

There have been endless debates in eastern European countries about the style and pace of privatization programmes. All have agreed on the need to go much faster than, for example, the British programme, which succeeded in transferring some 7 per cent of gross national output from the public to the private sectors over a period of some ten years. In the case of the eastern European economies, they had to achieve 50 per cent of total output in the space of five years at the minimum in order to have any visible impact upon the extent of their problem. People soon realized that the precedent of the large western privatization programmes led by the British was not a suitable one for eastern European conditions. There were no developed stock markets and many of the businesses to be privatized needed, and need, thorough restructuring, having been unprofitable for many years. Hungary began with the privatization of Ibus along traditional British lines, offering shares for sale in a profitable enterprise at a reasonable price, and capturing some stock exchange enthusiasm for them. Real attention, however, has had to turn to case-by-case restructuring and to mass privatization by different means.

Each privatization directorate or ministry has had to begin by compiling a survey of what the state currently owns. This is no easy task as good financial record-keeping was not a strong point of the Communist regimes. Once there is a list of all the state enterprises with a rough estimate of their assets and trading performance, it is then possible to group them loosely into different categories. In each country there is a large category of businesses suitable only for closure. They may be making things that nobody wishes to buy, their equipment may be so out of date that it has no chance of competing, or it may just be that the business totally lacks any kind of leadership and is difficult to rebuild in time. The second category would include those businesses where there is a potential market for their wares and where there is merit in soldiering on, but where fundamental changes are required. They may require completely new management, they may need new technology and equipment, and they will almost certainly need to slim down their work-force in relation to the size of output they are achieving. A third category would include those businesses that are already more commercial, profitable and enterprising, and suitable for traditional western-style privatization as soon as possible.

Each country has had to debate the balance of its privatization programme between foreign and domestic investors. Many have felt it would be wrong to allow the foreigner to gain access to cheap assets in the early days of privatization. This is an understandable but mistaken notion. Unless foreigners are allowed to obtain the property and production assets it is very difficult to attract the inward investment these economies are going to need on such a huge scale to rebuild them. It is especially difficult for foreign investors when so much of the land and buildings is owned by the state, as they need land and buildings to begin their new ventures and will naturally be attracted to the idea of owning freehold to provide them with some collateral to offer their backers and some stability for their business. Not many companies are going to want to risk their own money in a hotel venture if they cannot own the site and look forward to some appreciation in its capital value to offset the trading risks.

In order to solve the problem of carrying the public with them in their massive enterprises some countries have turned to vouchers. The idea behind the voucher is that every citizen receives one which gives him or her an entitlement to trade its shares at some later date in a range of ventures that are covered by the privatization voucher scheme. The voucher, in a way, is an unnecessary complication in what amounts to a system of free gifts of privatized assets to individual citizens, or deferred purchase.

Retaining political support for the privatization process is vital if it is to have any chance of success. The danger for eastern Europe is that privatization will be associated with asset speculation, massive redundancies and closures. A large number of people were brought up on the idea that everyone had a job and that one of the purposes of state factories was to maintain employment. Because the system declined over many years, gradually impoverishing people, it did not create the same trauma as a rapid move to the market in the form of redundancies and unemployment does.

Perhaps more important in eastern Europe's privatization programme than the actual transfer of existing state assets to new owners will be the attitude the eastern European countries strike towards liberalization and deregulation. A good paradigm case is that of telecommunications. The question of who owns and runs existing assets is not terribly important as the existing assets do not amount to very much. When fewer than one in ten people are connected to the telephone system and when the system is incapable of handling the more sophisticated services like data, video conferencing and value added services owing to technical and capacity constraints, it is immediately apparent that the future of telecommunications in these countries rests not on the existing investment but on the new investment. Each of these countries will have to embark upon a crash programme of telephone investment. They will have to leapfrog technologies. Many are discovering that the best way of getting some telecommunications into place in their countries is to back mobile and radio technology which is quicker to install than conventional hardwire systems.

If all of the new investment is made by a variety of new private sector companies, the telecommunication system will be substantially privatized over the next decade in each of the countries embarking upon this course. To allow this to happen requires the right legal framework. Sufficient controls have to be placed upon the existing state monopoly to prevent it stifling the new competitors at birth. The legislation has to be enabling, facilitating new investors and new technologies and allowing them the conditions in which they can start to trade successfully. In Czechoslovakia the Minister of Telecommunications was well aware of the opportunities that mobile technology offers to his country and sees that it could be a way of accelerating telecommunications investment and development. Unfortunately, the issue was clouded by the dispute between Czechs and Slovaks with worries about which type of technology implies Czech or Slovak domination.

What is true of telecommunications is true of many other sectors. With the right regime for foreign investors and with the right legal framework permitting competition and new developments it will be possible to privatize substantial sectors of the eastern European economies by the pressure of new investment alone. Crucial to success will be the attitude of the new governments to small enterprise. The biggest difference between the shape of eastern and western European economies is the complete absence of a thriving sector of small entrepreneurs in the East. This is most marked in services where the eastern European economies have failed to develop, owing to the planning system, and where the western economies have sprinted ahead in the last twenty years. Two-thirds of all employees in the west in a typical country now work in services, and only one-quarter in manufacturing. The successive application of more and more capital to the manufacturing process means that there will continue to be a reduction in the proportion working in manufacturing in the successful economies.

Each eastern European country is trying to lay down a legal framework permitting contract, company formation and small business development. In the early days it may create merely a frontier or Arthur Daley culture. Politically, it is difficult for these countries to live with some of the youthful excesses of capitalism without resorting to too many controls in response to the worries of electors about these early developments. Speculation is bound to be rife. Indeed, speculation is a necessary lubricant of the wheels of enterprise when getting off the ground or rebuilding the machinery. Unemployment is bound to rise substantially as the dislocation will be very great.

When I first visited Rumania one of the most persistent questions was: 'why do people in the West bother to work?' They found it very difficult to understand how it was that the West worked so hard and achieved so much when reports and rumours told them that failure to work did not lead to heavy fines or a prison sentence in the way in which it had under Ceauşescu in Rumania. The suggestion that some people actually enjoyed their work was a strange perception to most Rumanians. The idea that people worked for extra money was a bit more intelligible to them, but they had no direct experience of an incentive-based system where people are paid much more for longer hours or extra effort or superior achievement. One of the difficulties in explaining the concept was that in Rumania had you succeeded in working harder and earning more money as a result – which was more or less impossible in their system – there would have been no point because there would have been nothing to buy with the money you had acquired. It takes a visit to the West to understand the attraction of earning more money if you come from a closed society where there is nothing on offer whatever the price.

Countries further west understood it all too well, having been more exposed to the consumer advertising on western television and in western magazines which circulated lawfully or illicitly in their countries. They fully understood the advantage of more cash in the hand if it were dollars or deutschmarks, and were better equipped to get on with working out overtime, bonus and incentive pay systems.

There is not necessarily a skill shortage in eastern and central Europe. In some countries education has been extremely good. For example, in Hungary there are a number of well-trained, computer-literate scientists, and in the former Soviet Union there is a great repository of scientific skill, particularly in the nuclear area. I was interested in meeting economists in Hungary and Czechoslovakia. I asked them how they would adjust to capitalist economics, assuming that they had been trained on a diet of Marx and the Marxists. I soon discovered that their reading lists were very similar to those in the West. They explained that in the latter days of the Communist system as long as a student put in the first paragraph the point that all the capitalist views he was about to reveal had been disproved by Marx, he could then for the rest of the answer discuss the capitalist economists in a perfectly normal western way.

There is a hunger for knowledge and for western influences, more marked the further east you go, as the further east you go the more closed society has been. The British library in Bucharest set up by the embassy is besieged by readers who are particularly keen on the business and economic sections. There has been a strong surge in demand for English language courses since people recognize that English is the language of business and the language of world capitalism, and they wish to be able to discuss matters with Americans in their own language. As soon as the Russian empire fell so did the demand for Russian courses.

Dealing with the problems of unemployment and poverty are going to be the most important political questions for many of these countries. They have never before faced long periods of unemployment for large numbers of people. It was an old Communist joke that 'we pretend to work, and they pretend to pay us'. It meant that no one was well off, but that everyone did have the basics for at least one meal a day and was housed and clothed. Some of these guarantees from the all-embracing state have now been withdrawn. It is important that each of these countries puts in place some kind of a welfare net and speeds the retraining and new investment programmes to create required jobs. Everyone can see that the current balance of employment is wrong and unsustainable, but that is no comfort to the many millions who lose their jobs.

All of these countries desperately need growth in their gross national product. The beginning of the periods of reform was far from auspicious as you would expect. It is much easier to identify those parts of the economy that do not work and close them down than it is to create the conditions in which new business starts up. In the first full year of reform the Polish economy lost 12 per cent of their total outputs. Over an eighteen-month period the former Soviet economy and the Czechoslovak economy lost 15 per cent of their total output, and even Hungary, a bit better adjusted and nearer to western standards, had two years of losing 5 per cent of its output in each year.

The Hungarian and Polish economies are now showing signs of picking up and growing. The Russian and Ukrainian economies seem to be getting worse at an alarming rate.

Breaking into the cycle of decline and decay is not easy. When everything is broken everything needs fixing at once, but there is no one to fix it. You cannot have a competitive economy without free enterprise. You cannot have free enterprise without privatization and liberalization. You cannot attract foreign investors without stabilizing the currency. It is difficult to stabilize the currency without decontrolling prices and triggering major price increases. Something has to be done about the overhang of worthless currency and a decision made about who is going to lose what in the redistribution. Above all, there are powerful forces of dislocation in rising unemployment and factory closures, as many factories are rendered obsolete by the competitive pressures of the world market and many more have to be closed down for health and safety and environmental reasons.

To date, Hungary has made the best job of controlling inflation, stabilizing its currency and moving a bit nearer to western systems. Poland has battled bravely against the odds and Czechoslovakia has decided on a dramatic privatization programme through vouchers and free share issues after a protracted debate. Progress has been much less notable the further east one goes. The pace of economic reform, and its success, will in part depend on the resolution of many political conflicts, and on the constitution and political structures which emerge.

Too many civil wars or nationalist uprisings could destroy hopes of necessary inward investment and divert too much attention from the functioning of the prosperity machine. It is these wider political issues we should now examine.

NINE

Nationalism, Civil War and the UN – Pax Americana and the Rise of Germany

Berlin is equidistant from Minsk and Paris. As the 'plane flies it is a little further to the Urals than it is to Lisbon from the new capital of Germany. To Crete from Berlin is about as far as to the northern tip of Norway. Geography has determined that the new Germany will look eastward to a much greater extent than West Germany did, and has determined that at the centre of Europe will lie a large, powerful Germanic bloc. The German-speaking peoples of Austria, western Czechoslovakia and Bohemia, western Poland and Hungary in part look to the new Germany for trade, prosperity and growth.

The boundaries of the Balkans were not clearly or well drawn at the end of the Second World War. Poland, for long a buffer state fought over by Russians and Germans alike, lies within slightly more generous borders than history has often accorded. Czechoslovakia remains a divided kingdom, deeply split between the Czechs and the Slovaks. Hungary and Rumania dispute their frontiers and argue bitterly over the future of Transylvania. Rumania in its turn is not enamoured of its own frontier with Moldavia, once part of the Soviet Union. European history well knows the troubles that can descend from Balkan conflicts. The Yugoslav civil war has already shown the dramatic and explosive power which lies behind Slavic tensions. Western Europe has already found that it gets drawn into these conflicts and has also discovered that the main countries of western Europe are not always at one in their view of the future.

The case of Yugoslavia illustrates the dangers and the tensions. It shows powerfully that far from history having drawn to a close, history has been reborn with the ending of the Cold War. It was traditional French policy to back Serbia, and traditional German policy to back Croatia. Arguments within the European Community have surfaced for a wider audience as Germany has shifted EC policy in favour of recognizing Croatia and giving her support against Serbian ambitions. France argued to keep Yugoslavia whole, and to accept the strong influence of the Serbs in the Federation. Gradually, week by week, month by month, German argument and power moved the EC position towards the recognition of Croatia, towards acceptance that the Yugoslav Federation has broken down irretrievably. Endless EC peace initiatives have failed to produce a worthwhile cease-fire. The moderating influences of some other countries kept troops from western European member states out of the arena for many months. The decision to back the UN humanitarian relief effort enabled agreement without having to resolve the rights and wrongs of the combatants' positions. Geography and history have changed dramatically now that the old Prussian heartlands of Germany have been reunited in the new greater Germany. Between 1945 and 1989 Germany, divided on itself, and within shrunken frontiers, was a very different country. West Germany retained little of the mighty north German plain, its lowland area confined to a small region around Hanover and Bremen, and the Rhine valley. Now the new Germany contains the bulk of the German plain around Berlin, Magdeburg and Brandenburg, and looks eastward beyond Stettin into Poland. In the post-war period Germany has briefly flirted with an eastern policy. With reunification it was able to pursue a strong and determined policy towards the Soviet Union and now towards Russia, which is at one with its past. Germany was happy to do a deal with the Soviet Union to encourage more trade and to offer more aid in return for agreement that the Soviet troops would leave East Germany and the two Germanies would be allowed to reunite. The acquiescence of the Soviet Union in this fundamental change at the centre of Europe was a sign of how demoralized and weakened the Soviet regime had become. Russia's past and that of the Soviet Union pointed in the direction of the USSR wanting to maintain a weakened, western-looking Germany. Her acquiescence has strengthened eastern-looking Germany and was a sign of Soviet desperation.

Germany's priority will now be the reconstruction of the five East German *länder*. The choice of a conversion rate of one or two ostmarks to the deutschmark has burdened East Germany with great difficulties. Over half the work-force has lost its jobs as a result of its inability to withstand the competitive pressures imposed by the single currency, whilst the consequent overheating of the West German economy desperately trying to keep up to supply the new 15 million people in the East has precipitated an inflationary problem and led to the sharp rise in deutschmark interest rates. Overcoming these difficulties is Germany's first main task and has led to a slowdown in the West as the interest rate policy makes its impact.

In the meantime, Germany will be conscious of the commercial opportunities that lie elsewhere in eastern and central Europe, especially in the German-speaking parts. All of the central European countries are aware of the magnetic power of Germany, and although some are wary of it all take the view that if German businesses and capital are available to do the job and no one else is, then they would be foolish to forgo the German opportunity. Germany will be spurred on in her wish to see trade and prosperity spread into these countries by the ever-present threat of mass migration. Already large numbers of people are battering at the gates of Germany for access, from Poland, Rumania and elsewhere. As the dislocation from the former Soviet Union spreads, and as it becomes easier for citizens of the new sovereign states of the old Union to leave their countries, so the numbers will swell massively.

This poses an enormous problem for German policy makers. Many people in Germany wish to run a tight immigration policy, believing that there are limits to the number of people that the country can successfully absorb from the East. However, Germany feels constrained by her past about the lengths to which she can go to resist the immigrant tide. Geography again dictates the problem. Germany's land frontiers are extremely long. There are many crossing points into the West, official and unofficial, and now that the barbed wire and the watch towers have been pulled down, now that the ideological iron curtain has been removed, it is extremely difficult to police the border effectively. The border only worked in the 1960s and 1970s because the brutal Communist regimes of the East were prepared to shoot anyone who tried to cross without permission. Germany would not wish to, and could not afford to undertake such a heartless policy to stem the new tide of immigration. The result will be immigration settlement camps and large numbers of displaced people swimming the rivers and taking to the roads at night, making their way steadily westwards.

The imperative for Germany must therefore be to bring prosperity and stability to the new democracies along her borders by helping wherever she can. She will wish the immigration issue to be tackled in partnership with other western European countries. None of the courses likely to be adopted will be effective. The borders will continue to leak, people will continue to move westwards in search of Utopia. The only thing which will deter the travellers is success in creating some prosperity and stability east of the Elbe.

The position of the new Commonwealth of sovereign states to the East is the most difficult and dangerous of all. The ending of Russian and Soviet supremacy within a strong union means the end of the balance of terror, the mutually assured destruction that kept the peace for more than forty years between East and West. No sooner had the celebrations finished than strategists and policy planners realized the implications of four new nuclear powers arising in the East. President Gorbachev, in the last days of office, warned the West as clearly as he could that there could be difficulties between the new states emerging, and that it was in the West's interest to use whatever bargaining power they had to try and insist upon a common control and command system for the nuclear forces, and on the establishment of a unified body with which the West could deal in any further strategic arms limitations talks. For the time being a loose control system has been introduced between the four nuclear republics, but the fact remains that the nuclear weapons have been spread amongst four different countries, that those four countries are relatively poor and unstable, and that at any point the common command system could be replaced by single command systems in each of the four republics. The inability of the four countries to agree on common conventional forces illustrates just how deep is the distrust between the member states of the new union, and shows that the West should treat seriously the possibility of future conflicts and disputes between constituent parts of what was the USSR.

Russia has traditionally had two aims. The first has been to preserve its windows on the West through the Baltic Sea, and the second to preserve its access through the Black Sea into the Mediterranean. Whilst it had been interested in driving eastward, in the most active periods of its history it has been to the West and to the West's technology that Russia has looked. The secession of Latvia, Lithuania and Estonia has removed much of Russia's window on the Baltic, which has now narrowed to St Petersburg (formerly Leningrad) and the small hinterland around it. Through the secession of the Ukraine and Belorussia, Russia has lost its direct access through the Crimea and Odessa to the Black Sea. The capital of the new confederation has moved westwards to Minsk in the heart of the plain of Belorussia. The task of keeping even the reduced but vast Russian Federation together is going to be no easy one during the long, cold and difficult winters that lie ahead for this former Soviet republic.

Rebuilding the seventeen republics of the old Soviet Union is a task of heroic proportions. It is as grave and as difficult as that confronting western Europe from the ruins of the Second World War. The Soviet economy has collapsed. The introduction of price reform has sent inflation spiralling. The breakdown of the old Comecom trade and barter system has led to a reduction in incomes per head from the already very low levels they had reached under the Communist system. The ethnic tensions are quite considerable. One of the pressures leading to the break-up of the USSR and its army was the reluctance of Muslims and other non-Russians from the South and the East to serve in distant provinces and republics at the request of Russian officers, commanders and senior politicians. Lenin and Stalin's great successes in brutally suppressing nationalist sentiment throughout the republics, or in providing the greater ideal to which they could appeal, was overwhelmed in the latter days of the Soviet Union by the disparate forces of regionalism and nationalism in the varied provinces that made up the Union. Religion too is a force for change and conflict. Soviet ideology attempted to suppress churchgoing and downgraded religion. Countless churches were converted to civil uses and no active party supporter would be seen anywhere near a church. The introduction of *glasnost* made church-going respectable again and opened up the old conflicts between the Muslim South and the Christian West.

This explosive mixture has been made more dangerous by the pains of transition and the complexities of reform. The inability of any elected politician to find an easy way of delivering more goods to the shops and more money to the pay packets has created the preconditions for further revolutionary change. The presence of hundreds of thousands of former troops disbanded from the army with no homes or jobs to go to is a potential threat. The uncertainty about the disposition of the small firearms and portable weapons that the disbanded troops should have handed in adds fuel to the flames.

The territory of the former Soviet Union has been debauched. Large areas of it have been laid waste by over-intensive collective farming with too much fertilizer turning the once fertile soils into dust bowls. Over-farming and the diversion of river courses has turned areas in the Central South into arid and unusable land. The nuclear reactor programme led to the disaster at Chernobyl. Around other Soviet reactor sites leakage has occurred and whole settlements are affected by heavy doses of radiation. The city where the Soviet nuclear weapons grade plutonium was made has succeeded in dumping large quantities of radioactive material and turning a very large area of terrain into a highly radioactive and dangerous piece of real estate. The oil fields have been neglected and overworked, so that they now require massive investment in new technology to contain the oil leaks, to drill new wells and to provide the pipelines necessary to transport what oil remains to market. Industrial and factory areas in the Soviet Union have belched lethal fumes and leached heavy metals and other dangerous pollutants into the water courses. All of these things need effort, energy and money to tackle, commodities not in over-plentiful supply in the demoralized republics.

The republics look to the West for help and assistance. They are realistic enough to know that the bulk of the capital resources and many of the ideas and technology required to build them a better tomorrow must come from the West. They also feel strangely vulnerable, given the impressive display of American superiority in the Gulf. That is why they do not regard it as entirely fictitious to see some or all of the republics of the West and North applying to join NATO and become part of the western defence establishment. Indeed, some of their planners might foresee the day when the southern republics of the USSR under Muslim control form allegiances and alliances with the Muslim states to the south like Iran and Iraq. The Ukraine, Russia and Belorussia might well wish to be part of the western community being out of sympathy with the Islamic states to the south.

The West has a great deal of hard thinking to do about the future role of NATO and its own defence arrangements. Peace in western Europe and peace between western and eastern and central Europe has been maintained since the Second World War only by the balance of terror and by the presence of sizeable American ground forces and nuclear weapons on western European soil. Although the American presence has always been contentious, especially in the Low Countries and more recently in Germany, it was the willingness of the Americans to commit their troops to western Europe and form part of the combined NATO defence that prevented any Russian or Soviet expansion during the period of dynamic Soviet world colonization. At exactly the time when the Soviet tentacles were stretching out to Cuba, through South-East Asia and into Afghanistan and the Middle East, western resolve prevented the Soviets from thinking about expansion westwards into the rest of Europe. It may seem now that it was a natural dividing line to stop at the West German frontier and to stop at the Yugoslav coast, but there was nothing God-given about those geographical limits to the Russian empire when the Soviets themselves could and did exercise influence as far away as North Korea, North Vietnam and other parts of the Pacific littoral.

Western preparedness to site cruise missiles as a response to the Soviet deployment of SS20s demonstrated continuing resolve at a crucial time. Reagan's experimentation with Star Wars was the final denouement which precipitated Soviet collapse. The fact that American troops were in forward positions along the line where any invasion might have come was comforting to western countries who knew that without American fire power, finance and support, western Europe was indefensible against the might of the Soviet army.

NATO's future course is more difficult. There are those who

now believe that because the ideological challenge of communism is over and the Cold War has been rolled back, that NATO should effectively be disbanded. The so-called peace dividend has been spent many times over by the fashionable commentators in the media and by several political parties. They should appreciate that far from the world becoming a safer place as a result of the collapse of the Soviet Union and its ideology, it has in some ways become more dangerous. Recent years have seen a number of limited and localized conflicts that were none the less important to the principles of self-determination, democracy and freedom which are central to the western way of life. British troops had to be committed to recovering the Falkland Islands from an aggressive tyrant in Argentina; they had to be committed, with American troops, to defeating a demented tyrant in Iraq; and United Nations forces are being deployed in Yugoslavia.

One of the biggest dangers now facing the world is the spread of nuclear technology. Four nuclear nations have been created overnight out of the remains of the Soviet empire. Worse still, many accomplished nuclear scientists are now redundant or footloose. Which countries might bid for their skills? How soon might it be before the unstable countries of the Middle East have developed powerful atomic weapons in their own right? How long before countries like Argentina, Brazil, India and Pakistan, as well as Israel, have nuclear weapons? How long before China develops the missile capability to deliver her atomic weapons over long distances? These are the issues which matter to the security of the West as we approach the twenty-first century. It is not a background against which people should be contemplating wholesale disarmament and the removal of all nuclear weapons from western soil.

It is possible from this position of strength, where the West temporarily has hegemony and superiority, to negotiate lasting and worthwhile reductions in the number of weapons. The resumption of the weapons limitations and control talks with the inheritors of the Soviet empire is encouraging. The fewer weapons there are lying around, the less temptation in people's way, and the less risk of an accident or of loss. Any country embarking on a nuclear weapons programme, legally or illicitly, should also know that the West has the continuing will, as well as the continuing technical superiority, not to be defeated in conflict so that were tension to develop it would not be worthwhile for any emerging nuclear power to go to war.

An important element of British foreign policy in the next few years must be to maintain the American link and presence in western Europe. Western Europe is still not capable of defending itself against a concerted attack from nuclear powers with large armies. After all, only France and Britain have nuclear weapons. The centre of the European continent is wide open to threat. Military strategists over many years have realized that only by maintaining a nuclear capacity could the peace be maintained and the long border protected. It is quite possible to reduce the strength and fire power of the Americans in western Europe as part of the general relaxation of tension, and as part of the planned reductions in armaments on both sides. It would be wrong to conclude that all threats have been removed and that the Americans could therefore leave altogether.

British foreign policy has traditionally had an interest in the continent of Europe. The main British concern has been to avoid any one power dominating the rest of the continent. This was the policy Britain pursued against Spain in the sixteenth century, when she stood with the Netherlands against the might of the Spanish empire and the Catholic forces. It is a role England took up in the seventeenth century against the Dutch who had developed great commercial and maritime strength based upon their excellence as seafarers and their trading ambitions. In the eighteenth and nineteenth centuries it was the turn of Britain to construct alliances against France who had emerged as the most dangerous and powerful nation in Europe. In the twentieth century Britain had to stand with her allies against the force of the enlarged and united Germany in two world wars.

The relaxation of tension in the West since 1945 has been noticeable and most welcome. The closing years of the twentieth century are not likely to see a resurgence of militarism and the wish for military expansion by any of the leading western countries. There will, however, be substantial commercial rivalry and attempts by countries to outdo each other in the spheres of political and commercial prowess. French policy is dictated by a nervousness about Germany. France, under President Mitterand, has been pursuing an agenda to try to 'bind Germany in' to the European Community in the belief that France could then control the direction and use of German power. Edith Cresson, once France's European Minister and then Prime Minister, saw France as the rider and Germany as the horse: Germany provided the motive power, France told the horse where to go. This is surprising as when you look at all the important decisions made in the European Community in recent years you can see much greater German influence in the direction of events than French. Whilst France has had considerable influence through the skills of its civil service and through the presence of Delors as the President of the Commission, on many crucial issues the German view has prevailed. France had no distinctive position or influence when it came to the vital question of German reunification. France had no influence over the decision to grant to the united Germany more members of the European Parliament. France opposed this but lost. France saw her foreign policy over Yugoslavia being dragged in a pro-German direction by the strength of the German position. France discovered that her views on monetary union were watered down and amended as a result of German pressure and German fears about the dilution of the deutschmark.

Some senior officials and politicians in France think that French policy is based upon a false premise. There can be no 'binding Germany in'. Germany is an important, mature power in her own right. Germany will decide what is in Germany's best interests and Germany will have a very influential impact on many aspects of the European Community's life. Germany is the most important paymaster of the Community, and Germany is the largest country in terms of population and gross national product.

In a way the Community is waiting for French foreign policy to shift. It has a feeling of impermanence and instability about it at the moment, but a change of government is probably required for the policy itself to alter fundamentally. A right-of-centre French government would be much keener to defend French national integrity and independence. It would be much keener to ally with the United Kingdom, seeing the need to form an alliance of the second and third largest countries in the European Community, and seeing the common interest there could be between those two countries acting together. Half, or even more, of French society has felt very let down by the lack of an independent vigorous French foreign policy in recent years and by the attitudes taken by the French administration in European negotiations. In the meantime, the French Right keeps its lines open to London and watches with dismay as the French people move further towards the extreme Right under Le Pen, who offers the direct slogans of national identity and independence to an audience all too willing to listen as they see themselves being sold out by the French socialist administration.

American foreign policy has been dominated until recently by its response to the Soviet Union. In an age of two superpowers there was an uneasy balance. Every problem in the world was of interest to the United States of America as it was part of the bigger picture of whether Soviet or American influence would be dominant in different regions of the world. In the 1960s, the doctrine of the domino theory held sway. Many American strategists and politicians feared that if they allowed one more country to pass from democracy and capitalism to communism it would lead to a whole series of other countries falling. That was why the American administrations dug in over Korea in the 1950s and Vietnam in the 1960s, and why they were nervous about the spread of communism, particularly in Latin America, in Africa but also in all parts of the world. In the 1990s American foreign policy is going to have to adjust to the fact that each of these world conflicts is unrelated to the old central struggle between democracy and communism. Each one will have to be judged on its merits in relation to American interests and America will have to decide just how far she wishes to use her unique superpower status to become the world's policeman. The United States is in a position now where she could stop any aggressor indulging in conventional military activity. What she could not do, and would not wish to do, is to impose her will upon peoples in different countries. The 1950s and 1960s showed that however much military might and financial muscle you have, it is not possible to conduct a successful war in all circumstances against guerrillas and against determined fanatical opponents on the ground.

There are those in the United States of America who would like to see Uncle Sam rein in his ambitions and his obligations abroad. These belong to the depressing 'realist school', who argue that

American power is more apparent than real, that American GDP and position in the financial world is not what it was, and who see Japan as the rising commercial threat. To these people there would be much to be said for the United States withdrawing entirely or almost entirely from western Europe and leaving its defence to the European countries who are, after all, comparable in riches with the United States of America in aggregate. They might like to see a curtailment of American involvement in the Gulf and certainly are sceptical about American involvement in Africa and much of Asia. They would be happy to see America defend its trade routes and its essential commercial interests, to pursue some of its interests in the oil-producing areas of the world, and to maintain sufficient strategic nuclear defence so that America was without threat or challenge from anywhere in the world. They would be happy to see America forgo the pleasures of policing Asia and Africa, and even Latin America and Europe.

To date, wiser counsel has prevailed in the White House. The policy establishment has accepted that there is a special duty upon the American peoples and government now that it has established such supremacy. Whilst accepting that the American economy has not performed as well as the Japanese in recent years, they recognize the colossal accumulated wealth and economic success of the United States and believe that some portion of that can still be spent for military purposes to have a benign impact on world events. The establishment is proud of the efforts the United States is making to mediate between the Arabs and Israelis in the Middle East. They are understandably proud of the stance America took against Hussein in the Gulf and would see America having legitimate business interests in the oil-producing regions of the Middle East, in Latin America, America's own commercial backyard, and in parts of Asia and Europe. They do not believe that all of the tensions with the nuclear weapons powers of the Soviet area are behind them necessarily. America has to guard against the day when those weapons fall into the hands of less well-disposed regimes, or become the playthings of tyrants or fanatics.

Some see problems emerging both with the Spanish-speaking peoples in Mexico and beyond, and, more fundamentally, with the Islamic peoples of the Middle East. American democracy and capitalism might not be entirely safe as long as the Spanish world endures greater poverty than America and as long as values and views hostile to Christian democracy persist in the Middle East.

A great deal of American attention is devoted to Japan, an intriguing country since much of its success as a nation comes from its adoption of the American system. It is ironic that America's most successful client state should now be perceived as the biggest threat to her prosperity. Post-war Japan set diligently about the task of learning from the American conquerors how democracy could work and, more importantly, how a capitalist economy could generate the range of goods and services people wanted. The massive success of the Japanese prosperity machine in recent years has propelled Japan to the status of world economic power in a single generation, despite having a population under half of the United States of America, one-third of the European Community, and one-third of the former Soviet Union.

Many business people in the United States see the penetration of the American market by more and more Japanese imports as a sign of the unfairness of Japanese trading practices and the weakness of the American competition. They seek regularly to find means of holding back the tide of Japanese imports and are constantly sending their politicians and advisors off on missions to Japan to rattle the sabres and to demand fairer trade.

American and western attitudes to Japan and to Germany, the vanquished powers of 1945, are riddled with ambiguities. There is a jealousy that these two powers escaped the burden of defence expenditure imposed upon the victorious powers of America, France, Britain and the others by the peace treaties. Yet those peace treaties prevented German and Japanese rearmament on a large scale for the understandable reason that people immediately after the war feared a resurgence of militarism in those countries and saw the control of weapons as a method of preventing any resurgence of military ambitions. The West was very keen after the end of the war to see Japan and Germany rebuild themselves by their own efforts. Now that they have succeeded so well it is curious to note the jealousy that that success has aroused, despite it being the sincerest form of flattery.

The United States has become extremely worried about Japan but has been more enthusiastic about Germany. The United States' attempts to escalate the trade war spirit against the Japanese may be good domestic politics for presidential and senatorial candidates alike, but it does not relate to the underlying realities of international trade. When President Bush visited Japan early in January of 1992 he and his advisors tried to extract concessions from the Japanese about alleged unfair trading practices. The Japanese saw the President's collapse at a state banquet as a symptom of the sickness of the US economy. The US President came urging the Japanese to buy more American-designed and produced motor cars. It was the wrong product at the wrong time for the wrong people. The Japanese live on a crowded island. They have little space for parking cars and an aversion to using large amounts of gasoline in vehicles. American cars designed for the open highways and freeways and the rolling acres of the American countryside would be ill-suited to Japanese streets and Japanese mentality. The US does have a considerable number of products it can and should sell in Japan, but the gas-guzzling American mid-range and large car is unlikely to figure prominently. The Japanese are ambivalent towards the Americans. On the one hand, they deeply admire the United States of America, having learnt a great deal from her in the post-war period, and having seen the Japanese economy and constitution rise on American lines out of the rubble of the war. On the other hand, Japan now sees that she has a financial might that can challenge or rival that of the United States, and is not happy about the way the United States is now crying foul.

The USA sees the changes in eastern Europe as an opportunity to scale down its commitments to the defence of the western European countries. There are many politicians, especially in California and on the Pacific littoral in the United States, who favour a major reorientation of American strategy and a return to isolationism. The East Coast policy establishment and the clarity of the Republican view of America's world role have so far restrained them. None the less, the United States of America has been impressed by the rise of Germany, and has given support and succour to Germany in its ambitions to reunify and to develop its own eastern policy. The United States has also given, from time to time, encouragement to the process of European union.

There is an ambiguity in the American position. America, in one mood, tells western Europe to get its act together, meaning that it wishes to see a more united Europe so that it can just deal with one superpower. In another mood she argues strongly against the attitudes and views expressed by the European Community when it does act with a single purpose. America has not enjoyed the European Community negotiating line on the General Agreement on Tariffs and Trade, especially on agricultural protection and on industrial policy. US policy makers are going to have to get used to the idea that if they encourage further political union in western Europe, and they are successful, they are just as likely to encourage the growth of the very attitudes and policy stances they dislike, than to encourage something more favourable to their own position.

The immediate post-unification phase in American German policy was one of great friendship and support. The American government and President decided that Germany was the superpower in Europe, that the rest of western Europe could form a federation with Germany, and that Germany could give direction to the task of forming a solid western European policy. It was the speed of Chancellor Kohl's moves to develop an independent German policy towards the Soviet Union which caused America to rethink her stance. At a critical time in the evolution of the Soviet Union and in negotiations between the superpowers, the Germans made their own independent approach to buy *rapprochement* with the Soviet Union and to buy the withdrawal of troops from eastern Germany. In so doing, American policy-makers felt that the Germans paid insufficient attention to the great role the United States had played in encouraging the reunification of Germany, and consulted too little with American allies over how far and how quickly Germany should move in developing its own separate Soviet policy.

This cooling of relations was reinforced in the run-up to the Gulf War. The Gulf War showed yet again, as had the Libyan bombing raids, to the American policy makers and public that western Europe was an unreliable ally when it came to taking military action. In the approach to the Gulf War the United Kingdom made it clear that she unequivocally supported the American position and was prepared to commit her own troops alongside the American forces and under American command. France also made it clear that she too thought there were important principles at stake and that aggression should be resisted. She was prepared to make a military contribution but was not prepared to accept common command and control under American leadership. This reflected the position the French had had towards NATO over many years. Germany made it equally clear that, despite being the richest of the major European countries, she was morally and constitutionally unable to make any military commitment to the Gulf task force. Instead of debating firmly the principles of autonomy and the right to self-determination of peoples, Germany looked inwards and discussed the limits of German action given the constraints of her constitution. Lesser European countries like Belgium even refused ammunition to supply the armies that were committed to the Gulf war and were using common NATO-procured weapon systems.

This rang the alarm bells in Washington, reminding policy makers that western Europe had a long way to go before it had a united voice and that there was no reason why that united voice should be a strong voice for freedom and democracy in support of American actions. American policy then became less relentless in the pursuit of European unification, and in the critical discussions over Maastricht and the new treaties the US did not play an important part, appreciating that the politics were extremely delicate and the sensitivities highly attuned.

The United States of America has decided in the post-Gulf War world that its prime policy interests lie in the Middle East. For the time being, Cuba and Latin America are relatively quiescent and the United States is prepared to leave the problems of eastern and central Europe to others.

Those tensions and problems do not have the same immediate relevance that they had when they could lead inexorably to confrontation and conflict with the Soviet superpower. In the Middle East America sees an immediate problem arising out of the Gulf War and the run-up to that war. The United States would dearly love to broker a peace between the Arabs and Israelis. Israel has been caught a little unawares by the strength of the American regime and its preparedness to challenge the old assumption of American policy in the Middle East that the US always has to back Israel. The United States administration has made it clear that it wishes to see a movement by both sides and that it would like to see a negotiated peace settlement between the Arabs and Israelis.

This is naturally taking up a great deal of America's diplomatic capability at a critical time in the evolution of Europe.

The United States played little role in the gathering Yugoslav conflict. It has left attempts to bring the two parties together in discussion to the European Community and, latterly, to the United Nations. It is a sign that the United States of America accepts limits to its role in the world and that its attitude to European issues has shifted perceptibly as a result of the end of the Cold War.

The United States is not, however, prepared to ignore the massive changes in the former Soviet Union. Rightly, it perceives the need for considerable attention and diplomacy to be given to the rise of new nuclear weapons powers in the East. There are times when watching the news and listening to the debates between Russia, the Ukraine, Belorussia and Kazakhstan over the disposition of the mighty forces of the former Soviet Union, that spectators could be forgiven for thinking it has an air of unreality. Yet, underlying it, there is a desperately important reality. The question of how many strong military powers there are going to be in the East, and what their attitude to each other and to the countries of the West might be, has to be settled. If a large number of ships from either the Baltic or the Black Sea fleets pass to a power other than Russia, it gives that power significant strength in the world. It is quite possible to construct the second, third and fourth largest navies in the world out of the remnants of the Soviet Navy. Similarly, it is possible to divide up the airforce to provide colossal forces at the disposal of more than one power in the East.

We need again to turn to history to see what the ambitions of these emerging states are likely to be. In each case there is a history of fierce nationalism, and of expansionism, especially westwards. In each case there has been a history of expansion towards the sea with states seeking warm-water ports for the conduct of their trade and business. Whilst in an age of air communications this is less crucial, the general trend of these countries to look westwards and to seek to expand is one that needs to be fully understood.

A bigger question that all western policy-makers will have to address in the last decade of the twentieth century is the rise of Islam. Whilst the West may well celebrate its momentous victory in the Gulf, it was a victory for western principles and one which has a cost in terms of its impact upon fundamentalist

Islamic peoples who disagreed with the American action. Many Islamic peoples resent the intrusion of powerful western military forces into their lives. Many Islamic peoples now living abroad in western countries are seeking to respond to the pressures of the fundamentalist Islamic revolution. Nineteen ninety-two dawned with the establishment of the separate Muslim Parliament in the United Kingdom, the growing worries in France about the development in Algeria of a fundamentalist Islamic movement not that far away from the South of France, the growing tensions in the Middle East about how far the fundamentalists might run, and growing signs of disagreements amongst the Arab states between those fully committed to capitalism and many of the values of the West on the one hand, and those, on the other, who seek an alternative Islamic way. The Gulf War was a stunning military victory. It was certainly a victory against Soviet weapons which had considerable consequences. It may prove to be one chapter in a more difficult history in the relationships between Islam and Christianity.

The quiet commercial expansion of Germany in the centre of Europe, alongside the restrained but effective use of American power as world policeman, could provide a good background for the eastern European economies to join the global market. Their progress is likely to be disrupted and jolted by nationalist movements, border disputes and migrations of peoples. There is the ever-present danger of the rise of neo-fascism, and the threat that politics will be bestialized by conflicts and aggression. The UN has to rise to the occasion and the US has to take a world view if global capitalism and democracy are to build on the revolutionary progress they made in the late 1980s.

TEN

The New Socialism

The intellectual decline of Marxism was swift and to some surprising. A pseudo scientific doctrine that had dominated socialist and left-wing thinking for over one hundred years collapsed with few shots being fired at the end of the 1980s. For years left-wing parties had turned to the class war analyses of Karl Marx for their speeches and rallying cries. For years they have seen capitalism as the enemy of progress for working men. For years they had tried to impose their view of the political process as a struggle for the emancipation of workers on a recalcitrant society and on the recalcitrant facts of economic and social life. What was surprising was the length of time that Marxist contradictions and antiquated rhetoric held sway. Many are now wise with hindsight, but to Marxism's critics it had always seemed implausible and somewhat anachronistic.

The Left were at a loss in their thinking when Marxist rhetoric and analysis disappeared. They have now plunged themselves into a long period of either ignoring the new reality or attempting valiantly to grapple with it. What are they to think about working people who object to the penal levels of taxation that Marxism recommended allegedly for the benefit of the poor? What are they to think about the new style of service sector and high technology business that erodes the distinction between blue and white collar and enlarges the middle class from which Marx himself sprang and which he spent most of his life attacking? What are they to think about people who far from seeing government and local government as the natural ally of progress and improvement see it, in part, as a threat or a worry where it becomes too dominant or overreaching?

In Britain the socialist debate has been fairly sterile. The Labour Party under Neil Kinnock understood what it had to try to ditch, but found it much more difficult to discover what it needed to believe in to attract voting support. Over the 1980s the new model Labour Party gently and quietly distanced itself from the proposition that it should also always impede the purchase of individual council houses by the people living in them. It gradually moved away from the idea that it should resist every attempt to raise standards and encourage greater choice in education. It quietly dropped the proposition that every privatized industry had to be renationalized. Almost imperceptibly it tried to change itself from being a party that stood against shareholders to being a party that wanted to champion the rights and the causes of the small shareholder where he purchased stock.

Over the course of the 1980s the attempt to leave behind the extreme left-wing conceptions of progress through mass movements on the streets, through strikes and other unparliamentary activities, went on. Whilst the party had only limited success in changing its views on competition and choice in a range of public service areas and was still on whole the party that defended every vested interest in every public sector trade union, it did have greater success in distancing itself from the more absurd and damaging undemocratic processes recommended by the hard Left of the middle 1980s. The Labour leadership could see that association with Arthur Scargill and the crack troops of the miners' dispute was unhelpful to their aim to govern the country. They perceived that backing and underwriting the antics of the hard Left councillors in Liverpool City Council did not underwrite their new image of themselves as responsible men in grey suits awaiting the task of government. They recognized that always demanding more law and more public money to solve every problem laid them open to the charge that they were too interventionist in their approach and that their sums did not add up to an acceptable level of taxation.

The central conundrum that they could never solve was what they should do about the wish of people in a free society to see some balance preserved between the amount of money that the state controls and the amount that the people have a choice in deciding how it should be spent. Bryan Gould in 1992 asked the Labour Party too difficult a question even for the more enlightened era of the early 1990s. He wanted to know what the Labour Party's attitude should be when many voters, far from seeing government and local government action as friendly, saw it as a possible threat to their freedoms and their lifestyle. The Labour movement found this difficult to envisage, heavily entrenched as it is in the public service employee union nexus and committed as it has been to believing that there are few problems which cannot be solved by the application of a little more money to the public sector. They were flat-footed in their response to the citizens' charter movement and to the idea that standards could be set, contracts awarded and greater efficiency achieved in the interest of both the service user and the tax-payer. To the Labour mind it was natural to equate more money with better service and less money with 'Conservative parsimony'. There was a reluctance to accept that sometimes money can be better spent and that efficiency can ally with quality and improved service.

The relationship between public sector trade unions, the Labour Party and left-wing political thinking in Britain is the reason why the Labour Party finds it so difficult to make changes in this crucial area of its approach to problems. Improvements in efficiency and in service quality may well require substantial changes in working practices. These will often be opposed by shop stewards and union leaders, who believe, perhaps incorrectly, that their members wish to see every Spanish practice defended rather than working methods improved. The revolution in employee/employer relationships in the private sector and the rapid advances in productivity achieved in the 1980s and now the 1990s, especially by industry, have not always been replicated by similar progress in the public sector. It has been in the public sector unions, the Confederation of Health Service Employees, the National Union of Public Employees and the National Union of Teachers in particular, that there have been persistent tensions between employer and employees as expressed by shop stewards and union motions. There have been frequent demonstrations and objections to changes designed to raise standards and improve quality.

The besetting problem of the Labour Party is that such a large proportion of its money comes from trade union subscription, yet many of the opinion polls show that the British public would be happier to vote for the Labour Party if it did not have these strong connections and wasn't so influenced in its policies by the trade union movement. At the very time when the Confederation of British Industry was strongly attacking the Conservative government, making clear the distance between the government and the CBI on many issues, the trade union movement was snuggling closer to the Labour Party and underlining the importance of trade union funding to political action. The decline of the large nationalized industry and industrial unions through the productivity revolution and economic change meant that even greater reliance came to be placed by the Labour Movement on the Transport and General Workers Union, NUPE, COHSE and the other large unions representing wholly or primarily public service employees.

The Left, unable to rise to the challenge of the new world of quality and contracting out, turned instead to the development of a new constitutional agenda. Intuitively sensing that they were on weak ground both on democracy and on the advances in prosperity that popular capitalism could bring, they tried to out-manoeuvre the Conservative administration by pressing for large constitutional changes which they claimed would be more democratic.

They turned to the idea that the United Kingdom needed regional government as well as national, county and district government. They proposed a central bill of rights that would take precedence over parliamentary legislation or parliamentary debates and would bind successive parliaments and governments. They proposed more freedom of information, an assault upon secrecy in government generally and campaigned on a range of civil rights issues.

Where they were campaigning for openness and pluralism their case had some force which was already being met by government reforms. Where they were campaigning for more bureaucracy, more government in general and more control they were out of sympathy with the spirit of the times. The bill of rights itself is a difficult concept in the evolutionary British constitution. One Parliament cannot bind its successor. It would not be sufficient for a bill of rights to be proposed in one Parliament and then to be expected to be carried out by all subsequent Parliaments. It would naturally lead to successor Parliaments, especially where party control had changed, proposing amendments to the bill of rights, thus removing the idea that there are immutable truths that can be embodied in the constitution above the law makers for all time.

If the bill of rights was something that had to be based on cross-party support, a charter hammered out by agreement between the major political parties, then it could end up as a very anodyne document. Operating at a very high level of generality it would have little importance. It would then be up to Parliament and the courts to interpret its general propositions. If the bill of rights said that everyone was innocent until proved guilty and that everyone had the right to a fair trial it would have done nothing more than endorse long-standing English judicial practice. If the Labour Party tried to introduce the proposal that no matter relating to an industrial dispute could become a matter for the criminal law, it would not meet with the general approval of other parties and many people in the country. If the Conservative Party tried to introduce the principle that local councils should always put their work out to competitive tender to guarantee high performance and good value for money the Labour Party might regard that as a political act and oppose it vigorously. The floor of the chamber in the House of Commons provides a cockpit for the nation to see principles, philosophies and policies opposed and argued over. To try to replicate that in a universal bill of rights could cause great difficulties for the draughtsmen and could end up with little agreement.

It would be possible to draw up the general principles, perhaps with cross-party agreement, at the instigation of the government, with an eye to removing the more obviously political ideas which could then be put to the people in a referendum. This would establish the sovereignty of the people over their Parliament and might deter subsequent governments from attempting anything similar on too regular a basis. Were a bill of rights to be drawn up on recommendation through a popular vote governments would think twice about proposing amendments, running the risk of losing the vote and then perhaps having to contemplate resignation because of failure to carry the country in an important constitutional amendment.

Whilst this is the best variant of the idea of bill of rights it is difficult to see how it can avoid the problem already identified of, on the one hand, being too general and not having an impact or, on the other, of becoming too political to run the risk of it not being passed with a sufficient majority in the country or becoming permanent. It is difficult as well to see what a bill of rights adds to the evolving rights created by case law in the courts, by frequent amendments and changes to statute law in parliament and by the natural pressure of public opinion. How accommodative would a bill of rights be to the rapid pace of social change and would this matter? Had a bill of rights been drawn up forty years ago it may have contained passages about the sanctity and importance of the married family unit. Now that a large number of people form single parent households and one in three of all marriages end in divorce what relationship with social reality would the strongly defined rhetoric of a bill of rights from an earlier era enjoy? A bill of economic rights drawn up in an era of floating exchange rates might look a little strange in a world of managed or fixed currency rates. The advantage of the parliamentary process is its interaction with public opinion and the ability of Parliament to encapsulate the view of the nation and to take the action that the nation thinks appropriate. If Parliament loses touch or fails to perform then the people reassert their sovereignty by changing the MPs and parties they represent at subsequent by- and general elections.

The pursuit of greater openness in government is a natural cry of Oppositions who always feel starved of the information they require in order to attack the government strongly. Experience shows that the Opposition have often been well served by the cult of secrecy in government, as in a free society they usually get access to leaked documents from sympathizers within the administration. This gives the item more publicity than if it had not been secret in the first place. It is difficult to be badly informed as a Member of Parliament. A huge amount of information is published and produced by way of answers to parliamentary questions, ministerial statements and replies to debates and the regular round of publications and annual reports emanating from government departments, executive agencies, nationalized industries and the like. The problem for the Opposition Member of Parliament is not a lack of information but the ability to cut his way through it, to winnow out the significant and to use it well.

The classic system for openness in British government is based on the combination of Green Paper consultation, White Paper consultation, bill drafting, parliamentary debate and the final passage of the legislation. Whilst there may be early scare stories about what the government is thinking up or plotting, when the system works well it is open and consultative in its nature. The government publishes a Green Paper outlining a problem and some suggested options for change. It may have a strong preference or it may be more relaxed about the possibilities. This is then followed by a period of consultation and reply leading to the production of firm proposals of the government in the form of a White Paper statement of its anticipated policy. This too may well be followed by a period of consultation on the details leading up to the drafting of the legislation. During the passage of a bill back-bench MPs, lobbyists, interested parties and others have their say about whether the legislation fully reflects the detailed presentation made in the White Paper and the Opposition has another opportunity to attack the whole strategy if it is in strong political disagreement with it. During the committee stages of a bill the committee can work word by word, line by line, on the drafting of the legislation to try and perfect it.

These procedures at their best produce an open participative system of policy formation and of legislation. The Opposition argues that more of the working papers should also be made available. Members would like to see the policy submissions of the officials that went to the ministers before they came to their conclusion on the Green or White Paper line. They would particularly like to see any papers highlighting grave problems or difficulties that the government may wish to pause over before tackling or even may wish to see given little prominence in view of their sensitivity.

There do have to be some things that are kept secret. Most people in the secrecy debate would agree that the work of the intelligence services and information relating to the defence of the realm should be kept safe and understood by only a few. There is always the Privy Council system for briefing the leaders of the Opposition on these sensitive issues to make sure that they understand what they could be inheriting and to see if there is some cross-party agreement about these crucial matters. Many people agree that decisions to discipline individual members of staff or sensitive issues affecting individuals or groups in the government's employment should also be protected from the public gaze. The question of how open the government should be in policy formation is a more debatable issue where different departments and different ministers do have different styles of approach.

When the Conservative government decided to reform social security the then Secretary of State Norman Fowler agreed to a particularly open style of proceeding. He set up a number of review committees which were open for the submission of external evidence and included external advisors in the discussions and debates. The press was able to witness at close quarters the arguments going on and the documents being submitted. Only at the very end of the process was government collective secrecy reasserted when the Secretary of State, and his immediate advisers, pulled together the strands from the enquiries he had held and prepared his draft proposals for publication as a consultation document. It was a model of how open government can work well whilst preserving the need for a period of internal government reflection on the best way forward in order to obtain the necessary cross-departmental clearances between colleagues.

The Left has extended the language and argument about rights into more positive rights to certain benefits and the public service. They argue that if people should have a right to choose between different public sector schools or if they have a right to purchase their council house then maybe they should be granted matching or comparable rights to receive a certain level of benefit, to maintain a certain standard of living whatever their circumstances or a right to a home in the first place.

Some of these rights are an extension of opposition by other means. Where there is a debate about the right level of public expenditure, the Opposition might then dress up higher public expenditure as the offer of some right to individuals to benefit. In other cases there is no disagreement between the parties. Both Conservative and Labour accept that the unemployed have a right, if they have made the necessary national insurance payments, to unemployment benefit for a specified time period. Both parties agree that people in need have a right to income support payments as long as they fulfil the eligibility criteria. Both parties agree that there is a duty upon local authorities to house the homeless although there is disagreement about whether being on a waiting list for better housing is the same as being homeless.

We have already seen how constitutional argument has extended into voting systems and into the debate over regional government. The Left is particularly reluctant, however, to debate what people in the public services should be doing. Ever happy to debate how many more people there should be and how much more service should be provided, they become extremely coy when people wish to get down to the nuts and bolts issues of what the service providers are doing and what the impact of the services is upon the complex pattern of incentive and need throughout the recipient communities.

The balance between individuals acting as individuals and individuals acting as members of the community in 'a social way' is the central political dilemma that separates Left from Right. The Left argue that the new politics based upon a twin belief in popular capitalism and democracy is too self-centred and individualistic. They dislike the idea of a policy based upon competing individuals looking after themselves. They have a notion of a community-based politics founded upon mutual care and provision financed from taxation. In practice, the divide between the major parties of Right and Left in advanced countries is not nearly as severe as this crude caricature would suggest. Right-wing parties accept the role of taxation in redistributing income and in financing public services for those in need. The new left-wing parties are coming to accept the need to leave some incentive for individuals to encourage effort and enterprise. The debate is over degree and the correct mix.

Conservative thinking fully accepts that people live in communities and accept a range of obligations to each other. Right-wing thought tends to concentrate more on the family as the unit, left-wing thought upon the social community. Right and Centre thinking prefers to see care for grandparents based upon a mixture of attention and support in the family and upon pension, insurance and saving provision made in earlier years. Left-wing thought concentrates on seeing the problem of ageing relatives as being one that resides not with the family but with the community at large, urging ever more expenditure financed by the tax-payers for care for the elderly either in their own homes or in residential care. So far in the United Kingdom parties of the Right and Left have agreed that where an individual has assets of his

own these should be used first to pay for the care costs before
the care costs are assumed by the state. The practical distinction
between left-and right-wing policy is therefore rather limited as,
in practice, Conservative policy accepts that where elderly people
need care in residential homes this should be ultimately paid for
by the tax-payer if they have no other means, and parties of the
Left have accepted that where people do have resources of their
own these should be used to finance their care. The Left have
suggested that those caring for family and neighbours should be
recognized through payments from the state. The Government
has countered with radical proposals for care in the community,
extending the range of provision of ancillary and support services
to elderly and disabled people in their own homes to help relieve
the work of unpaid carers or to supplement and strengthen it.
The Left has felt uneasy trying to live with competition. As
we have seen, they opposed competition for the provision of
public services and opposed too much competition in areas like
education. The agenda of the Right has concentrated upon the
striving of individuals in school to win prizes, to pass tests, to excel
themselves. The philosophy of the Left, which imbued a great deal
of teacher-training practice in the 1960s and 1970s, concentrated
instead upon equality, the wish to avoid divisive distinctions being
made between pupils by testing and by competition and the belief
that creating a pleasant social environment in the classroom would
by osmosis produce good results in the children.

There has been a reaction against left-wing, equality-based
thinking in education. People have seen that too much child-
centred learning fails to deliver the results. You cannot have a
good school sports day if no one is allowed to win the races. It
is difficult to get children to learn and remember the basics if no
one ever checks up or tests them. There are now three broadly
competing models for educational advance. The socialist model
argues that the expenditure of more money on more teachers and
more facilities and better equipment in schools will produce its
own benefits. Children have to work in a relaxed atmosphere,
they have to work at their own pace, they need to work largely
in groups and they will find out a great deal for themselves. The
back-to-the-basics model, believing education was a lot better in
the past, is based on a rigorous regime of class teaching, learning

by rote, testing and fierce competition. In the middle lies a model which believes there is something to be learnt from both schools of thought but argues that at the moment the balance, if anything, needs to go in the direction of teaching, testing and measurement of results.

This third group accepts that learning through play, project work and the development of pupils' interest can be important in aiding learning and leavening the heavy diet of tables and spelling tests. However, these exponents are critical of the socialist theory that there should never be very much formal instruction or testing, as good project work and good group work require individuals to pitch in, having already mastered the basic skills to understand the subject of the project and to write well about it. The difficulty with the grammar school selection system did not lie with the grammar schools: most people agreed that they were fine schools which achieved good academic results. Many of their pupils went on to make an important contribution to the economic and social life of the nation. The problem lay in some secondary moderns where too many parents and pupils felt written off and dissatisfied by an educational standard and interest level which were not high enough, often giving them difficulties in later life.

Educationalists are now to some extent trying to solve this problem by balancing selection on academic grounds with a range of schools offering different facilities and opportunities for those who cannot achieve the highest academic standards. Because someone is not successful at Latin grammar or the theory of relativity does not mean they should be discounted from all other types of achievement. There can be schools which specialize in music, the performing arts, technology, the application of practical science, sports, engineering and crafts to complement those schools which provide a firm academic background. It is important that education releases the talents and excitements of every child wherever they may lie. We wish to create a community in which people do appreciate success, but where success and opportunity are open to all prepared to make a commitment. It should be possible for children with the determination and the talent to travel from schools specializing in sport to the Olympics, to move from schools specializing in music to performing in the Royal Albert Hall, to advance from schools specializing in electronics engineering to running their own computer software businesses, and progress from schools specializing in handicraft and design to the drawing boards and management offices of the best companies in the land. Magnet schools and technical colleges provide the natural foil to the academic stream of the grammar school.

Socialist thinking still finds the possibility of choice potentially divisive. Socialists do not like to recognize that there are different types of poverty. Some people are poor because they are disabled or elderly or incapacitated. Some people are poor because they fritter away their chances, they make wrong decisions and mistakes on too large a scale. Both types of poverty may need relief with state help and both types usually attract it. But it may be necessary to send different signals through the system, in the first case showing unalloyed generosity and in the other offering incentives for individuals to rebuild and recreate their own independence. For example, family credit gives cash support to those on low incomes who would otherwise find it better to stay on benefit than to work. Similarly, an educational system based upon choice and variety does permit very different outcomes. Some athletes will pound the county track for years doing reasonably well but only one or two will go to the Olympics. This is not an argument for abolishing the Olympics but an argument for recognizing that a large number of people are not suited to undertaking athletics on a full-time basis but may find their working opportunities elsewhere. The fact that only a few people will be able to conduct a concert at the Royal Albert Hall should not put others off studying music. It is necessary in life to be realistic about whether a particular skill or opportunity will satisfy your need for wages as well as your more spiritual needs.

Socialism has always had to face the dinner-jacket dilemma. Socialists campaigners begin by championing the cause of the under-dog and the under-privileged people they like to call the under-class. Championing is the modern version of the sans-culottes: they try to bring together an army of minority groups and protest movements from amongst the urban poor, the dispossessed and the special interest groups. Should this be forged into a political force that can win political power how then can the leaders of this force make sure that in accepting the restrictions and the privileges of government they do not lose contact with the very radical force that had put them in power in the first place? Should elected socialist politicians wear dinner jackets and attend feasts with grand people? They always do and argue that they should do as they are the people's chosen representatives and should keep up the standards of government activity. Yet the honest ones would admit there is always a tension. The party that represents people who fear the arrival of men in suits, who feel they belong to another culture that is not at home with bureaucratic argument in offices becomes represented by the men in suits who form the new administration. There is a growing awareness in socialist circles of the way in which state provision can often benefit the well educated, the middle classes, the intelligentsia rather than the poorer members of the community it was primarily designed to help. Who is best able to get good quality service out of a publicly provided health care system? The answer is usually those who are best able to argue their case, to write letters to Members of Parliament, to work with opposition spokesmen and to play the bureaucratic game within the administration of health care. It is rarely those who have least income, least education and least control of language.

The new emphasis in the British Labour Movement is on co-operation or what left-wing socialists might call collaboration. Labour may need to don grey suits to be at all electable but if elected it would have to try to remember the origins of its success and the need to do something about those least able to look after themselves. It would need to try to do this whilst not alienating the majority who would have to pay for the dearer services and more generous benefits and who would look askance upon a system which rewarded lack of effort too liberally at the expense of those who worked hard and did well.

One way socialists try to stay true to their principles is by looking carefully at the social origins of each of their leading spokesmen. Some socialists even go so far as to try to establish that they are 'working class'. It is not surprising that this interest in where MPs come from led to the charge and counter-charge of the Michael Meacher libel case, at the root of which was the question of how humble Mr Meacher's origins actually were.

It is one of those ironies of British political history that very often a public school boy from a relatively privileged background can face across the dispatch box a grammar school boy who has worked his way up from very little, the former a socialist and the latter a Conservative, and not vice versa. This should not surprise people, as the modern Conservative Party has become the party of opportunity and openness and the Labour Party has become the province of the middle class, public sector élite. Labour stands behind those school teachers, university teachers, doctors, dentists and senior administrators who favour a planned monopoly system and are against trusting people with too much information or choice. Conservatives stand for giving individuals, whatever their origins, more say over their futures and more individual rights to assert what they want from the public service.

In other parts of the world socialist parties have overcome the dilemma by strongly embracing the new mood of the times and voting for privatization, wider ownership, popular capitalism and the rest of the reforming agenda. It is partially a question of who was in power at the time these ideas evolved and became powerful. In New Zealand, to some extent in Australia, in Portugal, in Spain and in several other countries, socialist governments were in power when the private capital revolution started to sweep the world. Those socialist parties which were alert enough to pick up some of its rhetoric and some of its ideas often as a result enjoyed enhanced political popularity and renewed mandates. Where socialist parties were out of power or were backward in adopting the new agenda they have often remained out of power as with the Labour Party in Britain.

Quite rapidly the Communist Parties of western Europe had to break the umbilical cord with the Soviet Union as the Soviet Union Communist system collapsed in chaos. Gradually the Marxist Communist magazines had to rework their passage towards a more democratic socialism, no longer very red and with few teeth and claws left. The Left turned instead to the new range of protest issues, which we have already examined, picking up the interest of minorities and the themes of green issues, civil rights and empowerment. It was possible at the height of the power of factory-based modern capitalism for Labour to unite and for it to weld a substantial political movement based on the voting strength of employees in factories. That age is now dead. The natural base of support for a party like the Labour Party in

Britain has seen itself undermined. Traditionally supported by the industrial factory-wage employee living in a council house with no assets, it has seen such people transformed over the last two decades into skilled workers with more varied employment in small working units, usually owning their own house and now also joining the ranks of the shareholding population. Prosperity has become the deathwatch beetle in the timbers of socialism as people come to recognize that choice in capitalism can deliver more than socialism and planning.

In advanced western societies there will never be enough people on income support, enough people from ethnic minorities, enough homeless, to forge a winning coalition from policies that try to deal with their specific interests. A winning coalition requires the vote of many who go to work on time, who pay their taxes, who save for their old age, who do not wish the state to be too intrusive. This is the challenge for the new socialism: how to have something relevant to say to these people and how to respond to the coming of global capitalism. They also need to recognize that many unemployed people who want a job rather than a benefit cheque often fear socialism would make jobs even more elusive. The traditional socialist response to global capitalism has been to decry it. They have concentrated their attack upon the alleged failings and malpractices of the multinational corporations. They have drawn attention to the growing power of the multinational corporation, capable of mobilizing resources, providing jobs and influencing the futures of many thousands of people around the world. They have pointed out how sometimes these multinational corporations can be mightier than the governments of individual countries trying to regulate their affairs. They have underlined any alleged corruption or malpractice which these multinationals may perpetrate. If a multinational supplying oil to millions of cars and households across the world over many years has one tanker spill it leads to outpourings in the socialist magazines and press about the inequities and malpractices of the large oil companies. If petrol prices go up, perhaps because there has been some interruption to supply through war in the Gulf, the oil companies are blamed for racketeering and profiteering. If a pharmaceutical company infringes environmental regulations, the fact that its work is relieving pain and suffering is forgotten in the rush to condemn.

Socialists attack the secrecy of multinational enterprises and the way they are trying to make profits so that they have money to invest: in their eyes, the lack of concern for communities, the environment and social justice.

Another strand of international socialism has seen some merit in the globalization process. They have sought to counteract by globalizing organized labour, creating links between unions across national frontiers and attempting to provide a counteracting force to the mobilization of international capital. This reflects the old disunity in the Communist movement between those who favoured revolution in one country and those who favoured global revolution spreading from the Soviet heartlands. So often socialists want jobs, willing the end but not liking the means to get them.

As a society gets more prosperous the concepts of injustice have to be slowly adjusted to see injustice in things that would seem perfectly normal a few years earlier. The Labour Party in Britain now believes it is morally outrageous if people are not rich enough to own a television and a telephone. Some have sought to create a citizens' right to a telephone with suitable subsidies to guarantee that people can afford one. Thirty years ago few homes had telephones and many of us were still without televisions. They were then luxury items that no one would have dreamt of asserting should be supplied by the state if the individual was unable to afford them. If the prosperity machine makes rapid progress over the next twenty years are we then to hear socialist politicians saying that people should have a right to a dishwasher, a high-definition television and the full range of cable and satellite services? These luxuries, which are not yet the experience of the majority, will by then presumably be commonplace and might form part of the new sense of social injustice on the part of those who do not enjoy them.

The original idea behind Herbert Morrison's great dream of welfare provision was that people should be assured of protection against the basic evils of poverty, sickness and old age. His revolutionary national insurance scheme, combined with the health service, did remove many financial fears bought about by the onset of old age, sickness and disability. His concept is now being carried much wider. When one injustice is struck down two new ones are created to take its place.

There is some logic in this, as poverty is relative. If you earn £2000 a year in India you feel rich, whereas on £2000 a year in England you would find it hard to manage. But to some extent poverty is an absolute condition. If I have shelter and a reasonable amount of food to eat and can keep myself warm the things above that which require the expenditure of money are desirable but not essential. It might be nice to have state-financed tickets to Disneyland for entertainment, but maybe reading the newspapers in the local library and listening to the radio can provide a modest substitute and the tax-payer can be spared the extra.

Successful socialist parties are the ones which have adapted, seen the way in which class-based analysis has been removed, and have turned instead to some of the programmes and ideas of popular capitalism. Other socialist parties have failed to move with the changing theories and times and find themselves ignored by the electorate whose ideas have moved on. In advanced western democracies left-wing parties are no longer going to be elected because they represent blue-collar workers in factories or because they represent people in rented houses or those who are unemployed. They need to appeal more widely. To do so they need to understand that balance is required between the claims of individualism and a sense of community, and between the claims of state provision and the need to leave something in people's pockets for them to spend themselves. Self-help has an important role to play in politics and large areas of life have to be left outside the clutches of government. In turn, Right or Centre politicians have to acknowledge that there is some role for collective provision and that some people who are old, ill or disabled require help which only the state can supply.

ELEVEN

Conclusions

Karl Marx had many dubious ideas, but in his belief that technology was important in the course of history he did express a partial truth of some general value. The pace of technological change undoubtedly is an important influence over the pace of growth in prosperity. The style and nature of technology undoubtedly has a strong influence over social and economic organization in the communities and countries adopting it. The pace of technological change also has a strong impact upon the lifestyles of people determining much of the pace of change in general in their employment and living patterns. When great industries go into sharp decline often through change in tastes and technologies on the part of their consumers, areas of a country can move from prosperity to depression relatively quickly. Large numbers of people may ultimately have to pack their bags and move elsewhere to where the new growth industries are developing. In the United Kingdom there was a surge in people moving to the mining areas of Wales, Yorkshire and the North when coal-based industry powered the growth of Victorian and Edwardian prosperity. In the 1930s the first phase of decline in the large steel, shipbuilding and coal-based industries led to great unemployment and deprivation in many urban communities and led to a new surge in migration towards the industrial parks of Slough and the Great West Road where the 1930s electrical and consumer products businesses were flourishing. In the 1980s a further decline took place in the old metal and steel-based industries which was matched by a surge in investment along the Thames Valley and in Silicon Glen in the new high technology industries of the 1980s and 1990s.

Politicians, according to John Maynard Keynes, are often slaves to the theory of some defunct economist. They are also often the flotsam and jetsam on the tide of technological development. A politician representing a community in decline as technologies change will usually have very different attitudes and approaches to problems from the politician representing the vibrant society benefiting from the expansion of the new. The sunrise country or county has a very different attitude to the sunset country or county.

Secular trends in technology can also have a profound impact on politics. The politics of the mass labour movements of the 1920s and 1930s were geared to a world in which most people were working class. Then, working class meant blue-collar employment mainly in factories, and being herded in large numbers to carry out repetitive tasks in large-scale enterprises based in a single property. Everyone thought that the best way of protecting working men's interests was through solidarity, union action and socialism.

The world has changed dramatically since those days. In place of people carrying out repetitive tasks in factories, we have a culture based largely upon service activity and new style manufacturing with large numbers of people carrying out very different tasks, differently remunerated, facing different problems in their daily lives, and having to show flexibility. In place of a large blue-collar manual work-force, we have a predominantly white-collar work-force living by brain more than brawn, needing skills and flexibility. Where the prime way of looking after people who were paid a basic wage for carrying out repetitive tasks may well have been through organization – it certainly seemed so to those faced with that problem – the requirement is hardly the same when a large number of people are remunerated differently, often related to performance and sometimes through partial stakes in the firm or small business for which they work.

The tide of social change has converted the United Kingdom, formerly a country of tenants, into a country predominantly of home-owners. It has converted a large number of people who saw profits as the money they should have earned but didn't into seeing that profit provides the ability to invest in the new technology for the future and the dividends to pay their pensions through their pension funds in retirement. It is difficult to build a successful socialist policy based upon the principle of organized blue-collar labour when most people no longer live only on the product of what they can make with their hands and their tools.

Conclusions

The ability of politicians to recognize secular changes in technology and mood is one of the distinguishing characteristics between the successful and the unsuccessful. Harold Macmillan's great 'wind of change' speech and policy to allow the African countries a rapid move to independence was a feat of understanding which showed his recognition of the strong nationalist feelings and change of mood in the British colonies and Commonwealth, rather than a heroic act of leadership which tried to take people in a direction they themselves would not have grasped. Winston Churchill's speech on the Iron Curtain coming down across Europe was an early and brilliant perception of fundamental change brought by the presence of Communist dictatorships in eastern Europe and beyond. These politicians understood the mood of the times and understood the significance of events, and in that lay their genius.

A different kind of leadership was offered by Winston Churchill during the war when he demonstrated that a country ill-prepared for war, with modest armaments compared with Germany, could stand alone and could develop the spirit to buy the time necessary to stop the German war machine. Margaret Thatcher in peacetime demonstrated that it was possible to draw the public's attention to the logic of technical and social change and to welcome and further it in the interests of greater prosperity, rather than to continue speaking the political language of the past, keeping Britain in thraldom to old ideas and outmoded methods of organization.

The great leader can be more than the foam on the tide of technology and history. But the great leader will make more progress if he understands the strength of the tide and the time when it may turn of its own volition. Today, technology, ownership and choice all point in the direction of more devolved power and a smaller role for government. Large government was the natural reaction of people to the mass organization of labour for wages that characterized mid-twentieth-century capitalism. Later twentieth-century capitalism is based upon the global company and the global market, but also upon differentiation and skills of individuals, small company suppliers and the fracturing power of modern technology against great monopolies. The new generation is based upon open systems, networking, and new communications technology. It all points in the direction of work being increasingly divorced from the work-place, fashions, fads and messages passing round the world rapidly, and successful business being able to customize for the mass consumer. The politics for such a world are very different from the politics pioneered to meet the challenge of mass factory organization of the mid-twentieth century.

The island of Hong Kong and its shoreline is a living monument to enterprise capitalism as it has no natural resources. For years it faced hostility or indifference from communist China across its borders. It lived and thrived on the talents of its people, trading with the world through its busy port and from the runway of Kai Tak airport. Before the end of the century capitalist Hong Kong and Communist China will merge again. Some believe two systems can co-exist in one country, that China will see Hong Kong as a unique prosperity machine capable of earning China the hard currency it needs. Some believe Hong Kong's expansion through Kowloon into Canton is a sign that Hong Kong will lead a drive to liberalize, industrialize and modernize the whole Chinese economy. Some think the leadership will change in Peking in due course, and communism will pass into history. Pessimists worry that China will swallow Hong Kong and will destroy it. They see many more businesses and people leaving for Singapore or Australia.

Whatever happens to Hong Kong, Taiwan will be the main bearer of global capitalism in the Chinese world in the next millenium. Already, with a tiny fraction of the population of the People's Republic, Taiwan has almost reached the same GDP as mainland China. Taiwan has declared herself ready to do business with the world, and prepared to spend her 100 billion dollars of foreign exchange reserves on massive improvements on roads, railways, education and technology. The aggressive economies of the Pacific, the Asian tigers of Taiwan, Singapore, Thailand and the others will ensure eastern dominance in many areas as the next century dawns.

The pressures in the Pacific for greater capitalist success are strong and are reinforced by the apparent ease with which South Korea, Taiwan and the others have grown in recent years. In Asia there have been many democratic stirrings, but some territories have succeeded in combining light government intervention in the marketplace with authoritarian policies in other fields. Where they have kept taxes low enough and economic freedoms great enough they have succeeded in creating the preconditions for enterprise and prosperity.

The Olympic games in Barcelona in 1992 illustrated how far the global market has come, and how people will react to it. The best seats and places were reserved for the television cameras of the world as the main revenue came from rights sold to television. World companies like Coca-Cola paid large sums of money to be international sponsors, and used the fact as part of their world brand advertising throughout the summer. People from Honolulu to Moscow, from Rio to New York watched the best sportsmen and women in the world compete in games, many of which were first formalized in Britain. The idea of amateur sportsmen and women performing in their spare time is being replaced by a professional partnership between athletes, sponsors and trainers. The world market wants its say in the running and nature of the games.

It also demonstrated the strength of national and regional passions which underlie this world event. Everyone cheered on their national athletic champion. The games are now presented as struggles between mighty sporting nations. The opening ceremony contained different displays to represent Catalonia and Spain. Each announcement had to be made in four languages – not just French, Spanish and English, but Catalan as well. The games were a homage to Catalonia as much as a celebration of Spain. The more people feel their identity under threat from supranationalism the more they wave their flags and cling on to their own languages and dialects. English may be the ubiquitous language of airlines, hotels and business, but beneath a thousand local languages flourish with passion and fluency.

Special language betrays special thoughts. If an Englishman enters a shop in Welsh-speaking parts of Wales the locals are likely to switch promptly to speaking Welsh. Thus the Englishman cannot be sure whether they are talking about him. As businessmen from Germany or Britain move south to set up businesses under EC rules in Greece or Spain, they sometimes discover that local discriminatory rules seem to take precedence over the EC idea of the Single Market. When a consultant is advising governments he may be able to produce his report in English, but if he wishes it to go further he would be wise to understand the local language and way of thinking first.

People who dislike each other the strongest are usually those who live closest together or have most dealings with each other. British people do not have strong views about Mexican migration because it does not affect them. The USA does. South Africans have little interest in the conflict between the two Koreas; Norway is not unduly concerned about the Falklands and Argentina. The world market places a new strain on peoples – suddenly almost everyone has to have an attitude towards Japanese, American and European companies. Some see it as a new colonial era which should be opposed. Some see it as the rise of irreligion, threatening their fundamental beliefs. Many see it as economic salvation, in an age which praises material things highly.

Those who are worried about its economic as well as its cultural impact respond with protection, pronouncing statements such as, 'Let's stop this product coming in – we can make it here; Let's stop this man or firm setting up in business – our own could do it safer or better; Let's give advantages to our own producers to stave off the competitive challenge.' There is a grave danger that too many countries will take this line.

Those who are worried primarily about its moral and spiritual impact will try to close the eyes and ears of their people to the new materialism. They will denounce and attack it, associate it with American imperialism, lambast it as a corrosive and decadent cocktail. They will stand for a rival, more spiritual creed.

The next few years will see these issues worked out, as nations and people reassert their independence and identity, as great religions reject the all-conquering yen and dollar, and as others seek the rewards of belonging to the global market. History has a new beginning in the wake of communism's collapse. Let us hope it yields greater spiritual and material enrichment rather than too many corpses on the battlefields of religious and national identity.

Index